A NORWICH CITY FACT FILE

The Canary Companion

ROGER SMITH

RJS Publishing

Published by RJS Publishing
C/O The Driftway, Rectory Road, East Carleton, Norwich NR14 8HT

© 2004 Roger Smith

ISBN 0-9548287-0-4

Cover designed by Richard Smith.

Printed and bound by Norwich Colour Print Limited,
Drayton
Norwich
NR8 6RL

The majority of photographs in this book are supplied by kind permission of Archant Norfolk Limited.

Some photographs from handbooks and programmes are reproduced with permission from Norwich City Football Club.

A few pictures are the author's own.

ACKNOWLEDGEMENTS

This is the first book I have produced and I am indebted to several people for making the publication possible.

I would like to extend my sincere thanks to the following: -

Archant Norfolk Limited, for not only supplying most of the photographs, but also for allowing me access to their records and files in the sports department, library and archives. The staff in the library have been most helpful and I am very grateful.

Norfolk Museums and Archaeology Service (Bridewell Museum), for permission to photograph the character models of Canary and Dumpling and The Nest, in their Football Exhibition.

Richard Smith for cover design and tips on presentation.

The ' Coachmakers' crew' for all their encouragement, ideas and critique.

Norwich City Football Club for permitting use of some pictures from handbooks and programmes and their general support.

Mike Davage, the statistical oracle behind the club and instigator of the 'Canary Citizens' book. He has been superb in book advice and for readily giving permission to refer to his records.

Richard Balls of the Eastern Daily Press, for helping to promote interest in the book's publication.

Duncan Forbes, for his enthusiasm as always, in kindly agreeing to write the foreword.

The printers for their co-operation and willingness to cope with the last minute changes.

Last, but not least, for my wife Carol for her patience and understanding of the countless hours I have spent compiling this edition.

Finally, it needs to be acknowledged that all comments and views are my own and may not necessarily be those of the Club.

CONTENTS

Contents (continued)

FOREWORD BY DUNCAN FORBES

When this book was brought to my attention and I was asked to 'Do the Forward', I replied 'Yes, I had plenty of experience of that in my playing days.' Then I realised what was meant.

I served 33 years with this Football Club from 1968 until 2001. My first 13 years was spent as a player and captain, my last 13 as Chief Scout and the middle seven, working in the commercial department, organising away travel and overseeing the club shop. During this time I met so many supporters who never ceased to amaze me with their dedication, passion and knowledge. When I used to lead the team out at Carrow Road, the first sight was the packed terraces of the old South Stand. The roar and noise was spine tingling. In those days, if I won the toss we always kicked towards the Barclay as it meant we would kick downhill in the second half.

This year when I stood on the balcony of the City Hall looking out over the sea of yellow and green, it brought a lump to my throat to recall how proud I had been standing there 32 years previously collecting the Second Division trophy. It was a dream come true to play at so many famous stadiums, in front of huge crowds and against so many talented players. Although I had a reputation as a hard man, I can say I was never sent off, nor injured anyone badly. My most serious injury was when we beat Arsenal at Highbury 3-0 in the League Cup and I suffered a blow to my ribs, which caused me to have a collapsed lung.

I was fortunate also to appear at Wembley twice. The first time, I felt disappointed that I had missed an opportunity to score and I wondered if I would ever have another chance. The second time was perhaps more of a downer, as we really expected to win. Still, I was lucky enough to play in the top flight for over half my career with Norwich.

The book has jogged my memory on so many things. Perhaps our best ever signing was Martin Peters, whose class stood out a mile and he played 232 games for Norwich. Then there was Ted MacDougall, goal scorer supreme. 'Charlie' Boyer used to all the running for him, give him the ball and he would score.

When I joined Norwich in 1968 I didn't know what to expect, sometimes it 'happens' at a club and sometimes it doesn't. I was fortunate to be part of a big 'happening', with gaining promotion and playing in the top division of the day. I believe it has started to happen again, only this time it could be bigger.

This book is a wonderful collection of facts and records for supporters, which will resolve many an argument on the long away journeys. All the records and achievements are here in one book, it is well organised, like our defence, with any fact easy to look up. I hope all the many supporters of Norwich City enjoy this compilation and enjoy reminiscing as I have done.

Duncan Forbes

INTRODUCTION

This book is a lifetime's ambition. I've kept my own records since I started watching City, as I have always been passionate about football statistics and would now like to share these with other fans. I've seen nearly 1000 games over the last 43 years and have lived through a lot of the facts documented in this book.

I found topical information always appeared in the press, but other facts never seemed to be available when you wanted them. Hopefully, this book enables the reader to find out any information about Norwich City in one volume.

I have every book issued about Norwich City and they all cover various angles, with 'Canary Citizens' being the prize volume. I was an initial advance subscriber, no.179 in that book. It covers the history and players in full detail. However, the Canary Companion is different as it analyses and organises all the facts and records in an easily referenced format and doesn't attempt to cover player profiles. I have included a raft of statistics that haven't been shown before, such as televised matches, transfers, unusual incidents, ground development, great escapes and vital matches. The appendix includes all City's results, against every team, with a performance summary for each.

It is inevitable in a book with this number of facts that there may be the odd challenge or anomaly. I am grateful to Mike Davage for his initial scrutiny, which prevented several errors and with the intense checking I have since carried out I trust that those remaining are minimal.

I believe any glance in the book will trigger so many memories. All supporters have their own recollections and will now be able to clarify the facts more fully.

I have called this reference and record book 'The Canary Companion', because I see it as a book you can pick up and always find something of interest. The Canary & Dumpling characters, who used to walk around the pitch before games wearing the costumes shown on the cover, used to fascinate me and seemed an ideal choice.

I wish you many happy hours reminiscing.

Roger Smith
Author

ABANDONED MATCHES

Opponents	V	League / Cup	Date	Reason	Score	Minute Aban'd
Kirkley	H	Norfolk & Suffolk	29.11.02*	Bad light	1-1	78
Leicester Fosse	A	FA Cup	11.01.13	Snow	0-0	65
Plymouth Argyle	A	Division Two	14.01.39	Snow	0-1	66
Bristol Rovers	A	Division Three Sth.	17.02.51	Waterlogged	1-2	45
Newport County	A	Division Three Sth.	23.03.51	Waterlogged	1-5	70
Mansfield Town	A	Division Three	29.11.58	Fog	1-0	33
Manchester City	A	Division Two	08.09.65	Waterlogged	1-1	45
Chelsea	H	League Cup	20.12.72	Fog	3-2	84
Brighton & Hove Albion	H	FA Cup	04.01.03 **	Floodlights	-	37

* 1902
** 2003

The most important match above was against Chelsea in the semi-final of the League Cup, which put a temporary stop to City's first trip to Wembley. They had already won the first leg 2-0 and were leading 3-2 in the second, when the fog that had been threatening all evening closed in and caused the game to be abandoned with just six minutes remaining. After an agonising wait over Christmas, justice was done when the re-match saw them win 1-0, (3-0) on aggregate, to secure their first ever appearance at Wembley.

The Cup match against Leicester in 1913 was replayed five days later with City winning 4-1.

Surprisingly, two matches were abandoned in quick succession in the West Country in 1951. One of these was on Good Friday although City did manage to play the next day in another fixture away at Bournemouth

The biggest turnaround in fortunes was in the fixture at Newport in 1951. Losing

1-5 when the first match was abandoned, City managed to salvage a 1-1 draw in the rearranged game later in the season.

The abandoned game due to fog, against Chelsea in 1972.

The most bizarre instance was not really an abandonment, as the match never started. This occurred in 2003 against Brighton & Hove Albion in the FA Cup. With the crowd already assembled, the match was delayed due to floodlight failure. Even the back up generator was not working, leaving no alternative but to postpone the match after 37 minutes into the scheduled time. The crowd of nearly 17,000 was the biggest to be turned away from Carrow Road without seeing a ball kicked.

AGGREGATE SCORES

The highest aggregate of goals scored in a match involving City is shown for Cup-ties of eight goals and over and for League games of nine goals or more.

Note the 13 against Preston was City's record for a tie over two legs

Event	Goals	Opponents	Result	V	Date	League/Cup
Overall	18	Brighton & HA	18-0	H	25.12.40	War League
FA Cup	9	Brighton & HA	7-2	H	30.11.46	First Round
League Cup	13	Preston N.E.	3-3	A	29.09.84	Second Round
			6-1	H	10.10.84	Two Legs
	8	Halifax Town	7-1	A	27.11.63	Third Round

Event	Goals	Opponents	Result	V	Date	League/Cup
League Cup	8	Wrexham	6-2	H	10.10.73	Second Round
	8	Chester	5-3	H	21.10.64	Second Round
	8	Bradford City	5-3	A	07.11.95	Third Round rep
League	12	Coventry City	10-2	H	15.03.30	Division Three S
	12	Swindon Town	2-10	A	05.09.08	Southern
	10	Southampton	3-7	A	14.12.57	Division Three S
	9	Southampton	4-5	H	09.04.94	Premier
	9	Coventry City	4-5	A	27.12.77	Division One
	9	Notts County	7-2	H	17.11.34	Division Two
	9	Middlesbrough	5-4	H	09.12.61	Division Two
	9	Liverpool	4-5	A	13.01.62	Division Two
	9	Bristol City	7-2	H	28.08.33	Division Three S
	9	Plymouth A.	3-6	A	16.01.26	Division Three S
	9	Brighton & Hove Albion	3-6	A	07.09.29	Division Three S
	9	Shrewsbury T.	8-1	A	13.09.52	Division Three S
	9	Southend Utd.	7-2	H	17.12.55	Division Three S
	9	Walsall	3-6	A	26.01.57	Division Three S
	9	Shrewsbury T.	5-4	A	09.03.57	Division Three S

Brighton & Hove Albion

18 goals is easily the highest aggregate of any game involving Norwich although it took place in a wartime competition on Christmas Day when circumstances were far from normal. Brighton arrived with only four players, plus two 16-year-old juniors. To enable the game to go ahead the team was made up of five Norwich reserves, a Bolton player on loan to Norwich and a forward from the crowd. Centre forward Fred Chadwick scored six goals for City.

City have met Brighton in the FA Cup on more occasions than any other club and this includes their highest FA Cup aggregate of nine goals. The game was played in pouring rain with City coming from 1-2 behind although Brighton lost a player at half time. Leslie Eyre, scored five, with three coming in the last eight minutes.

League Cup

City met Preston North End four times in the League Cup in the 1980's, all over two legs. The 1984 results, of 3-3 at Preston and 6-1 at home, produced the highest Cup aggregate in a City match of 13 goals.

When City beat Fourth Division Wrexham, they had only won one of their first ten league matches.

League

Thomas Hunt scored five goals in City's biggest win, against **Coventry City** 10-2. The score at half time was 4-0 with eight goals following in the second half. It's a pity that a crowd of only 8000 witnessed the game.

City's record defeat, 2-10 at **Swindon Town,** was in only the second game of the season, having already lost 0-4 in the opening match at Luton three days earlier.

AMATEUR

Norwich entered the Amateur Cup competition in the first two years of their formation. In 1902, they progressed to the second qualifying round before losing at Lowestoft 2-4, having beaten Lynn Town 5-0 at home in the first round.

In 1903-4, City performed much better and reached the third round before going out to Ealing despite bringing them back to Newmarket Road for a replay. From 1904-5 they were excluded due to professionalism.

Round	Opponents	Result
First Qualifying	Bye	Not applicable.
Second Qualifying	Harwich & Parkeston	H .. 5-1
Third Qualifying	Leiston	H .. 5-1
Fourth Qualifying	Kirkley	A .. 2-0
First	Lowestoft Town	H .. 3-0
Second	Ilford	H .. 3-1
Third	Ealing	A .. 0-0
Third - replay	Ealing	H .. 1-2

This Cup exploit had repercussions for City. An FA Commission met at the Bell Hotel in December 1904 with their findings published in January 1905.

This removed the Club's amateur status due to certain excessive payments and expenses. Three prominent officials were suspended until the end of the season.

During a meeting at the Agricultural Hall on 4 March 1905, it was agreed that Norwich City would turn professional with John Bowman as manager and Wilfred Burgess as chairman.

This also had an affect on their league situation. From their formation in 1902, City played in the Norfolk and Suffolk League against other teams from East Anglia. They finished third in their first two seasons and were champions in 1904-5, despite being prevented from fielding any of their professional players.

Following the decision to turn professional, City sought election to the Southern League. Four clubs applied for the two places available and after lobbying and the selling of the City they were successful in the ballot with 21 votes received. This put them into second place, ahead of the 18 received by Crystal Palace.

ANGLO-SCOTTISH CUP

This was a pre-season competition for teams not eligible for Europe and replaced the Texaco Cup. It was played on a group basis with the winner progressing to meet Scottish opposition. Norwich failed to win a single game and never qualified from the group matches to meet any Scottish teams.

Year	Opponents	Result	Attendance
1975	Fulham	H...1-2	6,054
	Chelsea	A...1-1	7,886
	Bristol City	A...1-4	3,823
1976	Orient	H...0-0	6.285
	Chelsea	A...1-1	7,130
	Fulham	A...1-1	4,525
1977	Orient	H...1-1	3,124
	Fulham	H...0-1	3,135
	Chelsea	A...2-2	6,858
1978	Notts County	A...1-2	4,091
	Mansfield Town	H...1-1	2,771
	Orient	H...0-0	2,870

APPEARANCES

Kevin Keelan

Kevin Keelan holds the record for the most appearances, made over 17 seasons. The breakdown is as follows: -

League 571
FA Cup 31
League Cup 57
Texaco Cup 14
Total **673**

A further eight appearances were made in Willhire Cup matches.

He scored one goal in a penalty shoot out against Leicester City in the Texaco Cup.

His final game was played at the age of 39, against Liverpool at home on 9 February 1980 when City lost 3-5.

Kevin Keelan surveys the crowded Barclay in the days when fences were the norm

Kevin's contribution to the game was recognised when he was awarded the MBE in June 1980.

Most Appearances

	Appearances	Player		Seasons
Overall	673	Kevin	Keelan	1963-80
League	590	Ron	Ashman	1947-63
FA Cup	56	Ron	Ashman	1947-63
	38	Ken	Nethercott	1947-59
League Cup	57	Kevin	Keelan	1963-80
	42	David	Stringer	1963-76
Consecutive	208	Barry	Butler	1957-61

Consecutive Appearances

After the league match at Brighton & Hove Albion on 21 September 1957, centre half Barry Butler did not miss another game for four seasons, until the second round League Cup tie at Lincoln City on 4 October 1961, and this was only due to playing in an FA XI representative match.

This run totalled **208** appearances including 25 cup games. Even then, the match missed at Lincoln was the only one in that season and he went on to make 219 successive league appearances. The sequence finally ended on 5 September 1962 when he missed the home game against Huddersfield Town.

Most Appearances for City to May 2004

	Player		Appearances	Seasons
1	Kevin	Keelan	673	1963-80
2	Ron	Ashman	662	1947-63
3	David	Stringer	499	1965-76
4	Bryan	Gunn	477	1986-98
5	Joe	Hannah	427	1921-35
6	Roy	McCrohan	426	1951-62
7	Ian	Crook	418	1986-97
8	Ken	Nethercott	416	1947-59
9	Mark	Bowen	399	1987-96
10	Terry	Allcock	389	1958-69
11	Bernard	Robinson	380	1932-49
12	Ian	Culverhouse	369	1985-94
13	Duncan	Forbes	357	1968-80
14	Daryl	Sutch	352	1990-2002

APPEARANCES

Player			Appearances	Seasons	
15	Barry	Butler	349	1957-66	
16	Graham	Paddon	340	1969-73 ..	1976-81
17	John	Gavin	338	1949-54 ..	1955-58
18	George	Martin	337	1913-27	
19	Iwan	Roberts	306	1997-2004	
20	Robert	Fleck	299	1987-92 ..	1995-8
21	Ian	Butterworth	293	1986-94	
22	Craig	Fleming	289	1997-	
23	Tommy	Bryceland	284	1962-69	
24	Terry	Anderson	279	1965-74	
25	Tony	Powell	275	1974-81	
26	John	Polston	263	1990-98	
27	Chris	Woods	267	1981-86	
27	Peter	Mendham	267	1978-86	
29	Dale	Gordon	261	1984-91	
30	Dave	Watson	256	1980-86	
30	Bill	Lewis	256	1949-55	
30	Bill	Punton	256	1959-66	
33	Sandy	Kennon	255	1959-64	
34	Denis	Morgan	250	1946-56	
34	Bobby	Brennan	250	1953-60	
36	Rob	Newman	249	1991-97	
37	Joe	Mullett	248	1961-68	
38	Don	Pickwick	244	1947-56	
39	Noel	Kinsey	243	1947-53	
39	Colin	Suggett	243	1973-78	
41	Reg	Foulkes	238	1950-56	
41	Jerry	Goss	238	1984-96	
43	Martin	Peters	232	1975-80	
43	Malky	Mackay	232	1998-	
45	Bryan	Thurlow	224	1954-64	
46	Mark	Barham	223	1979-86	
47	Doug	Lochhead	220	1929-35	
48	Ruel	Fox	219	1986-94	
48	Andy	Marshall	219	1994-01	
50	Matt	Crowe	214	1957-62	
51	Charlie	Dennington	209	1922-29	
52	Greg	Downs	206	1977-85	
52	Neil	Adams	206	1994-99	

APPEARANCES

Player			Appearances	Seasons
54	Mal	Lucas	204	1964-70
54	Darren	Eadie	204	1993-99
56	Alan	Black	203	1966-73
56	Tom	Halliday	203	1933-38
56	Mick	McGuire	203	1976-83
59	Leslie	Eyre	201	1946-51
59	Ken	Foggo	201	1967-72

Above appearances exclude minor matches - Anglo-Scottish, Group, Simod, Willhire & Zenith Data Cups and League Trophy.

The shortest first team playing career for City, was for just ten minutes, by 17-year-old Mark Metcalf as a substitute at West Ham United on 13 November 1982.

Most Substitute Appearances

Daryl Sutch	61	1990-2003
Trevor Howard	45	1968-74

Norfolk born Trevor, was for some time the most used City substitute throughout his six seasons with the club. He was also the first substitute to score (in a 1-0 win at Hull on 26 December 1968).

Nearly a third of his 156 total appearances were as substitute and on a further 20 occasions he was not called on from the bench. This was in the days when only one substitute was permitted. Once the number allowed was increased, to first two, in 1987 and then three, by 1998, other players had more opportunity to beat his record. Eventually Daryl Sutch did so in 2002, making 15 substitute appearances in his last season, to total 61 in all.

Players used in a Season

Most	37	Division Three South	1946-7
Least	19	Division. One	1988-9

In the 1946-7 season, just after the war, Norwich used five goalkeepers and kept the same team in successive matches on only five occasions. As a result of such chopping and changing it was no surprise that the club finished in the bottom two.

In Division One in 1988-9, City only used 19 players. Nine made over 40 appearances and six made less than ten. This settled situation contributed to one of the best seasons City has ever enjoyed, when they finished fourth.

Ron Ashman was an ever present in six seasons and Kevin Keelan for five.

ATTENDANCES

Attendance figures stated in this section are as recorded by the Football League. They may vary, in some instances, from other reportings. This is due to amendments after the event for corrections or to reflect paid numbers rather than those actually attending. The practice of counting has varied through the years.

Currently attendances are declared at home matches with also the percentage present. The actual attendance is often around 10% less than the declared figure due to non-appearance, but the paid figure is usually the attendance published.

HIGHEST ATTENDANCES

Occasion	Attendance	V	Opponents	Result	League / Cup	Date
Wembley	100,000	N	Tottenham Hotspur	0-1	League Cup Final	03.03.73
	100,000	N	Aston Villa	0-1	League Cup Final	01.03.75
	100,000	N	Sunderland	1-0	Milk Cup Final	24.03.85
European	30,000	A	Inter Milan	0-1	Third Round 2nd leg	08.12.93
	20,829	H	Bayern Munich	1-1	Second Round 2nd leg	03.11.93
FA Cup	67,633	A	Tottenham Hotspur	1-1	Fifth Round	14.02.59
	43,984	H	Leicester City	0-2	Sixth Round	30.03.63
League Cup	58,010	A	Man. Utd.	2-2	Semi-Final	15.01.75
	35,927	H	Chelsea	0-1	Fourth Round	17.11.71

ATTENDANCES

Occasion	Attendance	V	Opponents	Result	League / Cup	Date
Premier*	44,694	A	Man. Utd.	0-1	League	04.12.93
	21,843	H	Liverpool	1-2	League	29.04.95
Division One	54,356	A	Man. Utd.	2-2	League	23.10.76
	36,688	H	Crystal Palace	2-1	League	24.04.73
Division Two	56,202	A	Man. Utd.	1-1	League	15.03.75
	35,943	H	Aston Villa	1-4	League	30.04.75
Division Three South	37,863	H	Notts County	0-1	League	28.04.48
	36,285	A	Cardiff City	1-6	League	28.12.46
Newmarket Road	11,500	H	Tottenham Hotspur	4-1	League	14.04.06
The Nest	25,037	H	Sheffield Wednesday	0-1	FA Cup Fifth Round	16.02.35
Youth	20,652	A	Everton Youth	1-0	FA Youth Final 3rd game	09.05.83
	10,569	H	Everton Youth	3-2	FA Youth Final 1st leg	25.04.83
Reserves	15,247	H	Plymouth A. Reserves			17.01.59
Texaco Cup	35,798	H	Ipswich Town	1-2	Texaco Cup Final	07.05.73
	29,698	A		1-2		04.05.73

* *The highest Premier attendances are sure to be exceeded during the 2004–5 season. The away game at Manchester United should set a new record of over 67,000 and some home attendances are likely to exceed 25,000 once the infill connection to the Jarrold Stand is completed.*

Leicester City

The attendance of 43,984 is the highest ever recorded at Carrow Road and with the ground then being mostly terrace, is unlikely to ever be bettered. The game was disappointing with City, then in Division Two, losing 0-2 to First Division Leicester City. Terry Allcock missed a penalty and Leicester went on to lose in the final to Manchester United.

The packed terraces can be seen in the record attendance against Leicester City.

Crystal Palace

The final home game of their first season in the top division required a victory to avoid relegation. David Stringer headed a last minute winner after City had fallen behind, to send Palace down instead.

Aston Villa

The Division Two fixture against Aston Villa was the final match of the season. Both clubs were already promoted and it was the last game before seats were installed in the South Stand.

Notts County

The highest ever league attendance at Carrow Road was in Division Three South and was boosted by the appearance of England international Tommy Lawton, playing for Notts County at the time.

Youth

When City beat Everton in the Youth Cup it took a deciding tie, attracting over 20,000 at Everton, after the first two legs had resulted in a 5-5 aggregate. The attendance for the three games to see City triumph totalled over 45,000.

Reserves

It was the practice to sell cup tickets at reserve games at the time and the impending visit of Cardiff City in the FA Cup fourth round. boosted the crowd against Plymouth Argyle Reserves to over 15,000.

Texaco Cup

The Texaco Cup games usually had the novelty value of playing Scottish teams. However, when City met Ipswich Town in a two-legged final, both attendances were some of the best in the competition. Unfortunately City lost both legs (1-2), which took some of the shine off surviving in their first season in Division One.

LOWEST ATTENDANCES

Occasion	Attend-ance	V	Opponents	Result	League / Cup	Date
Neutral (Both Second replays)	Nil		Bradford City	0-2	FA Third Round	03.03.15
	6,238		Manchester City	1-6	FA Third Round	29.01.75
European UEFA	9,133	A	Vitesse Arnhem	0-0	First Round 2nd leg	29.09.93
	16,818	H	Vitesse Arnhem	3-0	First Round 1st leg	15.09.93

LOWEST ATTENDANCES (continued)

Occasion	Attendance	V	Opponents	Result	League/ Cup	Date
FA Cup	1,500	A	Lowestoft Town	1-1	Fifth Round	20.09.02 *
	3,919	H	Tunbridge Wells Rangers	0-2	Sixth Round	13.01.06
League Cup	2,886	A	Charlton Athletic	2-0	Second Round 1st leg	09.10.91
	5,429	H	Barnet	2-1	First Round 1st leg	12.08.97
Premier	7,206	A	Wimbledon	1-3	League	05.03.94
	12,452	H	Southampton	1-0	League	05.09.92
Division One	3,531	A	Wimbledon	1-3	League	05.10.91
	10,514	H	Luton Town	1-0	League	26.10.91
Division Two	2,907	A	Carlisle United	4-0	League	12.10.85
	7,305	H	Barnsley	0-1	League	01.05.37
Division Three South	1,115**	A	Merthyr Town	5-1	League	07.12.29
	6,697**	H	Gillingham	0-0	League	24.02.54

* 1902
** *Lowest attendances since 1929, as previous years often estimated.*

FA Cup

The third round Cup-tie against Bradford City had already been replayed once and so the third match was played on neutral territory, which was the practice at the time. However, the FA decided to play the tie at Lincoln during a wartime afternoon behind locked gates to prevent nearby munitions workers from being attracted to the game. Although the official attendance was nil, a few hundred spectators did try to break in and at half time the gates were opened to let them watch City lose 0-2.

The tie versus Manchester City had also gone to a second replay, which was held at Chelsea where City were hammered 1-6.

Gillingham

The match against Gillingham in 1954 is the lowest Carrow Road league attendance. It was played on a mid week afternoon before floodlights had been installed. Ironically, the previous Saturday had seen City lose at home to Leicester City in the FA Cup fifth round before a crowd of nearly 40,000.

Division Three South

Some crowds were lower in earlier years as estimates were often made. A crowd of 3,500 was recorded at The Nest against Swindon on 21 January 1922, which was typical of many at that time.

Willhire Cup

Although a secondary competition, the game at home to Colchester United on 31 July 1980 attracted the smallest ever attendance at Carrow Road for a competitive game, of just 1,744.

AVERAGE LEAGUE ATTENDANCES - HOME

	Average	Division	Season
Highest	18,625	Premier	1994-5
	28,652	Division One	1972-3
	24,451	Division Two	1960-1
	26,402	Division Three	1959-60
Lowest	16,302	Premier	1992-3
	13,858	Division One	1991-2
	13,385	Division Two	1934-5
	8,317	Division Three South	1930-1

In 1992 Carrow Road was converted to an all seated stadium. However, in that season, the average attendance was the lowest they recorded in the Premier League. This was despite City's finishing third and qualifying for Europe.

AVERAGE LEAGUE ATTENDANCES – AWAY

	Average	Division	Season
Highest	23,217	Premier	1994-5
	27,200	Division One	1972-3

Highest Average League Attendances – Away (continued)

Average	Division	Season
17,377	Division Two	1971-2
15,995	Division Three South	1949-50

Lowest	Average	Division	Season
	20,768	Premier	1992-3
	11,964	Division One	1995-6
	8,058	Division Two	1985-6
	6,119	Division Three South	1930-1

HOME AVERAGE LEAGUE ATTENDANCES

The full list of average Home League attendances since 1929, when records were more reliable, is as follows: -

NB These are as published in the press or handbooks at the end of the season, but may have been subsequently revised for amendment after the season's reporting.

Average	Position	Division	Season
10,037	8	Division Three South	1929-30
8,317	22	Division Three South	1930-1
10,848	10	Division Three South	1931-2
10,895	3	Division Three South	1932-3
13,524	1	Division Three South	1933-4
13,385	14	Division Two	1934-5
16,603	11	Division Two	1935-6
16,030	17	Division Two	1936-7
16,136	14	Division Two	1937-8
14,252	21	Division Two	1938-9
17,135	21	Division Three South	1946-7
21,452	21	Division Three South	1947-8
24,334	10	Division Three South	1948-9
23,266	11	Division Three South	1949-50
24,404	2	Division Three South	1950-1
21,837	3	Division Three South	1951-2
21,121	4	Division Three South	1952-3
18,582	7	Division Three South	1953-4
16,056	12	Division Three South	1954-5
15,596	7	Division Three South	1955-6

ATTENDANCES

Average	Position	Division	Season
12,856	24	Division Three South	1956-7
20,294	8	Division Three South	1957-8
21,101	4	Division Three	1958-9
26,402	2	Division Three	1959-60
24,451	4	Division Two	1960-1
20,202	17	Division Two	1961-2
19,713	13	Division Two	1962-3
17,031	17	Division Two	1963-4
18,777	6	Division Two	1964-5
15,724	13	Division Two	1965-6
15,545	11	Division Two	1966-7
16,901	9	Division Two	1967-8
14,559	13	Division Two	1968-9
13,980	11	Division Two	1969-70
13,265	10	Division Two	1970-1
23,295	1	Division Two	1971-2
28,652	20	Division One	1972-3
23,410	22	Division One	1973-4
22,858	3	Division Two	1974-5
23,336	10	Division One	1975-6
22,928	16	Division One	1976-7
19,947	13	Division One	1977-8
18,512	16	Division One	1978-9
17,892	12	Division One	1979-80
17,724	20	Division One	1980-1
14,841	3	Division Two	1981-2
17,676	14	Division One	1982-3
16,432	14	Division One	1983-4
16,058	20	Division One	1984-5
14,528	1	Division Two	1985-6
17,913	5	Division One	1986-7
15,764	14	Division One	1987-8
16,785	4	Division One	1988-9
16,737	10	Division One	1989-90
15,527	15	Division One	1990-1
13,856	18	Division One	1991-2
16,302	3	Premier	1992-3
18,164	12	Premier	1993-4
18,624	20	Premier	1994-5

ATTENDANCES

Average	Position	Division	Season
14,581	16	Division One	1995-6
14,719	13	Division One	1996-7
14,444	15	Division One	1997-8
15,771	9	Division One	1998-9
15,539	12	Division One	1999-2000
16,525	15	Division One	2000-1
18,738	6	Division One	2001-2
20,353	8	Division One	2002-3
18,986	1	Division One	2003-4

First Home Attendance Over 10,000

FA Cup   10,366 .... Sheffield Wednesday 11.01.08

First Home Attendance Over 20,000

FA Cup   20,129 .... Corinthians 12.01.29

First Home Attendance Over 30,000

FA Cup   32,378 .... Chelsea 11.01.36

First Home Attendance Over 40,000

FA Cup   43,129 .... Portsmouth 12.01.50

HOME ATTENDANCES Over 30,000

Occasion	Attendance	Opponents	Date
FA Cup	43,984	Leicester City	30.03.63
	43.129	Portsmouth	12.01.50
	41,949	Sunderland	18.02.61
	41,000	Sheffield Wednesday	11.03.67
	39,973	Leicester City	20.02.54
	39,890	Ipswich Town	27.01.62
	38,930	Arsenal	12.01.52
	38,000	Manchester United	10.01.59
	38,000	Cardiff City	24.01.59

Occasion	Attendance	Opponents	Date
FA Cup (cont)	38,000	Tottenham Hotspur	18.02.59
	38,000	Sheffield United	03.03.59
	34,825	Newcastle United	13.03.63
	34,693	Liverpool	08.01.51
	33,346	Aston Villa	08.01.38
	32,378	Chelsea	11.01.36
	32,310	Leeds United.	13.01.73
	30,751	Blackburn Rovers	05.03.66
	30,108	Bolton Wanderers	04.02.37
League Cup	35,927	Chelsea	17.11.71
	34,731	Ipswich Town	04.12.74
	34,265	Chelsea	03.01.73
	32,000	Chelsea	20.12.72
	31,621	Manchester United	22.01.75
Texaco Cup	35,798	Ipswich Town	07.05.73
Division One	36.688	Crystal Palace	24.04.73
	36,500	Liverpool	28.10.72
	35,770	Manchester United.	02.12.72
	34,640	Ipswich Town	11.11.72
	34,445	Tottenham Hotspur.	14.10.72
	32,286	West Ham United	10.02.73
	32,170	Arsenal	23.09.72
	31,798	Leeds United	29.09.73
	30,993	Ipswich Town	09.04.77
	30,895	Q.P.R	17.04.76
	30,592	Ipswich Town	31.03.76
	30,032	Stoke City	30.08.72
Division Two	35,943	Aston Villa	30.04.75
	34,914	Bristol City	04.04.72
	34,160	W.B.A.	08.02.75
	33,999	Millwall	12.02.72
	32,619	Charlton Athletic	24.08.60
	32,232	Plymouth Argyle	07.09.60
	31,972	Sheffield. United.	20.08.60

ATTENDANCES

Occasion	Attendance	Opponents	Date
Division Two	31,634	Swindon Town	22.04.72
(continued)	31,304	Stoke City	10.02.62
	30,788	Charlton Athletic	27.12.71
	30,884	Ipswich Town	26.12.60
	30,342	Hull City	15.03.72
	30,160	Portsmouth	11.02.61
Division Three	37,863	Notts County	28.04.48
South	36,479	Barnsley	09.09.59
	35,933	Nottm. Forest	26.12.49
	35,361	Ipswich Town	12.03.49
	35,267	Newport County	26.03.51
	32,357	Ipswich Town	04.03.50
	32,130	Notts County	24.08.49
	32,008	Ipswich Town	26.12.51
	31,054	Ipswich Town	02.04.56
	30,575	Bristol Rovers	22.04.53
	30,052	Q.P.R	21.04.48
	30,003	Reading	14.04.51
Division Three	34,905	Southend United	27.04.60
	33,723	Grimsby Town	16.04.60
	33,232	Halifax Town	18.04.60
	32,243	Bury ..	23.09.59
	31,527	Tranmere Rovers	26.08.59

Away Attendances over 50,000

Occasion	Attendance	Opponents	Date
FA Cup	67,633	Tottenham Hotspur	14.02.59
FA Cup	65,125	Sunderland	10.02.51
FA Cup	63,500	Luton Town (at Tottenham)	15.03.59
FA Cup	63,405	Manchester United	19.02.67
League Cup	58,010	Manchester United	15.01.75
FA Cup	57,987	Chelsea	17.02.68
Division Two	56,202	Manchester United.	15.03.75
FA Cup	55,767	Arsenal	30.01.54
Division One	54,356	Manchester United	23.10.76
Division One	50,587	Manchester United	01.11.75

AWAY MATCHES

LEAGUE MATCHES

Most Away Wins in a Season

10	2003-4	Division One
9	1933-4, 1950-1,1952-3	Division Three South
9	1958-9	Division Three
9	1985-6	Division Two
9	1988.9	Division One
8	1992-3,1993-4	Premier

The nine wins in 1988-9 were achieved in only 19 away games.

The 2003-4 Championship team broke the record for away wins in a season.

Least Away Wins in a Season

0	1930-1	Division Three South
0	1978-9	Division One

In 1978-9, although City lost all their away league matches they did win two away League Cup matches.

Most Away Draws in a Season

13.....................1978-9 ....Division One

In this season, City created a Football League record of 23 draws.

Least Away Draws in a Season

0.....................1938-9 ....Division Two
0.....................1980-1 ....Division One

City did draw an away Cup-tie in 1980-1.

Most Away Defeats in a Season

20.....................1930-1 ....Division Three South

This miserable record was out of a total of 21 matches. The only match in which they prevented defeat was a 2-2 draw in their second game of the season.

Least Away Defeats in a Season

5.....................1932-3, 1933-4.....................Division Three South
5.....................1974-5 ....Division Two
5.....................1993-4 ....Premier
6.....................2003-4 ....Division One

Best Away Record per Division (Based on points won)

Played	Won	Drew	Lost	Season	Division
23	10	7	6	2003-4	Division One
21	9	5	7	1985-6	Division Two
21	9	7	5	1933-4	Division Three South
21	8	8	5	1993-4	Premier

Worst Away Record per Division (Based on points won)

Played	Won	Drew	Lost	Season	Division
21	0	1	20	1930-1	Division Three South
21	3	0	18	1938-9	Division Two
21	1	6	14	1973-4	Division One
21	2	5	14	1994-5	Premier

Most Away Goals Scored

Note the record of either Division Three or Division Three South has been shown for the Divisional figures below.

Goals	Season	Division
43	1952-3	Division Three South
39	1993-4	Premier
35	1996-7, 2003-4	Division One
33	1985-6	Division Two

Least Away Goals Scored

10	1930-1	Division Three South
10	1994-5	Premier
11	1938-9	Division Two
14	1972-3, 1983- 4, 1987-8, 1990-1	Division One

Most Away Goals Conceded

61	1938-9	Division Two
57	1956-7	Division Three South
48	1980-1	Division One
46	1992-3	Premier

Least Away Goals Conceded

20	1971-2	Division Two
24	2003-4	Division One
30	1933-4	Division Three
32	1993-4	Premier

AWAY SEQUENCES

League Away Games Without A Win

41 .... 1977-9 .... Division One

After defeating West Ham 3-1 on 20 August 1977, in the first away game of the season, City went an incredible 41 league matches, covering two years, without winning away. They went the rest of that season, the whole of the next and not until the first game, two years after the sequence started, did they manage to win away by beating Everton 4-2 on 18 August 1979. They did win two League Cup games away against lower opposition during this run.

All Away Games Without A Win

25........................... 1930-1 .... Division Three South

City beat Bournemouth on 21 April 1930 and it was not until 19 September 1931 that another away win was achieved, when they beat Clapton Orient 3-1. This run totalled 25 games, including one cup-tie.

League Away Games Without A Defeat

12........................... 1985-6 .... Division Two

City lost at Portsmouth on 31 August 1985 and then remained undefeated on their league travels for 12 games, before losing 1-2 to Wimbledon on 8 March 1986, although they had lost 0-5 to Liverpool in the FA Cup.

All Away Games Without A Defeat

10........................... 1950-1 .... Division Three South

After losing their first away game against Nottingham Forest on 26 August 1950, City went nine league and one FA Cup game away before losing to Leyton Orient on 11 January 1951.

League Away Games Without A Draw

37........................... 1980-1 .... Division One / Two

A 1-1 draw at Manchester City on 1 March 1980 was the last City achieved away in the league until drawing 0-0 with Charlton Athletic on 30 December 1981, a total of 37 games. However, two games were drawn away in the League Cup.

All Away Games Without A Draw

29........................... 1980-1 .... Division One / Two

After a 1-1 draw at Ipswich on 23 September 1980, City did not draw away again until a goalless draw with Charlton Athletic on 30 December 1981.

Successive Away Wins

5............................ 1988-9 .... Division One

The first five away matches of the season were won against: -

Middlesbrough 3-2

Newcastle United 2-0

Derby County 1-0

Manchester United 2-1

Wimbledon 2-0

The sequence ended at Everton, but City still managed a 1-1 draw.

Successive Away Defeats

22............................ 1930-1 .... Division Three South

After drawing 2-2 with Watford on 3 September 1930, City lost their next 21 away league games and 1 cup-tie, before beating Clapton Orient 3-1 on 19 September 1931 to end the year long sequence.

Successive Away League Games Scored

19............................ 1958-9 .... Division Three

After losing 0-2 at Bournemouth on 24 September 1958, City scored in every one of their next 19 away league games before drawing 0-0 against Tranmere Rovers on 31 August 1959.

Away Games Without Conceding A Goal From The Start Of A Season

4............................ 1989-90 .... Division One

This performance equalled a Football League record set by Leeds United.

Best Away Wins (5+)

Score	Opponents	Date	Division/ Cup
8-1	Shrewsbury Town	13.09.52	Division Three South

This record win was even more remarkable in that City lost Don Pickwick with a broken leg before half time although they were leading 4-1 by then. No substitutes were permitted at that time.

Score	Opponents	Date	Division/ Cup
6-1	Bristol City	15.01.49	Division Three South
5-0	Crystal Palace	18.04.51	Division Three South
5-1	Merthyr Town	07.12.29	Division Three South
5-1	Torquay United	30.12.50	Division Three South
5-2	Southampton	21.04.56	Division Three South
5-3	Coventry City	02.02.33	Division Three South
5-4	Shrewsbury Town	09.03.57	Division Three South
5-0	Sheffield Wed.	29.12.01*	Division One
5-3	Burnley	03.04.04**	Division One
5-2	Bury	18.09.65	Division Two
5-2	Sheffield United	22.03.86	Division Two
7-1	Halifax Town	27.11.63	League Cup
5-0	Blackpool	02.10.00**	League Cup
5-1	Stockport County	01.11.72	League Cup
5-3	Bradford City	7.12.95 aet	League Cup
5-1	Everton	25.09.93	Premier

City were a goal down, but came back to win with Efan Ekoku scoring four goals in 28 minutes.

Score	Opponents	Date	Division/ Cup
5-0	Tunbridge Wells R.	17.01.06	FA Cup

This early win in City's history remains as their highest away FA Cup victory.

Score	Opponents	Date	Division/ Cup
5-2	Southend United	30.10.09	Southern
5-2	Reading	26.04.13	Southern

*   *2001*
** *2004*
*** *2000*

Biggest Away Defeats (6+)

Score	Opponents	Date	Division/ Cup
2-10	Swindon Town	05.09.08	Southern

City were 1-6 down at half time at Swindon and finished up with their biggest hiding ever.

0-7	Walsall	13.09.30	Division Three South
1-7	Crystal Palace	30.10.26	Division Three South
1-7	Luton Town	29.03.32	Division Three South
1-7	Torquay Utd.	23.02.57	Division Three South
1-7	Brentford	11.01.58	Division Three South
3-7	Southampton	14.12.57	Division Three South
0-6	Brighton & H.A	03.12.55	Division Three South
0-6	Bristol City	11.10.47	Division Three South
0-6	Shrewsbury Town	29.08.55	Division Three South
1-6	Swindon Town	01.05.22	Division Three South
1-6	Millwall	28.08.26	Division Three South
1-6	Cardiff City	28.12.46	Division Three South
3-6	Plymouth A.	16.01.26	Division Three South
3-6	Brighton & H A	07.09.29	Division Three South
3-6	Walsall	26.01.57	Division Three South
0-7	Sheffield Wed.	17.11.38	Division Two
1-7	Sunderland	20.03.63	Division Two
0-6	Blackburn Rovers	03.12.38	Division Two
0-6	Millwall	04.03.39	Division Two
0-6	Crystal Palace	16.04.68	Division Two
2-6	Chesterfield	02.10.37	Division Two
1-7	Blackburn Rovers	03.10.92	Premier

City were top of the League prior to the Blackburn match.

0-6	Liverpool	21.02.79	Division One
1-6	Middlesbrough.	09.10.80	Division One
1-6	Port Vale	21.12.96	Division One
2-6	Liverpool	01.11.86	Division One

Score	Opponents	Date	Division/ Cup
0-6	Luton Town	10-12.27	FA Cup
0-6	Manchester City	24.01.81	FA Cup

The 0-6 loss against Manchester City was in the middle of seven successive defeats

1-6	Manchester City	29.09.75	League Cup

The League Cup second replay against Manchester City was played on neutral territory at Stamford Bridge, Chelsea

1-7	Reading	21.11.08	Southern
1-7	Swindon Town	28.12.09	Southern
0-6	Crystal Palace	28.10.11	Southern
1-6	West Ham United	10.02.06	Southern

Biggest Away Draws

4-4	Newport County	23.11.29	Division Three South
4-4	Mansfield Town	22.03.47	Division Three South
4-4	Reading	27.03.54	Division Three South
4-4	Burnley	13.09.75	Division One
4-4	Charlton Athletic	22.02.97	Division Two
4-4	Rotherham United	17.01.04*	Division One

*2004

BADGES

The original badge design, taken from the City of Norwich crest, depicting a castle with lion passant underneath, had become outdated for the Football Club in the 1970's. A competition was launched in 1972 to find a more modern design. This resulted in the current version of a canary perched on a ball.

On 24 October 1959, British Rail presented City with the green and yellow nameplate from the 1933 built locomotive named "Norwich City", one of many named

after football clubs at the time. This was in recognition of their great cup run earlier in the year.

The curved plate, above a football, has been restored and given pride of place over the entrance to the players' tunnel, in the City Stand at Carrow Road .

Iwan Roberts posing in front of the Norwich City nameplate after signing for the club in 1997.

BARCLAY

The Carrow Road ground was built in 1935 with a seated Main Stand and an open terrace on the other three sides. The Barclay Stand became the first terrace to be covered in 1937, named after Captain Evelyn Barclay, a vice president of the club, who helped finance the project. It remained the only covered terrace until 1960. Initially its capacity was as high as 10,000, but with the implementation of stricter safety regulations it was gradually reduced. During its lifetime it has accommodated the more vociferous supporters. Away fans were also housed there, with segregation introduced in the 1970's. The initial division soon proved inadequate.

The escalating violence required the installation of high fences, both between rival supporters and at the front to prevent pitch invasions. A no-mans pen was also established between home and away supporters to keep warring fans apart.

One incident after a City win, saw Manchester United fans climbing on to, and pulling tiles off. the roof to hurl at City supporters and police.

Coins and missiles were regularly thrown between rival supporters, but in February 1982, after a match against Queens Park Rangers in which the referee was hit by a cigarette lighter, an extra mesh net was installed behind the goal for the remainder of the season to prevent objects from being thrown on to the pitch.

The infamous Barclay fences.

Opinion started to change following the Hillsborough disaster and the Taylor Report, when first perimeter fencing was removed and then all seater stadia were demanded.

A new all seated Barclay Stand was built in 1992 at a reported cost of £2.8m with capacity of around 6,000. The stand housed players' lounges, pressroom, police control room with cameras and a broadcasting room as well as other large lounge areas. A restaurant and viewing area was provided between the two tiers and a connecting corner infill built in 1993, adding a further 650 seats.

With catering becoming more profitable, particularly after Delia Smith's influence, extra kitchen space was added to the back of the stand in 2000 to make the capacity of the restaurant the largest in the City. The facilities in the Stand will provide further use, when a proposed hotel is built in the corner between the Barclay and Jarrold Stands in 2005.

BEST PERFORMANCE AGAINST OTHER CLUBS

Successive Home Wins

Opponents	Number	Seasons	
Crystal Palace	11	1947-58	
Bolton Wanderers	10	1962-75	includes Cup
Watford	8	1949-56	includes Cup
Northampton Town	7	1905-12	
Leyton Orient	7	1929-48	
Shrewsbury Town	7	1951-58	
Southampton	7	1934-55	
Walsall	7	1949-56	

Successive Away Wins

Opponents	Number	Seasons
Crystal Palace	5	1990-96
Bournemouth	4	1933-49
Sunderland	4	1985-98
Derby County	4	1981-90

Without a Home Defeat

Opponents	Number	Seasons	
Watford	21	1905-30	
Gillingham	19	1905-28	

as (New Brompton) 1905-12

Leyton Orient	17	1929-62	
Cardiff City	16	1913-70	includes Cup
West Ham United	16	1973-	

Without a Home Defeat (continued)

Newport County .... 15 .... 1919-34 .... includes Cup
Bristol City 14 1965-
Grimsby Town 14 1920-
Merthyr Town 13 1912-30
Bristol Rovers .... 13 .... 1905-21 .... includes Cup
Exeter City 12 1909-24
Brighton & H.A 12 1952-86
Nottingham Forest 12 1934-81
Swindon Town .... 12 .... 1957-99 .... League only
Q.P.R 12 1957-79

Without an Away Defeat

Opponents	Number	Seasons	
Derby County .... 9 .... 1976-91 .... League only
Huddersfield Town 7 1960-67

Best Overall League Record Against Other Clubs

Club		Won	Drew	Lost
Merthyr Town	H	9	4	0
	A	5	5	3
	TOTAL	14	9	3
Shrewsbury Town	H	9	1	0
	A	6	1	3
	TOTAL	15	2	3
Grimsby Town	H	8	5	0
	A	5	4	4
	TOTAL	13	9	4
Leyton Orient	H	18	5	1
	A	7	7	10
	TOTAL	25	12	11
Derby County	H	16	3	5
	A	6	11	7
	TOTAL	22	14	12
Cardiff City	H	14	5	1
	A	6	2	12
	TOTAL	20	7	13

Club		Won	Drew	Lost
Bristol City	H	15	10	3
	A	13	5	10
	TOTAL	28	15	13
Watford	H	30	15	7
	A	12	19	21
	TOTAL	42	34	28

BOGEY SIDES

Successive Away Defeats

Opponents	Number	Seasons	
Coventry City	20	1937-80	includes Cup
Crystal Palace	14	1911-27	League only
Plymouth Argyle	9	1905-14	
Gillingham	8	1921-29	

Successive Home Defeats

Opponents	Number	Seasons	
Manchester United	6	1991-	includes Cup
Bournemouth	4	1953-57	
Charlton Athletic	4	1995-	

Without an Away Win

Opponents	Number	Seasons	
Northampton Town	25	1909-50	
Coventry City	22	1933-80	includes Cup
Plymouth Argyle	21	1905-30	
Manchester City	21	1965-98	includes Cup
Southampton	19	1956-85	
West Ham United	17	1905-74	
Brighton & H.A.	16	1922-49	includes Cup

Without a Home Win

Opponents	Number	Seasons	
Arsenal	10	1986-	includes Cup
Manchester City	10	1965-80	includes Cup
Bournemouth	9	1952-	includes Cup
Huddersfield Town	8	1961-68	includes Cup

Successive Away Draws

Opponents	Number	Seasons
Huddersfield Town	6	1960-66

Worst Overall League Record Against Other Clubs

Club		Won	Drew	Lost
Manchester City	H	5	13	6
	A	2	5	17
	TOTAL	7	18	23
Wolves	H	6	6	6
	A	1	3	14
	TOTAL	7	9	20
Wimbledon	H	5	2	7
	A	3	3	8
	TOTAL	8	5	15
Coventry City	H	22	19	9
	A	4	8	38
	TOTAL	26	27	47
Manchester Utd.	H	6	6	12
	A	3	6	15
	TOTAL	9	12	27
Liverpool	H	7	7	8
	A	4	4	14
	TOTAL	11	11	22

BROADCAST

The first radio second half commentary involving City was at Brentford on 3 September 1955 in a Division Three South game, which they won 2-1.

Norwich set up their own radio station, 'Radio Canary' on 1 October 1994 commencing with the home match against Blackburn Rovers. This was only the third one in the country at the time and was situated in a purpose built studio in the corner infill between the City and Barclay Stands. It had a transmission range of five to ten miles and broadcast at all home matches, from three hours before kick off until an hour after the end of the match. Full match commentary, interviews and discussions featured, but the main innovation was the live broadcast of the after match managers' press conference, believed to be the first radio station to do so. It was dissolved in 1996 and local radio stations filled the void with regular commentaries by Roy Waller of Radio Norfolk.

Radio Norfolk commentator Roy Waller.

BROTHERS

There have been six sets of brothers who have played for City, but only the Palmers, Lambertons and Duncans played together in the first team.

The most famous brothers were Justin and John Fashanu. Both were 'Dr Barnardo's Boys', brought up by foster parents near Attleborough. Justin was an effervescent character who played regularly in the first team from 18 years of age. He was made instantly famous by scoring a 'Goal of the Season' on 'Match of the Day' in 1981 and prompted Nottingham Forest to buy him for £1m. His career floundered after this move and sadly he took his own life in 1998.

His younger brother John didn't show as much promise at Norwich and was allowed to leave for Lincoln City for £15,000. He soon emerged as an even more flamboyant character than his brother and moved on to Millwall and Wimbledon to outshine Justin. He won an FA Cup medal, was capped by England, and became well known on TV as host of the "Gladiators" show.

John Fashanu signing for the club, watched by brother Justin and secretary Bert Westwood.

Brothers		Seasons	Appearances	Goals
Rowland	Palmer	1902-04	8	1
James	Palmer	1903-04	15	4
James	Lamberton	1906-07	6	0
George	Lamberton	1906-08	47	14
Jim	Bauchop	1907-09	24	12
Bill	Bauchop	1912-13	36	1
Bill	Duncan	1920	2	0
John	Duncan	1920	4	0
Reg	Cropper	1926-28	53	18
Arthur	Cropper	1928-30	23	3
Justin	Fashanu	1979-81	103	40
John	Fashanu	1981-82	7	1

CAPS

PLAYERS CAPPED WHILST AT NORWICH

FULL INTERNATIONAL CAPS

Most Capped Player

Mark Bowen ....Wales 1988-96 35

City's most capped player, Mark Bowen

First Full Cap

Mick O'Brien .... Eire .... 1930 .... v Belgium

First Full English Cap

Phil Boyer .... England .... 1976 .... v Wales

Caps won to July 2004

Country	Player	Caps	Years
England	Dave Watson	6	1984-6
	Chris Woods	4	1985-6
	Mark Barham	2	1983
	Kevin Reeves	1	1980
	Phil Boyer	1	1976
Scotland	Ted MacDougall	7	1975-6
	Bryan Gunn	6	1990-3
	Robert Fleck	4	1990-2
	Gary Holt	4	2002-
	Malky Mackay	3	2004-
	Jimmy Bone	3	1972-3
Northern Ireland	Martin O'Neill	18	1981-3
	Phil Mulryne	15	1999-
	Paul McVeigh	12	2002-
	Adrian Coote	6	1999-2000
	Jimmy Hill	4	1959-62
	Owen Madden	1	1938
Wales	Mark Bowen	35	1988-97
	David Phillips	24	1989-93
	Craig Bellamy	9	1998-2001
	Iwan Roberts	8	2000-2
	David Jones	8	1976-80
	Ron Davies	5	1964-6
	David Williams	5	1986-7
	Noel Kinsey	4	1951-2
	Trevor Hockey	4	1973
	Malcolm Allen	3	1989-90

Country	Player	Caps	Years
Wales (cont)	Ollie Burton	2	1963
	Chris Llewellyn	2	1998
Eire	Andy Townsend	17	1989-90
	Keith O'Neill	11	1996-9
	John Gavin	5	1950-7
	John Devine	5	1983-5
	Mick O'Brien	1	1930
Norway	Aage Hareide	4	1983
Canada	Jim Brennan	3	2004
Nigeria	Efan Ekoku	1	1994

Under 21/23 Caps

England	Chris Sutton	13	1993-4
	Kevin Reeves*	9	1978-80
	Dave Watson*	7	1980-1
	Darren Eadie	7	1994-8
	Justin Fashanu	6	1980-1
	Dale Gordon	4	1987
	Robert Rosario	4	1987
	Tim Sherwood	4	1990
	Daryl Sutch	4	1992-3
	Andy Marshall	4	1995-7
	Ian Henderson	2	2003-
	Louis Donowa	3	1985
	Chris Woods*	1	1984
	Lee Marshall	1	1999
Northern Ireland	Adrian Coote*	12	1998-2000
	Phil Mulryne*	2	1999
Scotland	Jimmy Bone*	5	1972-3
	Robert Fleck*	3	1988-9
	Paul Dalglish	3	2000

Country	Player	Caps	Years
Eire	Keith O'Neill*	1	1996
	Lee Power**	13	1991-4
Wales	Chris Llewellyn*	14	1998-2000
	Craig Bellamy*	8	1996-9
	Ron Davies*	3	1964-5
	Ollie Burton*	2	1963
	Ian Davies	1	1978
	Mark Walton	1	1981

Indicates also gained a full international cap
*** Lee Power holds the record for Eire under 21 caps*

CAPTAINS

FIRST OCCASION

Match

Bob Collinson, who had just joined City from local club C.E.Y.M.S, was captain in City's first ever match on 29 September 1902 in the FA Cup tie against Lowestoft Town. He also captained the side in their first Norfolk and Suffolk League match against Beccles Caxton.

Southern League

In their first professional match in the Southern League on 2 September 1905 against Plymouth Argyle, **Jimmy McEwan** was captain.

Football League

George "Pompey" Martin had the honour of captaining City on the Club's Football League debut in Division Three South. This was also against Plymouth Argyle on 27 August 1921.

Trophy Winner

Stan Ramsay was the first City captain to receive a trophy when they became champions of Division Three South in 1935.

Second Division

Tom Halliday was captain in City's first Second Division game against West Ham United on 31 August 1935, which was also the first game at Carrow Road.

Division One and Wembley

Duncan Forbes was captain in City's first game in Division One on 12 August 1972 against Everton. He was also the first City captain to receive the Second Division trophy in April 1972 and the first to captain City at Wembley when they reached the League Cup final in 1973.

Duncan Forbes with the Division Two trophy in 1972.

First Success at Wembley

Dave Watson was captain when City won the League Cup (Milk Cup) at Wembley in 1985.

Premier League

Ian Butterworth captained City in their first match in the Premier League against Arsenal on 15 August 1992.

Europe

John Polston was captain in City's first ever European match against Vitesse Arnhem on 15 September 1993.

Longest Reigning Captain

Ron Ashman first captained the side on 5 May 1951 against Crystal Palace, although he did not become first choice for the role until the 1954-5 season. He was captain for the last time on 19 December 1963 in his final match at Southampton.

Ron had been captain on 472 occasions in his 662 appearances. During this time City had won promotion to Division Two, had their most famous Cup run in 1959 and won the League Cup for the first time in 1962. He later became manager in 1963.

CARROW ROAD

The site for the present ground was offered to the club by J & J Colman Ltd in June 1935. The name Carrow was taken from the ancient Carrow Abbey that stood on the riverbank. Work commenced on June 11 and the ground was completed on 17 August in an incredible 82 days at a cost of £25,962.

A crowd of 29,779 saw the first game at home to West Ham United on 31 August 1935 when City won 4-3.

Floodlights were installed in 1956 and the ground was bought outright from the new owners, Boulton & Paul in May 1971 and initially valued at £136,000. Purchase of the car park followed in 1993 together with land at the rear of the South Stand. This enabled further development to be planned, in bringing the stadium up to the modern requirements.

During the years improvements were made and new stands were built to comply with the all seater needs. This commenced with the Norwich & Peterborough double tier stand at a reported cost of £1.7m replacing the old River End open terrace in 1979.

The Geoffrey Watling City Stand was built at a reported cost of £1m to replace the old Main Stand, destroyed by fire in 1984 and the Barclay Stand (£2.8m) replacing the old covered terrace in 1993.

Under-soil heating was added in 1990, a disabled stand in 1994 and extensive restaurant facilities in 2000/1.

The most recent development has been the erection of a new 8,000 seater (Jarrold) stand to replace the old South Stand in 2004. The corner infill, incorporating disabled facilities, is to be added in 2004/5. This was financed by sale of land for housing development at the adjacent Riverside complex.

Major improvements were made to the pitch during the summer 2004, to alleviate problems with drainage and wear. Under-soil heating was re-installed, the pitch re-sown with a mixture of artificial and natural material and re-positioned more centrally between the stands. Additionally, eight pits were created to allow cameramen to operate without impeding supporters' views.

The building of a top class hotel in the corner of the Barclay Stand in the near future will end the immediate projects and allow the club to move forward with a more satisfactory capacity of over 25,000.

CHAIRMAN

Chairman		Years
Robert	Webster	1902
Wilfred	Burgess	1905
John	Pyke	1907
William	Blyth	1917
Ernest	Morse	1920
William	Hurrell	1931
James	Wright	1935
James	Hanley	1948
Geoffrey	Watling	1957
Arthur	South	1973
The	Trust	1985
Robert	Chase	1986
Barry	Lockwood	1996
Bob	Cooper	1998
Roger	Mumby	2001-

In 1985 discord arose amongst the directors over the cost and plans for a new City Stand. The board resigned en-bloc and for two months, from 2 November, the reins were taken over by members of the "Trust", which had been formed following the crisis days of 1956. During the "Trust's" two month reign under the chairmanship of James Alston, all games were won. In January 1986 they handed over to a new board, chaired by Robert Chase.

The most unpopular chairman in the Club's history was probably Robert Chase. The club did enjoy success during his reign and he maximised the grants on offer at the time, to considerably progress ground development. However, his policy of selling players and spending money on property, angered many supporters. The halcyon days of Europe were replaced with relegation and his public disagreements, with first Mike Walker and then Martin O'Neill, caused unrest. Pressure groups tried to force Chase off the board, but he remained in control until the club nearly went bankrupt and were forced to sell Ashley Ward and Jon Newsome in the same week. Chase eventually sold his 34% shareholding in 1996 to Geoffrey Watling who then instigated a whole new board, including Delia Smith and her husband Michael Wyn Jones.

The longest serving chairman was Geoffrey Watling who held office for 16 years from 1957-73.

CITY STAND

In 1984 the Main Stand was gutted by fire. This was in some ways fortuitous as the insurance payout enabled a new City Stand to be constructed. Built at a reported cost of £1m, it was generously tiered with an uninterrupted view, contained a viewing gallery and lounges and was unique at the time in not having turnstiles. However, the total capacity of the stand was just over 3,000, until corner infills were added, to provide a further 1,300 seats. Although well equipped, the stand has always been on the small side and is now dwarfed by the surrounding larger stands. However, there is capability to add a top tier if required, as the foundations allowed for potential expansion and with traffic having now been routed away from the immediate vicinity of the ground, it may be a feasible proposition in the future if demand requires.

The City Stand was officially opened by the Duchess of Kent, on 14 February 1987, who then stayed to watch the 1-1 drawn game with Manchester City

CLUBS

League Clubs Never Played in any Competition to Aug 2004

Boston United   Kidderminster Harriers   Macclesfield Town
Rushden & Diamonds

Clubs Played Most Often

Club	League	Cup
Q.P.R	122	6
Crystal Palace	110	4
Watford	104	3
Coventry City	100	9
Swindon Town	98	9
Southampton	98	8
Millwall	88	6
Brighton & H A	86	14

Clubs Played Most Often in Cup Competitions

Ipswich Town	15	3 FA, 8 League, 2 Texaco, 1 Simod, 1 Zenith Data
Brighton & H.A.	14	11 FA, 2 League and 1 Zenith Data
Sunderland	12	7 FA, 5 League Cup

Non League Clubs Played in Cup since City joined the Football League

Bath City	1934-5	H	2-0
Bedford Town	1956-7	H	2-4
Chatham	1926-7	H	5-0
	1928-9	H	6-1
Corinthians	1928-9	H	0-5
Dagenham & Redbridge	2002-3	H	1-0
Dorchester Town	1955-6	H	4-0
Folkestone Town	1923-4	A	3-2
	1924-5	A	2-0
	1932-3	A	0-1

Gloucester City .... 1949-50 .... A .. 3-2
Hastings United .... 1953-4 .... A .. 3-3 .... H .. 3-0
Headington United .... 1954-5 .... H .. 4-2
Ilford .... 1922-3 .... H .. 5-1
                                        1958-9 .... H .. 3-1
Merthyr Tydfil .... 1947-8 .... H .. 3-0
Metrogas .... 1921-2 .... A .. 2-1
Oxford City .... 1921-2 .... A .. 1-1 .... H .. 3-0
Poole .... 1927-8 .... A .. 1-1 .... H .. 5-0
Redhill .... 1957-8 .... H .. 6-1
Rhyl .... 1950-1 .... A .. 1-0
Sutton United .... 1988-9 .... H .. 8-0
Tonbridge .... 1952-3 .... A .. 2-2 .... H .. 1-0
Wellington Town .... 1948-9 .... H .. 1-0
Wimbledon .... 1931-2 .... A .. 3-1
Yeovil Town .... 1953-4 .... A .. 2-0
                                        1979-80 .... A .. 3-0

CONSECUTIVE SEQUENCES

Successive League Wins

10 .... 1985-6 .... Division Two

From 23 November 1985 beginning with a 3-2 victory over Grimsby Town, until 1 Februray 1986, when they drew 2-2 with Barnsley, City registered ten successive league wins. However, they did lose in the FA Cup to Liverpool during this run.

Seq	Date	Opponents		Result		Pos	Attendance
1	Nov.23	Grimsby Town	H	3-2	W	5	12,108
2	Nov.30	Leeds United	A	2-0	W	4	11,480
3	Dec.7	Blackburn Rovers	H	3-0	W	3	12,820
4	Dec.14	Oldham Athletic	A	3-1	W	1	3,949
5	Dec.21	Millwall	H	6-1	W	1	12,349
6	Dec.26	Charlton Athletic	H	3-1	W	1	17,984

Seq	Date	Opponents		Result		Pos	Attendance
7	Jan.1	Fulham	A	1-0	W	1	7,463
8	Jan.11	Middlesbrough	H	2-0	W	1	13,730
9	Jan.18	Portsmouth	H	2-0	W	1	20,129
10	Jan.25	Crystal Palace	A	2-1	W	1	8,369
	Feb.1	*Barnsley*	*A*	*2-2*	*D*	*1*	*5,608*

Italics shows end of sequence.

Successive Wins in all Games

7...1950 .... Division Three South

City won five league games and two FA Cup ties between 4 November and 23 December 1950, before drawing 1-1 with Brighton and Hove Albion on Boxing Day.

Successive Draws

7...1978-9,1994....................... Division One, Premier

City have twice drawn seven successive games. Once, from 9 December 1978 until 2 February 1979, when they then crashed 0-6 at Liverpool and again when they drew seven games from 15 January 1994, before losing 1-3 at Wimbledon on 5 March 1994.

Successive Defeats

7...1957 .... Division Three South
7...1981 .... Division One
7...1995 .... Premier

From 12 January 1957, when they lost 1-2 at home to QPR, City then lost the next six games before beating Millwall 2-0 on 2 March 1957. During that run they conceded 29 goals.

From 10 January to 28 February 1981, City lost six league games and one FA Cup tie 0-6. From 1 April to 6 May 1995, City lost seven league games on the trot on their way to relegation. They managed to draw their final game of the season against Aston Villa.

CONSECUTIVE SEQUENCES

Successive Games Scored

31...................................1963-4................................ Division Two

After losing their first home game 0-1 to Bury on 28 August 1963, City then went 31 league and cup games continuously scoring, until a 0-4 defeat at Rotherham United on 1 February 1964.

Without a Win

26...................................1956-7................................ Division Three South

After beating Plymouth Argyle 3-0 on 15 September 1956, City did not win again for 25 League games and one in the FA Cup, until they beat Millwall on 2 March 1957.

Without a Defeat

23...................................1950-1................................ Division Three South

After losing 2-4 to Nottingham Forest, City then went 20 league and three cup games before losing 1-3 to Leyton Orient on 11 January 1951.

Without a Draw

18...................................1952................................ Division Three South

After drawing 2-2 with Newport County on 22 March 1952, City then went 18 games before drawing 1-1 at Crystal Palace on 24 September 1952.

Without a Defeat From the Start of Season

15...................................1971................................ Division Two

City started their promotion season 1971-2 undefeated for 13 league and two League Cup games before losing to fellow contenders Millwall 1-2. They had won eight and drawn five games.

Successive League Games Scored From the Start of Season

18...................................1992................................ Premier

In the first Premier League season, City scored in each one of their first 18 games before losing 0-1 to Manchester United on 12 December 1992. During that run they scored 34 goals.

Without Scoring

5...............................1992............................... Premier

Surprisingly, this sequence immediately followed the successive scoring above from 12 December 1992, ending with a 1-1 draw against Coventry City on 16 January 1993. Two of the games were drawn.

CRISIS

In 1917 the Club went into voluntary liquidation with debts of over £7,000. This wasn't surprising with the effect of wartime. After the war in 1919, a new Company was formed with William Blyth as chairman and Major Frank Buckley was appointed manager.

During the 1956-7 season, City faced a serious financial crisis, which was further exacerbated by the purchase of floodlights at a cost of £8,000. A public appeal was launched on 17 January to raise £25,000. The situation worsened in February 1957, with gates at an all time low and during a record run of games without victory, including recent home defeats of 3-6 and 2-5, the club was unable to pay the players wages. The Lord Mayor, Arthur South, was asked to promote the public appeal and the Norfolk News Company stepped in to pay the £500 outstanding wage bill. The club was rocked and it was hoped that the fund would raise the necessary money. An appeal friendly against King's Lynn attracted a crowd of 8,000, but only raised £588. Eventually, around £23,000 was raised from supporters rallying round. The board resigned en bloc, until a new one was elected with Geoffrey Watling as chairman. Local stalwarts formed a "Trust" with a substantial shareholding to ensure the future stability of the club. The club finished bottom of the Football League, but were successfully re-elected.

In 1996, following the loss of Premiership status the previous year, City found themselves struggling, both on the field and financially. The departure of manager Martin O'Neill, exits from both Cups, including a 1-2 home defeat by lowly Brentford, together with a fall down the table, brought demonstrations at each game from angry fans. On 14 March 1996 City were forced to sell off their two most prized assets, Jon Newsome and Ashley Ward, for a combined transfer of £2.7m to reduce their debts and stave off bankruptcy. Further cuts were made to non-playing staff and the mood amongst the supporters was sombre.

Mounted Police were also a feature at games and once had to charge down Carrow Road to disperse angry supporters. With pressure ever mounting Chase finally sold his shares on 2 May 1996 to Geoffrey Watling. The immediate crisis had come to an end and a new board, including Delia Smith, joined the club and harmony with the supporters was gradually restored.

Mounted police present at City games during the supporters' unrest in 1996

DEBUTS

Hat Trick on Debut

Scorer	Opponents	Date	Result
Percy Gooch	Lowestoft Town. H	19.09.03*	4-1
Roy Hollis	Q.P.R H	21.04.48	5-2
Laurie Sheffield	Derby County .... H	12.11.66	4-1

1903

David Hodgson	Millwall H	29.10.86	4-1

Although not on his actual debut, Dave Hodgson scored a hat trick on his full debut after making two substitute appearances previously.

Roy Hollis scored a hat trick on his debut.

DEBUTS

Quickest Goal on Debut

Marc Libbra.....................Manchester City. H .... 18.09.01**.........2-0

Marc Libbra scored in 19 seconds after coming on as substitute in the 74th minute.

Alf Moule.....................Crystal Palace ....H .... 27.08.27..............4-1

David Phillips...................Sheffield Wed.....A .... 19.08.89..............2-0

Both scored in the second minute, Alf Moule was 33 and had just been signed from Millwall. David Phillips scored in the first match of the season after being signed from Coventry City.

Own Goal on Debut

Stan Ramsay ....Watford..............H .... 27.08.32..............1-2

David Jones ....Newcastle Utd....A .... 18.10.75..............2-5

Steve Bruce.....................Liverpool. ....H .... 25.08.84..............3-3

Tony Spearing...................Tottenham H......A .... 12.05.84..............0-2

Stan Ramsay and Steve Bruce both conceded own goals in the first minute of their City debuts. Tony Spearing conceded a goal in the 78th minute of his first game. David Jones conceded a last minute own goal at Newcastle in a 2-5 defeat.

Sent Off

Mark Halsey ....Newcastle Utd....A .... 26.04.78..............2-2

Karl Simpson ....Torquay Utd.......H .... 20.09.95..............6-1

Both Mark Halsey and Karl Simpson were sent off in the 78th minute of their debuts for second bookable offences. The crowd at Newcastle was just 7,180, as a poor season in which they were relegated drew to a close.

Youngest

Ryan Jarvis.....................Walsall..............A .... 26.04.03***....... 0-0

Ryan Jarvis became the youngest player to make his debut for City, as a substitute in the 73rd minute at Walsall. He was 16 years 282 days.

Ken Shaw was only 16 years and one day old when he played against an RAF XI during wartime football in 1942.

** *2001* *** *2003*

DEFEATS

Most Defeats in a Season

Defeats	Season	Division
24	1930-1, 1938-9, 1946-7	Division Three South
24	1938-9	Division Two
21	1972-3	Division One
19	1994-5	Premier

Least Defeats in a Season

6	1933-4	Division Three South
6	1971-2	Division Two
8	1986-7, 2003-4	Division One
12	1992-3	Premier

Biggest Defeat Against each Club in terms of Goal Difference

Where biggest defeat was on more than two occasions these are not listed, but instead marked with the number of instances.

Only League and FA and Football League Cup results included (See section - Minor Cups)

In some cases a club's full name has had to be abbreviated to fit table.

	Home			Away			Cup FA / FL			
Aberdare	1-4	1922-3	D3	1-3	1925-6	D3				
Accrington	2-4	1958-9	D3							
Aldershot	1-3	1957-8	D3	1-4	1948-9	D3				
					1954-5	D3				
Arsenal	0-4	1973-4	D1	0-5	1988-9	D1	0-5	H	1951-2	FA
Aston Villa	1-4	1974-5	D2	0-3	1936-7	D2	1-4	A	1962-3	FL
					1977-8	D1				
Barnsley	0-1	1936-7	D2	0-2	1959-0	D3	1-2	H	1921-2	FA
Bedford T.							2-4	H	1956-7	FA
Birmingham	1-2	1972-3	D1	0-4	*3 Occ*		1-2	A	1995-6	FA
Blackburn	0-2	1999-0	D1	1-7	1992-3	PR	1-4	A	1911-2	FA
Blackpool	1-2	1936-7	D2	1-2	*4 Occ*		0-2	A	1961-2	FL
		1967-8	D2							
Bolton W.	2-3	1934-5	D2	2-5	1964-5	D2	0-2	H	1922-3	FA

DEFEATS

	Home			Away			Cup FA / FL			
Bourn'm'th	1-6	1946-7	D3	1-4	1930-1	D3				
Bradford C	1-4	2001-2	D1	0-2	1936-7	D2	0-2	N	1914-5	FA
Bradford P	1-3	1938-9	D2	0-3	1937-8	D2				
					1938-9	D2				
Brentford	0-2	1922-3	D3	1-7	1957-8	D3	1-4	A	1931-2	FA
Brighton	0-2	1926-7	D3	0-6	1955-6	D3	1-5	A	1954-5	FA
Bristol City	1-3	1925-6	D3	0-6	1947-8	D3	0-2	H	1908-9	FA
Bristol Rov	1-5	1947-8	D3	1-5	1949-0	D3	1-3	A	1963-4	FA
Burnley	2-3	2000-1	D1	0-3	3 Occ	D2	1-3	A	1977-8	FL
Bury	1-2	1937-8	D2	2-4	1963-4	D2				
Cardiff City	1-2	1970-1	D2	1-6	1946-7	D3				
Carlisle Utd				1-4	1965-6	D2				
Charlton A.	0-4	1997-8	D1	1-4	1935-6	D2				
Chelsea	1-3	1990-1	D1	0-3	1973-4	D1	0-4	A	2001-2	FA
Cheltenham							0-3	H	2002-3	FL
Chesterfield				2-6	1937-8	D2				
Colchester	0-2	1954-5	D3	0-3	1959-0	D3				
Corinthians							0-5	H	1929-0	FA
Coventry C.	1-4	1959-0	D3	1-4	1978-9	D1	1-3	H	1999-0	FA
Crewe A.	0-2	1997-8	D1	2-3	1998-9	D1				
Croydon C				1-4	1914-5	D3				
Crystal Pal	0-3	1990-1	D1	1-7	1926-7	D3	0-3	A	1933-4	FA
Darlington							0-5	A	1919-0	FA
Derby Co.	1-4	1968-9	D2	0-3	1962-3	D2	0-3	A	2000-1	FL
Doncaster R				0-3	1935-6	D2				
Everton	0-3	1987-8	D1	0-4	1986-7	D1	0-5	A	1994-5	FA
Exeter C.	1-3	1946-7	D3	1-4	1948-9	D3				
Folkestone							0-1	A	1932-3	FA
Fulham	0-4	1929-0	D3	0-4	1931-2	D3	0-4	H	1999-0	FA
					1974-5	D2				
Gillingham	1-3	1956-7	D3	0-5	1922-3	D3				
Grays				2-3	1904-5	SN				
Grimsby T				1-3	1963-4	D2	0-3	A	1997-8	FA
Hudder'fi'ld	0-2	1964-5	D2	0-2	1967-8	D2	0-1	H	1967-8	FL
Hull City	0-2	1970-1	D2	0-5	1966-7	D2	0-3	H	1971-2	FA
Ipswich T	1-5	1947-8	D3	0-5	3 Occs	D3	1-3	H	1980-1	FL
Leeds Utd.	2-3	1980-1	D1	0-3	1962-3	D2	0-5	N	1972-3	FA

DEFEATS

	Home			Away			Cup FA / FL			
Leicester C.	1-3	1984-5	D1	0-3	1969-0	D2	0-3	A	1978-9	FA
					1973-4	D1				
Leyton				0-2	1907-8	SN				
Leyton O	1-2	1963-4	D2	0-3	1946-7	D3	0-1	H	1977-8	FA
Liverpool	1-4	1978-9	D1	0-6	1978-9	D1	0-5	A	1985-6	FA
Lowestoft T							0-5	A	1902-3	FA
Luton Town	0-4	1937-8	D2	1-7	1931-2	D3	0-6	A	1927-8	FA
		1961-2	D2							
Man. City	1-3	1977-8	D1	0-5	1963-4	D2	0-6	A	1980-1	FA
Man Utd.	0-3	1990-1	D1	0-5	1934-5	D2	0-3	A	1905-6	FA
					1979-0	D1				
Mansfield T				2-5	1931-2	D3				
Merthyr Tn.				0-3	1921-2	D3				
Middlesbro'	1-3	1997-8	D1	1-6	1980-1	D1	0-2	A	1990-1	FL
Millwall	0-3	1968-9	D2	0-6	1938-9	D2				
Newcastle	1-5	1936-7	D2	1-5	1976-7	D1				
Newport Co	2-3	1955-6	D3	2-5	1919-0	SN				
Northamptn	1-4	1923-4	D3	0-4	1929-0	D3	0-1	A	2003-4	FL
Nottm Forst	2-6	1990-1	D1	0-5	1984-5	D1	0-1	A	1964-5	FA
							0-1	H	1990-1	FA
Notts Co	1-2	1982-3	D1	0-5	1949-0	D3	0-4	A	1924-5	FA
Oldham A.	1-2	1981-2	D2	2-4	1934-5	D2				
		1991-2	D1							
Oxford Utd	1-3	1998-9	D1	0-3	1987-8	D1	1-3	A	1985-6	FL
Plymouth A	0-3	1925-6	D3	0-5	1924-5	D3				
Port Vale	3-4	1998-9	D1	1-6	1996-7	D1				
Portsmouth	1-3	1965-6	D2	2-5	1968-9	D2	0-2	H	1949-0	FA
Preston NE	1-3	1967-8	D2	0-4	2001-2	D1				
Q.P.R.	0-3	1993-4	D2	2-5	1933-4	D3	0-3	A	1909-0	FA
Reading	2-5	1956-7	D3	1-7	1908-9	SN	1-2	A	1959-0	FA
Rotherham	1-2	1965-6	D2	0-4	1963-4	D2				
United					1964-5	D2				
Scunthorpe	0-1	1960-1	D2	1-3	1962-3	D2				
Sheff. Utd	1-3	1975-6	D1	0-4	1938-9	D2	1-3	A	1961-2	FA
Sheff. Wed	0-3	1987-8	D1	0-7	1938-9	D2	1-4	A	1998-9	FA
Shrewsbury				0-6	1955-6	D3	0-1	A	1960-1	FL
Southmptn	1-4	1956-7	D3	3-7	1957-8	D3	0-4	H	1968-9	FL

DEFEATS

	Home			Away			Cup		FA / FL	
Southend U.	1-5	1946-7	D3	2-5	1953-4	D3				
					1957-8	D3				
Stockport C.	1-3	1958-9	D3	1-2	2001-2	D1				
Stoke City	0-1	1975-6	D1	0-3	1962-3	D2	1-2	A	1965-6	FL
Sunderland	1-3	1984-5	D1	1-7	1962-3	D2	2-4	A	1955-6	FA
Swansea	1-4	1922-3	D3	0-4	1982-3	D2	0-1	A	1994-5	FL
Swindon T.	1-5	1929-0	D3	2–10	1908-9	SN	0-2	H	1987-8	FA
Thames				0-2	1930-1	D2				
Torquay U.	0-2	1933-4	D3	1-7	1956-7	D3	1-3	A	1948-9	FA
Tottenham	1-3	1976-7	D1	1-5	1992-3	PR	0-2	H	1992-3	FA
Tranmere	0-2	1997-8	D1	1-3	1996-7	D1				
Walsall	1-4	1927-8	D3	0-7	1930-1	D3	2-3	A	1947-8	FA
Watford	1-3	1986-7	D1	1-4	1946-7	D3				
W.B.A	2-4	1996-7	D1	1-5	1996-7	D1	0-3	A	1968-9	FA
West Ham	2-6	1938-9	D2	1-6	1905-6	SN	1-2	A	1984-5	FA
Wigan Ath.							0-1	A	1986-7	FA
Wimbledon	0-4	1990-1	D1	0-3	1992-3	PR				
Wolves	0-3	1965-6	D2	0-5	1997-8	D2	1-5	A	1970-1	FA
		2002-3	D1							
Workington							0-3	A	1964-5	FL
Wrexham							1-2	H	1969-0	FA
York City	2-3	1974-5	D2	0-1	1974-5	D2				

Key: -

PR = Premier, D1= Division One, D2 = Division Two, D3 = Division Three / Division Three South, SN = Southern League.

FA = FA Cup, FL = Football League Cup.

Other clubs not shown have never defeated City.

Biggest Defeats: -

City's biggest defeats have been: -

Score	Opponents	Venue	Occasion	Date
2-10	Swindon Town	A	Southern	05.09.08
0-7	Walsall	A	Division Three South	13.09.30
0-7	Sheffield Wed.	A	Division Two	17.11.38
1-7	Reading.	A	Southern	21.11.08
1-7	Swindon Town	A	Southern	28.12.09
1-7	Crystal Palace.	A	Division Three South	30.10.26
1-7	Luton Town.	A	Division Three South	29.03.32
1-7	Torquay United.	A	Division Three South	23.02.57
1-7	Brentford.	A	Division Three South	11.01.58
1-7	Sunderland.	A	Division Two	20.03.63
1-7	Blackburn.Rovers	A	Premier	03.10.92
3-7	Southampton	A	Division Three South	14.12.57

DEFENSIVE RECORDS

LEAGUE

Division Three included with Division Three South

Most Goals Conceded

Goals	Division	Season	Position
100	Division Three South	1946-7	21st
90	Division Two	1938-9	Relegated
73	Division One	1980-1	Relegated
65	Premier	1992-3	Third

Least Goals Conceded

36	Division Two	1971-2	Champions
39	Division One	2003-4	Champions
45	Division Three South	1950-1	Second
61	Premier	1993-4	12th

Most Clean Sheets

18....................Division One..................2003-4.....................Champions
17....................Division Two...............1971-2.....................Champions
17....................Division Two...............1985-6.....................Champions

DERBY MATCHES (IPSWICH)

Overall Record

		H	O	M	E		A	W	A	Y		Succ.
DIV	**Ply**	**W**	**D**	**L**	**F**	**A**	**W**	**D**	**L**	**F**	**A**	**%**
Div.3 South	20	4	1	5	13	16	4	1	5	11	20	43
Div.2	10	2	0	3	7	10	1	1	3	3	9	33
Div.1	36	7	6	5	17	15	5	3	10	16	36	40
Prem.	6	2	0	1	4	2	1	0	2	4	6	50
Lg Ttl	**72**	**15**	**7**	**14**	**41**	**43**	**11**	**5**	**20**	**34**	**71**	**41**
F.A	3	1	1	0	2	1	1	0	0	2	1	77
F.L	8	1	1	1	4	4	3	1	1	8	5	63
Texaco	2	0	0	1	1	2	0	0	1	1	2	0
Total	**85**	**17**	**9**	**16**	**48**	**50**	**15**	**6**	**22**	**45**	**79**	**45**

F.L = Football League Cup including its various sponsor names.

Biggest Wins against Ipswich

Home

3-0 .... Prem 1994-5
3-1 .... Div.1....... 1996-7
3-1 .... Div.1....... 2003-4
2-1 .... Div.2....... 1964-5
2-0 .... Div.3 Sth 1948-9,1951-2
1-0 .... FA Cup... 1982-3
2-0 .... FL Cup ... 1984-5

Away

2-1 ....Prem...................1994-5
2-0 ....Div.1 1999-2000
2-0 ....Div.1 2003-04
2-0 ....Div.2 1966-7
2-0 ....Div.3 Sth. 1951-2
2-1 ....FA Cup...............1961-2
4-2 ....FL Cup...............1968-9

Biggest Defeats by Ipswich

Home

0-2 .... Prem 1992-3
0-2 .... Div 1....... 1984-5,2002-3
0-3 .... Div 2....... 1960-1
1-5 .... Div 3....... 1947-8
1-3 .... FL Cup ... 1980-1

Away

1-3 ....Prem.................... 1992-3
0-5 ....Div 1 .... 1976-7, 97-8
1-4 ....Div 2 1960-1
0-5 ....Div 3 1946-7
0-1 ....FL Cup 1984-5

City have never lost to Ipswich in the FA Cup.

Martin Peters and George Burley in local derby action.

Longest without Win against Ipswich

7 1983-93

Most Games without Defeat by Ipswich

4 ....All 1998-2000

7 ....Home................. 1993-2000

4 ....Away................ 1998-2004 on going.

Doubles over Ipswich

4	1948-9,1951-2	Division Three South
	2003-4	Division One
	1994-5	Premier

Doubled by Ipswich

5	1956-7	Division Three South
	1960-1	Division Two
	1976-7..........1984-5	Division One
	1992-3	Premier

Most City Appearances in Derby Games

Kevin Keelan............... 23

Played for Both Sides (League Appearances)

		Ipswich Town Appearances	Goals	Norwich City Appearances	Goals
Clive	Baker	46	0	14	0
Bobby	Bell	32	1	3	0
Keith	Bertschin	32	8	78	17
John	Deehan	49	11	162	62
Allenby	Driver	86	25	49	19
John	Miller	50	2	9	0
Peter	Morris	206	13	26	1
Cecil	Potter	9	3	131	31
Trevor	Putney	103	8	82	9
John	Roy	15	2	6	0
Clive	Woods	268	23	24	3
Andy	Marshall	53	0	195	0

Several Ipswich players guested for Norwich during the war time matches with Fred Chadwick being the most notable, scoring six in the record 18-0 win against Brighton.

Trevor Putney, one of a select number who played for both City and Ipswich.

Finished above Ipswich

Incredibly in the 59 seasons since Ipswich joined the Football League in 1938, City have only finished above them on 17 occasions.

Season	Ipswich Position	Norwich Position	Division
1938-9	Div.3	Div.2	City in higher Div.
1949-50	17	11	Div.3 Sth.
1950-1	8	2	Div.3 Sth.
1951-2	17	3	Div.3 Sth.
1952-3	16	4	Div.3 Sth.
1965-6	15	13	Div.2
1977-8	18	13	Div.2
1986-7	Div.2	Div.1	City in higher Div.
1987-8	Div.2	Div.1	City in higher Div.

Season	Ipswich Position	Norwich Position	Division
1988-9	Div.2	Div.1	City in higher Div.
1989-90	Div.2	Div.1	City in higher Div.
1990-1	Div.2	Div.1	City in higher Div.
1991-2	Div.2	Div.1	City in higher Div.
1992-3	16	3	Premier
1993-4	19	12	Premier
1994-5	22	20	Div.1
2003-4	5	1	Div.1

DISABLED

Norwich were one of the first clubs to build a stand solely for disabled spectators. This stand, opened in March 1989 at a cost of £150,000, assisted by a grant of £100,000, was built between the Norwich & Peterborough and the South Stands. It was constructed behind glass and had space for 28 wheelchairs, which with seats for helpers had an overall capacity of 115. This was demolished when the South Stand was replaced in 2004. A two-tier corner infill between the Jarrold and Norwich & Peterborough Stands was built in 2004 with special facilities between the tiers to accommodate forty wheel chairs, plus over a hundred walking disabled.

DIVISION THREE SOUTH CUP

This was another minor Cup competition, for Division Three South clubs, but City only competed in 1933-4 before gaining promotion to the Second Division.

Season	Round	Opponents	Result	Attendance
1933-4	First	Gillingham	H...4-0	2,763
	Second	Clapton Orient	H ..3-0	2,561
	Third	Northampton Town	H...3-2	2,738
	Semi-Final	Torquay United	N...1-4	3,727

DOUBLES

Most Doubles Achieved in a Season

8........Division One...................... 2003-4
7........Division Two. 1985-6
7 ....Division Three South .... 1933-4 .... 1951-2 .... 1952-3 1959-60
7........Division Three 1959-60
6 ....Premier.............................. 1992-3

Least Doubles Achieved in a Season

0........Division Three South.......... 1922-3 1930-1
0 ....Division Two 1963-4
0........Division One...................... 1973-4 .... 1977-8 .... 1978-9 1991-2

Most Doubles over City in a Season

2 ....Premier.............................. 1992-3 1993-4
6........Division One...................... 1984-5
6........Division Two 1938-9
6 ....Division Three South.......... 1928-9 1946-7

Least Doubles over City in a Season

0........Division Three South.......... 1932-3 .... 1933-4 .... 1950-1 .... 1952-3 . 1955-6
0 ....Division Two 1971-2
0 ....Division One...................... 2003-4

Successive Doubles by City over Other Clubs

2 .... Several times

Successive Doubles Against City

3 ....Manchester United............. 1990-3

1990-1	1991-2	1992-3
H 0-3	H 1-3	H 1-3
A 0-3	A 0-3	A 0-1

City were also doubled by United again in 1994-5.

Highest Scoring Double by City

13...... Swindon Town .... 1932-3.... H ..5-2 .....A ..4-2 .....Division Three
13...... Bournemouth..................... 1933-4.... H ..6-1 .....A ..4-2   South

Highest Scoring Double Against City

13...... Nottingham Forest............. 1990-1.... H ..2-6 .....A .. 0-5 ....Division One

DRAWS

LEAGUE

Most Draws in a Season

23 ..... Division One 1978-9

This is a Football League record for draws in a season. Although this has been equalled, City's record was in only 42 games. During this season City did not win a single away game. They drew ten games at home and 13 away and once had seven draws in succession. Although City won just seven games in the season, they lost only 12 and finished in sixteenth place. Here is the seasons record.

Home   **Away**

Played 42 Won 7 Drawn 10 Lost 4   Won 0 Drawn 13 Lost 8   Points 37

1978-9

Date	Opponents	V	Result		Position	Attendance
Aug.19	Southampton	H	3-1	W		21,133
Aug.22	Bristol City	A	1-1	D	6	19,274
Aug.26	Coventry City	A	1-4	L	11	20,452
Sep.2	Manchester City	H	1-1	D	11	18,607
Sep.9	W.B.A.	A	2-2	D	11	21,947
Sep.16	Birmingham City	H	4-0	W	6	16,407
Sep.23	Bolton Wanderers	A	2-3	L	11	19,901
Sep.30	Derby County	H	3-0	W	8	16,585

DRAWS

Date	Opponents		Result		Position	Attendance
Oct.7	Liverpool	H	1-4	L	11	25,632
Oct.14	Middlesbrough	A	0-2	L	12	18,203
Oct.21	Leeds United	H	2-2	D	12	19,981
Oct.28	Chelsea	A	3-3	D	13	23,941
Nov.4	Tottenham Hotspur	H	2-2	D	13	25,695
Nov.11	Southampton	A	2-2	D	13	21,183
Nov.18	Coventry City	H	1-0	W	12	17,696
Nov.25	Everton	H	0-1	L	14	19,383
Dec.9	Arsenal	H	0-0	D	15	20,165
Dec.16	Aston Villa	A	1-1	D	13	26,366
Dec.26	Ipswich Town	A	1-1	D	14	26,366
Jan.13	W.B.A.	H	1-1	D	14	20,972
Jan.31	Q.P.R.	H	1-1	D	13	14,203
Feb.3	Bolton Wanderers	H	0-0	D	13	15,369
Feb.10	Derby County	A	1-1	D	12	20,837
Feb.21	Liverpool	A	0-6	L	15	35,754
Feb.24	Middlesbrough	H	1-0	W	14	13,886
Feb.27	Manchester City	A	2-2	D	14	30,014
Mar.3	Leeds United	A	2-2	D	15	23,038
Mar.7	Wolves	H	0-0	D	14	15,427
Mar.10	Chelsea	H	2-0	W	10	19,071
Mar.14	Nottingham Forest	A	1-2	L	10	24,046
Mar.17	Tottenham Hotspur	A	0-0	D	10	24,982
Mar.24	Bristol City	H	3-0	W	9	14,507
Mar.27	Birmingham City	A	0-1	L	10	12,168

Date	Opponents		Result		Position	Attendance
Mar.30	Everton	A	2-2	D	10	28,825
Apr. 7	Manchester Utd	H	2-2	D	11	20,077
Apr.13	Q.P.R.	A	0-0	D	11	14,659
Apr 14	Ipswich Town	H	0-1	L	12	21,325
Apr 16	Wolves	A	0-1	L	14	18,457
Apr 21	Aston Villa	H	1-2	L	15	15,061
Apr 25	Manchester Utd	A	0-1	L	16	33,678
Apr 28	Arsenal	A	1-1	D	14	28,885
May 5	Nottm. Forest	H	1-1	D	16	17,651

Most Draws at Home

12.......Division One...................... 1998-9

Most Draws Away

13 ......Division One 1978-9

Most Successive Draws

7 ....Division One 1978-9
7 ....Premier.............................. 1993-4

Successive Draws at Home

7 ....Division One...................... 1987

From 3 January until 11 April 1987, City drew six league and one FA Cup game.

Least Draws in a Season

5 ....Division Two 1938-9

Least Away Draws in a Season

0 ....Division One...................... 1980-1

Least Home Draws in a Season

1 ....Division One 1951-2

Longest Without a Draw

16.......Division One 1980

After drawing 1-1 with WBA on 22 March 1980, City did not draw again until the home match with Birmingham City on 27 September 1980, which was also 1-1

Longest Without an Away Draw

37.......Division One 1980-1

After drawing 0-0 with Manchester City on 1 March 1980, City went 37 league games before drawing again, against 0-0 Charlton Athletic on 30 December 1981. During this run, City managed to draw away in cup games and in all away games, City's record stands at **29**, from 23 September 1980 until 30 December 1981.

Longest Without a Home Draw

27.......Division Three South 1951-2

City drew 1-1with Exeter City 1-1 on 12 September 1951 and did not draw again until a 2-2 draw with Millwall on 4 October 1952, a total of 24 league and three cup games.

Highest Home Draw

4-4 ....Division Three South.......... Exeter City 18.09.26
4-4 .....FA Cup 2nd Round .... Q. P. R 14.12.46
4-4 .....Division One .... Southampton 09.09.89

Highest Away Draw

4-4 ....Division Three South.......... Newport County 23.11.29
4-4 ....Division Three South.......... Mansfield Town 22.03.47
4-4 .....Division Three South.......... Reading 27.03.54
4-4 .....Division One .... Burnley 13.09.75
4-4 .....Division Two .... Charlton Athletic.......... 22.02.97
4-4 .....Division One .... Rotherham United 17.01.04

GOAL-LESS DRAWS

Most in a Season

8.........Division Two 1965-6

Least in a Season

0 ....Division Three South.......... 1928-9 1946-7

0.........Division One....................... 1980-1

Most Goal-less Draws in Succession

4.........Southern League 1906

From 24 February until 10 March 1906, City drew four successive games 0-0. Strangely enough these were the only non-scoring draws they had in the whole season.

EUROPEAN MATCHES

Norwich first qualified for Europe on winning the League Cup (Milk Cup) in 1985, only to be denied entry following the ban imposed on English clubs, after the deaths in the previous final between Liverpool and Juventus, at the Heysel Stadium, Belgium. City technically qualified twice more on league position whilst the ban remained in force.

Eventual qualification was achieved in 1993, after finishing third in the inaugural Premier League. As there were only two places available, they only qualified by virtue of Arsenal's double cup victories over Sheffield Wednesday; releasing an extra place to the third league position.

As an un-seeded team, City had a series of difficult draws. In the first round they disposed of Dutch team Vitesse Arnhem 3-0 at home and 0-0 away. A number of bookings picked up in the second match proved a handicap in the later rounds.

Team: Gunn, Culverhouse, Bowen, Newman, Polston, Goss, Crook, Megson, (Eadie), Ekoku, Fox, Sutton, (Robins).

Gunn, Culverhouse, Bowen, Newman, Polston, Butterworth, Goss, Crook, Ekoku, (Megson), Fox, Sutton.

In the second round, City faced mighty Bayern Munich of Germany and unbelievably won away, 2-1 in the Olympic stadium, the first English side to do so. This match featured one of the most stunning goals ever scored in City's history, a 20 yard leaping volley by Jerry Goss. City then held the German champions to a 1-1 draw at home, despite going behind in the fourth minute, to progress to the next round. Bayern fielded three International captains, Lothar Matthaus, (Germany), Jan Wouters, (Holland) and Jorginho, (Brazil).

Jerry Goss scoring his wonder goal against Bayern Munich. He ended up as top scorer in the European matches with three goals.

Team: -Gunn, Culverhouse, Bowen, Butterworth, Prior, Goss, Crook, Newman, Robins, (Sutch), Fox, Sutton

Gunn, Culverhouse, Bowen, Butterworth, Polston, Goss, Crook, Newman, Eadie, (Akinbiyi), Fox, (Sutch), Sutton.

In the third round they were drawn against the favourites, the Italian giants Inter Milan. City lost the first leg at home to a late penalty scored by Dutch international, Denis Berghamp. In the second leg at the famous San Siro stadium, despite fielding a weakened side due to suspensions and injuries, City outplayed Inter, but having squandered chances to pull the tie round, lost to a late breakaway goal, scored again by Denis Berghamp. City's wonderful support that day remained in the ground singing long after the match had ended much to the bemusement of the Italian police.

Team: Gunn, Culverhouse, Bowen, Butterworth, Polston, Goss, Crook, Newman, Fox, Sutton, Sutch, (Power).

Gunn, Woodthorpe, Bowen, Newman, Prior, (Power), Ullathorne, Megson, Goss, Ekoku, Newman, Fox, Sutton, (Sutch).

Substitutes, shown in brackets, replaced the player immediately before in the list.

UEFA CUP

Rnd.	Date	Opponents			Attendance	Scorers
1	15.09.93	Vitesse	H	3-0	16,818	Ekoku,Goss, Polston
	29.09.93	Arhnem	A	0-0	9,133	
2	19.10.93	Bayern	A	2-1	28,500	Goss, Bowen
	03.11.93	Munich	H	1-1	20,829	Goss
3	24.11.93	Inter	H	0-1	20,805	
	08.12.93	Milan	A	0-1	30,000	

European Appearances

6............Gunn............ Bowen ....Newman....... Sutton..........Goss.......Fox
5............Crook.......... Culverhouse
4............Sutch .... Polston ....Butterworth
3............Ekoku .... Megson
2............Eadie........... Robins ....Prior .... Power
1.............Akinbiyi....... Ullathorne ....Woodthorpe

EXHIBITIONS

There have been two special exhibitions held for the Football Club.

On 4/5 January 1981, in aid of two local charities, a special exhibition of all the major trophies was held at Carrow Road.

These included: -

The Championship trophies for the First, Second, Third and Fourth Divisions

European Cup   FA Cup   League Cup

Charity Shield   Scottish FA Cup   Scottish League Cup

The Scottish Premier trophy

Combination League Cup   Central League Cup   Willhire Cup

In addition to the above trophies, all held by other clubs at the time, there were also all the tournament and tour trophies awarded to Norwich City.

The exhibition of football's major trophies at Carrow Road in 1981.

EXHIBITIONS

This unique exhibition was supplemented by a display of the private collection of Mr Geoffrey Watling, consisting of commissioned silver replicas and pieces to commemorate exceptional landmarks in the club's history, such as models of the stands at Carrow Road.

The second exhibition was held at the Castle Museum during the summer of 2002 to commemorate the Club's Centenary.

This showed the memorabilia and history through the years and included kit, programmes, photographs, written records and reports, sound audios of commentaries and videos of goals through the centenary. The most unusual exhibit was a model of The Nest, showing how this remarkable ground actually existed and was of much interest to the supporters who had only heard about it.

A model of The Nest at the Centenary Exhibition. Fences protect houses at the bottom, a stand is placed to the right of these houses and the infamous concrete wall is at the far end.

The Queen toured the exhibition on her visit to the City of Norwich in 2002.

A partial exhibition continued in the Bridewell Museum in 2004.

FA CUP

Furthest Reached in FA Cup

Semi-Final .... 1959 .... 1989 1992

Opponents	Result	Venue	Attendance
Luton Town	1-1 at	White Hart Lane	61,500
	0-1 at	St Andrews	49,500

In 1959, City were only the fourth Third Division side to reach the semi-final of the FA Cup. After a glorious campaign in which they had performed several giant killing feats, they eventually succumbed to Luton Town 0-1, in a replay at Birmingham. In the first match at White Hart Lane, City owed much to the heroics of Kennon in goal and Brennan's equaliser. In the replay, City dominated the game, but could not penetrate the Luton defence and fell at the last hurdle.

City defence under pressure against Luton in the 1959 Semi-Final.

Team: Kennon, Thurlow, Ashman, McCrohan, Butler, Crowe, Crossan, Allcock, Bly, Hill, Brennan.

Everton   0-1 at Villa Park..............................46,553

In 1989, City lost 0-1 to Everton in a drab match at Villa Park, lightened up by hundreds of inflatable canaries waved by supporters. City were without their star striker Robert Fleck, due to the sudden death of his father the night before. The match faded into insignificance when it was learned that in the other semi-final, one of the biggest tragedies in football was occurring with the deaths of several fans in the crush at the Liverpool v Nottingham Forest tie.

Canary waving fans at the FA Cup Semi- Final against Everton.

Team: Gunn, Culverhouse, Bowen, Butterworth, Crook, Linighan, Townsend, Gordon, Allen, (Fox), Rosario, Putney.

Sunderland   0-1 at Hillsborough........................40,462

In 1992, Norwich were clear favourites against Second Division Sunderland, but so poorly did City play that they went down by a solitary goal to a very ordinary Sunderland side at Hillsborough. Fleck, who had been out injured for several matches, returned to boost City, but he, along with the rest of the team, did not perform on the day.

Team: Walton, Culverhouse, Woodthorpe, Butterworth, Polston, Goss, Fleck, Newman, Sutton, (Sutch), Bowen, Fox.

CITY'S PERFORMANCE IN THE FA CUP

Biggest Win

8-0 ....Sutton United............................H......................1988

5-0 ....Tunbridge Wells Rangers.........A 1906

Biggest Defeat

0-5 ....Corinthians...............................H......................1929

Manchester City........................H......................1939

Arsenal ....H......................1950

0-6 ....Luton Town ....A......................1928

Manchester City........................A......................1981

Consecutive Wins

4........................... 1950-1

In the 1950-1 campaign, City won four ties straight off, before losing 1-3 at Sunderland in the fifth round. They defeated: -

Round	Opponents	V	Result
First ....Watford....................................H..................2-0			
Second ....Rhyl..A...................1-0			
Third ....Liverpool ....H..................3-1			
Fourth ....Newport County ....A..................2-0			

Consecutive Defeats

5...........................1968-73, 1997-2001

After beating Sunderland 1-0 away in the third round in 1968, City then lost five successive ties before drawing with Leeds United in 1973. Even then they lost the replay and two further ties, until eventually beating Rochdale in 1976, and that at the third attempt.

City also lost five cup games in succession between 1997 and 2001. They lost at Leicester City in the fourth round in 1996 and then were knocked out in the third round on each occasion in the next four years, to Grimsby Town (0-3), Sheffield Wednesday (1-4), Coventry City (1-3) and Sheffield Wednesday again (1-2).

The losing sequence was ended in the next season when they took Chelsea to two games, but still exited the cup in the third round.

It was not until 2002-3 that at last they progressed beyond the third round with home wins over Brighton & Hove Albion (3-1) and non–league Dagenham & Redbridge (1-0).

Longest Without a Win

12 games ....After losing in the fourth round at Chelsea in 1968, City did not win again until the third round second replay against Fourth Division Rochdale in 1976.

Longest Without a Home Win

8 games...............After beating Derby County in the third round in 1966, City did not win another home FA Cup tie until 1976 by beating Rochdale 2-1at the third attempt.

Longest Without an Away Win

11 games ....After beating Stoke City in the third round in 1982, City did not win away again until they beat Huddersfield Town 4-2 in 1987.

Longest Without a Defeat

10 games ....During the 1959 Cup run between the first round and the semi-final replay against First Division Luton Town, City went ten games undefeated.

Longest Without a Home Defeat

14 games............From their very first home tie against Lowestoft Town in the preliminary round in 1903, City didn't lose at home in the FA Cup until their fifteenth game in 1921 against Barnsley.

Longest Without an Away Defeat

6 games...............After losing to Grimsby Town in 1920, City did not lose away in the FA Cup until seven games later at Notts County in 1924.

Successive Home Ties

7.........................Fourth round 1990

Third, Fourth, Fifth & Sixth rounds 1991

Fourth & Fifth rounds....................................1992

Successive Away Ties

7.........................1983-7

During this run City drew in the first game on three occasions to bring their opponents back to Carrow Road.

Longest Without a Home Tie

5.........................1930-5, 1977-81

Longest Without an Away Tie

8.........................1990 Fourth round - 1992 Sixth round

Most Matches to Complete a Tie

4.........................1985

It took City four matches to beat Birmingham City in the FA Cup in 1985. This was before penalties were introduced to settle ties within two games.

Result	Attendance	Date
0-0 ....A.......................... 12,941 ....05.01.85		
1-1 ....H.......................... 11,883 ....23.01.85		
1-1 ....A.......................... 11,755 ....26.01.85		
1-0 ....H.......................... 12,396 ....28.01.85		

Best Period

During the four Cup campaigns between 1989-92, City reached the semi-finals twice and the sixth round once.

Worst Period

From 1969 to 1979, City failed to progress further than the third round except in 1976, when even then they were knocked out by Fourth Division Bradford City in the fifth round at Carrow Road. They had also taken three matches to defeat Fourth Division Rochdale in the third round.

FAMOUS VICTORIES

FA CUP

Opponents	Result	Round	Date	Attendance
Sheffield Wed.	H 2-0	First Round	11.01.08	10,366

This was City's major giant killing act at Newmarket Road. Facing the cup holders, they were given little chance, especially having just lost four matches on the trot. City were perhaps helped by the frozen surface, but goals from James Bauchop and Tommy Allsopp shocked the football world.

Team: Roney, Newlands, McEwen, Livingstone, Bushell, Hutchinson, Muir, Taylor, Young, Bauchop, Allsopp.

Opponents	Result	Round	Date	Attendance
Liverpool	A 3-2	Second Round	06.02.09	32,000

This was City's first giant killing performance away from home. The Canaries were in the lower half of the Southern League and were drawn against one of the country's leading sides at Anfield. Although Liverpool had the bulk of the play, City scored with the few shots they had through Tomlinson, Smith and Allsopp, to cause a major upset.

Team: Roney, French, Craig, Newlands, Wagstaffe, Whiteman, Long, Flanagan, Tomlinson, Smith, Allsopp.

Opponents	Result	Round	Date	Attendance
Leeds United	A 2-1	Fourth Round	30.01.35	27,269

An exciting first match at The Nest saw City come from 0-2 down to lead 3-2 before conceding a last minute equaliser. City were given no chance in the replay, but goals from Vinall, and Burditt saw them earn a splendid victory.

Team: Wharton, Robinson, Halliday, Lochhead, Burditt, Vinall, Houghton, Kirchen, Russell, Bowen, Scott.

Opponents	Result	Round	Date	Attendance
Brighton & HA	H 7-2	First Round	30.11.46	19,264

During heavy rain, City recovered from a 1-2 interval deficit, to storm back with six goals against ten men Brighton. Leslie Eyre scored five of the haul, including three in the last eight minutes.

FAMOUS VICTORIES

Team: Dukes, Flack, Taylor, Robinson, Low, Williams, Plunkett, Dutton, Johnson, Eyre, Jones.

Liverpool   H   3-1.....Third Round...................06.01.51 34,641

This was another classic giant killing performance, against the previous season's finalists. Tom Docherty scored two and Les Eyre the other, to give City a convincing win.

Team: Nethercott, Lewis, Pickwick, Foulkes, Ashman, Gavin, Kinsey, Eyre, Docherty, Duffy, Hollis.

Arsenal   A   2-1.....Fourth Round.................30.01.54 55,767

In front of a huge crowd, City achieved one of their most notable cup victories, despite missing an early penalty. This was followed by the sending off of Forbes (Arsenal) and Brennan for fighting in the 33rd minute. Arsenal scored early in the second half, but City replied through two goals by Johnston in the 56th and 74th minutes. City's resolute defence held out for the remainder of the game to send them into the fifth round.

Team: Oxford, Morgan, Lewis, McCrohan, Foulkes, Ashman, Gordon, Hansell, Johnston, Brennan, Gavin.

Man. United   H   3-0.....Third Round...................10.01.59 38,000

The famous "Busby babes" came to Carrow Road on the back of eight successive league victories. On the snow bound pitch, City coped admirably with the lethal United attack and went ahead through Bly in the 31st minute. Crossan nodded the second in the 61st minute and Bly scored again in the 88th minute for an unbelievable victory.

Team: Nethercott, Thurlow, Ashman, McCrohan, Butler, Crowe, Crossan, Allcock, Bly, Hill, Brennan.

Tottenham H.   H   1-0.....Fifth Round...................18.02.59 38,000

City were denied a victory in the first game at White Hart Lane by a last minute equaliser in front of a 67,633 crowd. In the replay at Carrow Road, urged on by a partisan crowd, City stormed forward and Bly's goal mid way through the second half took them into the sixth round for the first time in their history.

FAMOUS VICTORIES

Team: Nethercott, Thurlow, Ashman, McCrohan, Butler, Crowe, Crossan, Allcock, Bly, Hill, Brennan.

Man. United   A   2-1.....Fourth Round................19.02.67............63,405

Against the team destined to be champions and on their own ground, this was indeed a remarkable victory for City, despite the absence of their two best strikers, Sheffield and Curran. Both goals were the result of defensive blunders, with first Don Heath racing through in a potentially offside position, to score in the 26th minute and Gordon Bolland intercepting a back pass to put City into the lead again in the second half. This was after Denis Law had equalised with a blistering volley. Keelan made several important saves to keep City in the game before mass celebrations at the end from the 10,000 City fans.

Team: Keelan, Mullett, Stringer, Lucas, Brown, Allcock, Kenning, Heath, Bryceland, Bolland, Anderson.

Sutton Utd.   H   8-0.....Fourth Round................28.01.89............23,073

City achieved their biggest ever FA Cup victory against non-league Sutton who had already knocked out First Division Coventry in the third round. Norwich simply tore them to shreds. Putney opened the scoring in the 13th minute followed by Malcolm Allen and Robert Fleck scoring four and three respectively to complete the rout.

Team: Gunn, Culverhouse, Bowen, Butterworth, Linighan, Townsend, (Crook), Gordon, Putney, Phelan, Allen, Fleck.

LEAGUE CUP

Halifax   A   7-1.....Third Round ....27.11.63............4,822

This is still the second highest away win in the competition. Against lowly Halifax, City ran riot, Leading 2-1 at half time, they added five more in the second half. Ron Davies scored two with Bell, Bryceland, Kelly, Punton and Allcock adding the rest.

Team: Kennon, Kelly, Mullett, K Hill, Butler, Bell, Barnes, Bryceland, Davies, Allcock, Punton.

FAMOUS VICTORIES

Arsenal   A   3-0.....Fifth Round 21.11.72 37,671

An emphatic victory at high flying Arsenal saw City move into the semi-finals. On a night when Paddon scored a hat trick (17,28,50 minutes) and Forbes was taken to hospital with a collapsed lung, City showed tremendous character and skill to dismiss their illustrious opponents.

Team: Keelan, Butler, Black, Stringer, Forbes, (Howard), Briggs, Livermore, Bone, Cross, Paddon, Anderson.

Ipswich Town   H   2-0.....Semi-Final Milk............06.03.85 23,545

To reach a major cup final is a tremendous achievement, but to do so by beating your deadly rivals is more satisfying. After losing the first leg at Ipswich 0-1,City knew they had a battle on their hands. The tie was squared when Deehan scored from a deflected free kick after 35 minutes. It remained deadlocked with the prospect of extra time, when City scored a late winner at the death through a scorching header from Steve Bruce, to send City fans into ecstasy.

Team: Woods, Haylock, Van Wyk, Bruce, Mendham, Watson, Barham, Channon, Deehan, Hartford, Donowa.

LEAGUE

Coventry City   H   10-2...Division Three South.....08.02.30 8,230

This was City's record win, achieved against a side who had already beaten them twice during the season. Everything went right for Norwich, as they ripped Coventry apart with three goals coming in the first 14 minutes. They led 4-0 at half time and four more goals in the opening 16 minutes of the second half plus Coventry scoring their first, made the score 8-1 after just over an hour's play. Two more goals in the last seven minutes with Coventry's second sandwiched in between, completed the scoring. Half City's goals were headed and Thomas Hunt scored five.

Team: Jarvie, Hannah, Brown, O'Brien, Lochhead, Anderson, Scott, Graham, Hunt, Slicer, Potter.

Walsall H 8-0.....Division Three South.....29.12.51 18,561

This emphatic win was inspired by a superb individual display by Roy Hollis. He scored all four first half goals and added a fifth in the 77th minute with the last goal of the match.

Team: Nethercott, Morgan, Lewis, Dutton, Foulkes, Ashman, Jones, Kinsey, Hollis, Ackerman, Rackham.

Shrewsbury T. A 8-1.....Division Three South.....13.09.52 11,890

City recorded their biggest away victory despite losing Don Pickwick with a broken leg just before half time. However, by that time they were already leading 4-1. Despite the handicap of being a man short, they continued to dominate the game and added four more goals in the second half. Tommy Johnston scored four on the trot, with Rattray, Gavin, Summers and an own goal completing the tally.

Team: Nethercott, Duffy, Lewis, Pickwick, Holmes, Ashman, Gavin, Kinsey, Johnston, Rattray, Summers.

City in action against Orient in 1972 on their way to Division One.

Orient A 2-1.....Division Two 24.04.72 15,530

At the end of a long season, City finally achieved their long sought after promotion to the First Division in their penultimate game. The tension was relieved soon after half time when Foggo fired City into the lead. After Paddon converted a penalty in the 67th minute, City began to relax. Although Orient pulled one back in the last minute, City had already made the game safe. In the local pubs after the game, City fans celebrated and even a piece of turf with the penalty spot thereon was displayed as a trophy. It was a satisfying journey back to Norfolk for all the fans who had seen their cherished dream realised. Around 15,000 of them returned five days later, to see the Division Two championship clinched in a 1-1 draw at Watford.

Team: Keelan, Payne, Black, (Howard), Stringer, Forbes, Paddon, Brigs, Livermore, Bone, Cross, Foggo.

Crystal Palace   H   2-1.....Division One 24.04.73 36,688

A tumultuous match with both clubs having to win to avoid relegation and played before he second biggest league crowd ever at Carrow Road. City fans watched in horror as Palace took the lead through a penalty after 27 minutes, but City fought back to equalise through Suggett before half time to set up a tension filled second half. Locked in deadlock it seemed that the match would end in a draw, which neither side wanted, but with only two minutes remaining, Stringer headed home from a corner to save City and relegate Palace.

Team: Keelan, Payne, Black, Stringer, Forbes, Hockey, Livermore, Suggett, Cross, Briggs, Mellor.

Liverpool   A   2-0.....Division One 23.04.83 37,022

Given little chance, Norwich were facing a Liverpool side who needed to win to clinch yet another championship. However, City had other ideas and proceeded to outplay Liverpool. After going ahead through an own goal in the 52nd minute, they withstood tremendous pressure to clinch victory with a 30 yarder from Martin O'Neill in the 72nd minute. Not only were City the first side to beat Liverpool at Anfield that season, but the only side to do the double over them.

Team: Woods, Haylock, Downs, O'Neill, Walford, Watson, Barham, Channon, Deehan, Bertschin, Bennett.

Arsenal   A   4-2.....Premier 15.08.92 24,030

It is not often that the opening fixture of the season produces such a remarkable match. City looking down and out at 0-2, but brought on substitute Mark Robins, who immediately turned the game around by pulling a goal back with a close range header. Phillips then equalised, before first Fox put the Canaries ahead and then

Robins deceived Adams, before superbly chipping Seaman to complete a morale boosting start for City in the Premier League.

Team: Gunn, Culverouse, Bowen, Butterworth, Polston, Megson, (Crook), Fox, Newman, Sutton, (Robins), Goss, Phillips.

Everton   A   5-1.....Premier 25.09.93 20,531

Norwich's biggest Premier away victory was more remarkable coming as it was immediately before their first European away match. From being 0-1 down City came back strongly through Ekoku, who could do no wrong in scoring four goals in 41, 57, 63 and 69 minutes, with Sutton adding the fifth in the 77th minute

Team: Gunn, Culverouse, Bowen, Butterworth, Polston, Fox, Newman, Sutton, Goss, Phillips, Ekoku.

FATHER & SON

The following fathers and sons have played for City.

Father / Son	Seasons	Appearances	Goals
Terry Ryder	1925-26	3	
Terry Ryder	1946-50	51	12
Mike Cassidy	1937	1	
Nigel Cassidy	1968	3	
Derrick Lythgoe	1958-62	74	29
Phil Lythgoe	1978-79	12	1
Mike Sutton	1963-66	54	3
Chris Sutton	1991-94	126	43

The following sons also played when their fathers were Manager.

Kevin Bond	1976-81	161	14
John Bond	1973-80		
Kenny Brown	1986-88	28	
Ken Brown	1980-87		

Mike Sutton played in the 60's. His son, Chris, was the first £5m British transfer.

FINALS

Norwich have appeared in four League Cup finals, winning two.

Opponents	Result	Date	Attendance
Rochdale	A 3-0	26.04.62	11,123
	H 1-0	01.05.62	19,800

City won their first major trophy in the second year of the competition by beating Fourth Division Rochdale over two legs. With several First Division clubs not entering, City's task was made much easier. Having already won the first leg at Rochdale 3-0, City had an ample cushion in what was a disappointing return leg. It was not until the 74th minute that Hill scored the winner to complete a comfortable aggregate victory.

Team: Kennon, McCrohan, Ashman, Burton, Butler, Mullet, Mannion, Lythgoe, Scott, Hill, Punton.

Tottenham H.   0-1 .... 24.04.73 100,000

This was City's first Wembley appearance. They were clear underdogs and the occasion seemed to get to them in a disappointing final. The City defence with Forbes and Stringer resolute, held out until the 70th minute, when Spurs substitute Ralph Coates scored the winner. Forbes nearly equalised from a corner, but it was not to be and all City had were memories of treading the hallowed turf.

Team: Keelan, Payne, Butler, Stringer, Forbes, Livermore, Anderson, Paddon, Cross, Briggs, Blair, (Howard).

Aston Villa   0-1 .... 01.03.75 100,000

In their second Wembley final in two years, against fellow Second Division Aston Villa, City were expected to perform to their potential under flamboyant manager John Bond. However, they again failed on the big stage, much to the disappointment of their fans. City survived until the 80th minute when they conceded a penalty due to Machin handling a shot off the line. Keelan did manage to deflect the penalty shot against the post, the first save from a penalty in a Cup Final at Wembley, but Graydon followed up to score.

Team: Keelan, Machin, Sullivan, Morris, Stringer, Forbes, Miller, MacDougall, Boyer, Suggett, Powell.

Machin dives to palm the ball away and concedes a penalty in the 1975 League Cup Final.

FINALS

Sunderland   1-0 .... 24.03.85 100,000

At last City gave a Wembley performance to lift their supporters in their first triumph at the famous stadium, in what was known as the 'Friendly Final'. Having had the better of the first half, City scored immediately after half time. In the 46th minute Hartford's shot was deflected by a defender to give City a deserved lead.

With the fans still celebrating, Van Wijk handled in the area to concede a penalty. City's supporters were thankful when Walker's spot kick failed as it struck the outside of the post Although City continued to press forward and nearly scored a second from a volley by Barham, they had to be content with the one goal for their first success at Wembley. Ironically, both sides were relegated that season and even worse was to follow for City when the ban imposed following the Heysel tragedy denied them their first appearance in Europe.

Team: Woods, Haylock, Van Wijk, Bruce, Mendham, Watson, Barham, Channon, Hartford, Deehan, Donowa,

Asa Hartford turns away to celebrate his goal against Sunderland in the 1985 Milk Cup Final

FIRE

In the early hours of 25 October 1984 the Main Stand at Carrow Road was completely gutted by fire and reduced to a charred shell. Sadly, many of the club's trophies were destroyed. The insurance pay out enabled a new modern City Stand to be built.

A glum Ken Brown surveys the wreckage of the Main Stand after the fire.

FIRSTS

First Match

Occasion	Opponents		Result	Date	Attendance
Friendly	Harwich & Parkeston	H	1-1	06.09.02*	2,000
Norfolk & Suffolk	Beccles Caxton	A	4-2	27.09.02*	
FA Cup	Lowestoft Town	A	0-5	20.09.02*	1,500
Southern League	Plymouth Argyle	A	0-2	02.09.05	8,000
As Professional Home	Southampton	H	1-1	09.09.05	7,000
At The Nest (Friendly)	Fulham	H	2-0	01.09.08	3,300
At The Nest (League)	Portsmouth	H	1-0	12.09.08	6,700
Division Three	Plymouth Argyle	A	1-1	28.08.20	14,000
Division Three South	Luton Town	H	0-1	27.08.21	11,000
Division Two	Brentford	A	1-2	25.08.34	24,000
At Carrow Road	West Ham Utd.	H	4-3	31.08.35	29,779
Division One	Everton	H	1-1	12.08.72	26,028
League Cup	Oldham Athletic	H	6-2	26.10.60	13,080
Premier	Arsenal	A	4-2	15.08.92	24,030
Wembley	Tottenham H	N	0-1	03.03.73	100,000
Europe	Vitesse Arnhem	H	3-0	15.09.93	16,818
Play Off Match	Wolves	H	3-1	28.04.02**	20,127
Play Off Final	Birmingham City	N	1-1 (2-4)	12.05.02** after pens.	71,597

* 1902
** 2002

Note that the Third Division commenced in 1920-1 before being split into South and North sections in the following season. These sections remained until the top and bottom halves split to form new Third and Fourth Divisions in 1959-60. City have never played in the Fourth Division, but the records in these tables include performance in Division Three as well as Division Three South for completeness.

FIRSTS

First Win

Occasion	Opponents		Result	Date	Attendance
Norfolk & Suffolk	Beccles Caxton	A	4-2	27.09.02*	
FA Cup	Lowestoft T.	H	4-1	19.09.03*	4,000
Southern League	West Ham U.	H	1-0	07.10.05	6,000
At The Nest	Northampton Town	H	1-0	26.09.08	6,095
Division Three	Reading	A	1-0	06.11.20	8,000
Division Three South	Reading	H	4-1	29.10.21	7,500
Division Two	Bury	H	4-1	27.08.34	18,643
At Carrow Road	West Ham U.	H	4-3	31.08.35	29,779
Division One	Ipswich Town	A	2-1	15.08.72	29,828
League Cup	Oldham Ath.	H	6-2	26.10.60	13,080
Premier	Arsenal	A	4-2	15.08.92	24,030
Wembley	Sunderland	N	1-0	24.03.85	100,000
Europe	Vitesse Arnhem	H	3-0	15.09.93	16,818
Play Off Match	Wolves	H	3-1	28.04.02**	20,127

* *1902,1903*
** *2002*

First Scorer

Occasion	Scorer	Opponents		Result	Date
Friendly	Jimmy Shields	Harwich & Parkeston	H	1-1	06.09.02*
Norfolk & Suffolk	Jimmy Stoakes	Beccles Caxton	A	4-2	27.09.02*
FA Cup	Percy Gooch	Lowestoft T.	H	4-1	19.09.03*
Southern League	Fred Wilkinson	Southampton	H	1-1	09.09.05
At The Nest	John Smith	Fulham	H	2-1	01.09.08
Division Three	Viv Whitham	Plymouth Argyle	A	1-1	28.08.20
Division Three South	William Bertram	Plymouth Argyle	A	1-1	29.08.21
Division Two	Ken Burditt	Brentford	A	1-2	25.08.34

Occasion	Scorer	Opponents		Result	Date
At Carrow Road	Doug Lochhead	West Ham U.	H	4-3	31.08.35
Division One	Jim Bone	Everton	H	1-1	12.08.72
League Cup	Matt Crowe	Oldham A.	H	6-2	26.10.60
Premier	Mark Robins	Arsenal	A	4-2	15.08.92
Wembley	Asa Hartford	Sunderland	N	1-0	24.03.85
Europe	Efan Ekoku	Vitesse Arnhem	H	3-0	15.09.93
Play Off Match	Mark Rivers	Wolves	H	3-1	28.04.02**
Play Off Final	Iwan Roberts	Birmingham C.	N	1-1	12.05.02**

* 1902,1903
** 2002

Jim Bone scores City's first ever top flight goal against Everton in 1972.

FIXTURES

Most Games Played in a Season

61..................... **1972-3**

> 42......... League
> 3 .... FA Cup
> 8 .... League Cup including one abandoned after 84 minutes.
> 8 .... Texaco Cup

Congested Fixtures

City played 17 matches in 47 days between 14 March and 29 April 1959, including 11 in the month of April.

They won nine, drew five and only lost three games as they finished the season fourth following their wonderful Cup run.

1959

Opponents	Match	V	Result		Date
Luton Town	FA Semi-Final	N	1-1	D	Sat. 14 March
Luton Town	FA Semi-Final	N	0-1	L	Wed 18 March
Bradford City	League	H	4-2	W	Sat 21 March
Accrington Stanley	League	A	2-0	W	Mon 23 March
Hull City	League	H	3-3	D	Fri 27 March
Halifax Town	League	H	3-1	W	Mon 30 March
Halifax Town	League	A	1-1	D	Wed 1 April
Brentford	League	H	4-1	W	Sat 4 April
Mansfield Town	League	A	1-1	D	Mon 6 April
Notts County	League	A	3-1	W	Sat 11 April
Wrexham	League	A	2-1	W	Tue 14 April
Bury	League	A	2-3	L	Wed 15 April
Mansfield Town	League	H	1-0	W	Sat 18 April
Tranmere Rovers	League	H	0-0	D	Wed 22 April
Swindon Town	League	A	3-4	L	Sat 25 April
Chesterfield	League	H	2-1	W	Wed 29 April
Brentford	League	A	4-0	W	Thur 30 April

FIXTURES

City played five games in a week in 1906 in the Southern League.

1906

Opponents	Match	V	Result		Date
Watford	League	H	2-0	W	Sat 22 Dec
Northampton Town	League	H	3-1	W	Tue 25 Dec
Q.P.R	League	A	1-1	D	Wed 26 Dec
Northampton Town	League	A	1-1	D	Thu 27 Dec
Fulham	League	A	1-1	D	Sat 29 Dec

Cup Ties

City played five FA Cup matches in the month of March 1963 as they were required to catch up with the postponements caused by the bad weather

Opponents	Round	V	Result		Date
Blackpool	Third Round	H	1-1	D	Mon 4 March
Blackpool	Third Round	A	3-1	W	Wed 6 March
Newcastle United	Fourth Round	H	5-0	W	Wed 13 March
Manchester City	Fifth Round	A	2-1	W	Sat 16 March
Leicester City	Sixth Round	H	0-2	L	Sat 30 March

In addition to the cup games, City played four league matches, including a 6-0 win over division leaders Stoke City and a 1-7 defeat at Sunderland.

Earliest League Fixture

Aug 9 .... Aston Villa ....A ...0-1 1969

Latest League Fixture

May 21 .... Middlesbrough ...A .. 2-6 1963

In 1985 City were relegated. They had already finished their season on 14 May, but had to wait agonisingly while Coventry City won their last three games, completing their last fixture on 27 May to send Norwich down to Division Two.

Christmas Fixtures

Football was regularly played on Christmas Day until 1956 with City's last match being a 1-1 draw at Colchester.

FIXTURES

First Game Played on a Sunday

24 March 1985   Sunderland ....League Cup (Milk) Final ... 1-0

First Sunday League Game

22 January 1989   Millwall ....A .. Division One 3-2

First Sunday Home League Game

21 January 1990   Manchester Utd .H .. Division One 2-0

First Game on Match of the Day

11 March 1967   Sheffield Wed.....H .. FA Cup Fifth Round 1-3

First League Game on Match of the Day

26 August 1967   Q.P.R ....A .. Division Two................ 0-2

First Home Game on Match of the Day

11 March1972   Sunderland..........H .. Division Two................ 1-1

First Televised Live Match

24 March 1985   Sunderland.........League Cup Final 0-1

First Televised Live Match at Home

27 December 1988   West Ham Utd....H. . Division One 2-0

Repeat Meetings

Leeds United: four times in 16 days, January 1973

FA Cup Third Round	H	1-1	D	Sat 13 January
FA Cup Third Round replay	A	1-1	D	Wed 17 January
Division One	H	1-2	L	Sat 20 January
FA Cup Third Round 2nd replay Villa Park	N	0-5	L	Mon 29 January

Birmingham City: four times in 23 days, January 1985

FA Cup Third Round	A	0-0	D	Sat 5 January
FA Cup Third Round replay	H	1-1	D	Wed 23 January
FA Cup Third Round 2nd replay	A	1-1	D	Tues 26 January
FA Cup Third Round 3rd replay	H	1-0	W	Thur 28 January

Leicester City: five times in a Season, 1972-3

League Cup Second Round	H	2-1	W	6 September
Division One	A	2-1	W	21 October
Texaco Cup Second Round 1st Leg	A	0-2	L	24 October
Texaco Cup Second Round 2nd Leg	H	2-0	W	8 November
Division One	H	1-1	D	17 March

Preston North End: In the League Cup

Norwich were drawn against Preston in the second round of the League Cup four times in seven years, each over two legs. City won all the games over the two legs.

Season	V	Result		Attendance
1982-3	H	2-1	W	7,273
	A	2-1	W	6,082
1984-5	A	3-3	D	5,265
	H	6-1	W	13,506
1985-6	A	1-1	D	4,330
	H	2-1	W	11,537
1988-9	H	2-0	W	7,484
	A	3-0	W	7,002

FLOODLIGHTS

Norwich first installed floodlights in 1956 at a cost of £8,000. Sunderland provided the opposition for the opening ceremony on 17 October 1956, beating City 3-0 before a crowd of 23,094. These floodlights were upgraded in 1974 with new brighter halogen bulbs. When the new stands were built the floodlights were supported on much slimmer posts, fixed through the roof, rather than on free-standing pylons.

FOREIGN TEAMS

City have met many foreign teams on tours abroad. The following is a list of foreign clubs who have played at Carrow Road in friendly matches.

Date	Team	Country	Score
12.05.51	Servette	Switzerland	5-1
17.12.58	Rouen	France	3-2
29.11.61	Belgrade Sports	Yugoslavia	2-1
09.10.63	Sliema Wanderers	Malta	5-0
17.03.65	Nykobing Boldklub	Denmark	6-1
10.11.65	ADO (The Hague)	Holland	4-1
04.05.66	S.C.Telstar (The Hague)	Holland	2-1
28.02.68	Bratislava Slovnaft	Czechoslovakia	1-0
09.02.76	Red Star Belgrade	Yugoslavia	0-1
15.11.78	IFK Gothenburg	Sweden	3-0
22.10.79	New Zealand XI	New Zealand	5-0
30.09.81	Fort Lauderdale Strikers	USA	2-2
08.08.87	Real Sociedad*	Spain	2-0
01.03.89	Dynamo Moscow	Russia	0-2
09.08.89	Aris Salonika	Greece	1-2
16.02.90	Ferencvaros	Hungary	2-0
08.08.91	Otelul Galati	Rumania	4-0
28.01.92	Bayern Munich	Germany	4-1
10.08.92	Zenit St Petersburg	Russia	1-1
25.08.92	Kuwait	Kuwait	1-2
09.05.94	Genoa *	Italy	4-5
10.08.96	Sparta Rotterdam *	Holland	0-0
30.07.99	AZ Alkmaar *	Holland	0-0
29.07.00	Heerenveen	Holland	1-1
27.07.01	Ajax	Holland	0-1

Testimonials

FORMED

Norwich City Football Club was formed on 17 June 1902 at the Criterion Café in White Lion Street. The instigators were Robert Webster and Joseph Nutchey who had been associated with the principle Norwich Club at the time, CEYMS. Arthur Turner was appointed as first secretary / manager and was given the task of finding players for the coming season as an amateur side in the Norfolk & Suffolk League.

FOUNDERS

City were founder members of Division Three in 1920 after being elected en bloc with the other teams from the Southern League. The following season they became members of Division Three South when the North and South sections were formed. They were also founder members of the Premier League in 1992.

FULL MEMBER'S CUP

This was a cup competition for members of the First and Second Divisions. It was of no great interest until the later stages when a Wembley final was a prospect. In 1987, City were in minutes of reaching the final when they led Charlton Athletic 1-0. However, a last minute equaliser, followed by the winner in extra time, saw City cruelly denied. The competition was sponsored by Simod, with Zenith Data taking over in later years.

1986-7

Round	Opponents	Result	Attendance
First	Coventry City	H...2-1	6,235
Second	Southampton	A ..2-1	5,745
Third	Portsmouth	H...3-1	9,204
Semi final	Charlton Athletic	A...1-2	5,431

GATE RECEIPTS

Record gate receipts at Carrow Road have progressed since first reaching £5,000, as follows: -

Receipts	Opponents	Event	Date
£5,482	Arsenal	FA Cup third round	12-01-52
£5,693	Leicester City	FA Cup fifth round	20-02-54
£6,000	Tottenham Hotspur	FA Cup fifth round replay	18-02-59
£6,648	Sunderland	FA Cup fifth round	18-02-61
£8,183	Leicester City	FA Cup sixth round	30-03-63
£9,947	Blackburn Rovers	FA Cup fifth round	05-03-66
£15,448	Chelsea	League Cup semi-final	03-01-73
£20,853	Manchester United	League Cup semi-final	22-01-75
£26,845	Orient	FA Cup third round replay	16-01-78
£43,393	Wolves	FA Cup fourth round replay	30-01-80
£56,894	Ipswich Town	League Cup third round replay	08-10-80
£71,948	Tottenham Hotspur	FA Cup fourth round replay	01-02-84
£126,395	West Ham United	FA Cup sixth round replay	22-03-89
£173,570	Nottingham Forest	FA Cup sixth round	09-03-91
£261,918	Inter Milan	UEFA Cup third round	24-11-93
£339,005	Chelsea	FA Cup third round	05-01-02
£750,000*	Birmingham City	Play off Final, Cardiff	12-05-02

* City took the whole net gate allocation of around £750,000 from Cardiff as the losers in the Play off final. This was agreed with Birmingham before the game.

GIANT KILLING

FA Cup Games where City have beaten teams from a Higher Division.

As a Non-League Side

Opponents	Result	V	Round	Season	Status of Other Club
Sheffield Wednesday	2-0	H	First	1907-8	Division One
Liverpool	3-2	A	Second	1908-9	Division One
Sunderland	3-1	H	First	1910-1	Division One
Leicester City	4-1	A	First	1912-3	Division Two
Nottingham Forest	4-1	A	First	1914-5	Division Two

As a Non-League side (continued)

Opponents	Result	V	Round	Season	Status of Other Club
Tottenham Hotspur	3-2	H	Second	1914-5	Division One

As a Third Division side

Stockport County	2-0	H	Sixth Qualify	1923-4	Division Two
Liverpool	3-1	H	Third	1950-1	Division One
Arsenal	2-1	A	Fourth	1953-4	Division One
Manchester United	3-0	H	Third	1958-9	Division One
Cardiff City	3-2	H	Fourth	1958-9	Division Two
Tottenham Hotspur	1-0	H	Fifth	1958-9	Division One
Sheffield United	3-2	H	Sixth	1958-9	Division Two

As a Second Division Side

Leeds United	2-1	A	Fourth	1934-5	Division One
Liverpool	3-0	H	Third	1936-7	Division One
Ipswich Town	2-1	A	Fourth	1961-2	Division One
Blackpool	3-1	A	Third	1962-3	Division One
Manchester City	2-1	A	Fifth	1962-3	Division One
Manchester United	2-1	A	Fourth	1966-7	Division One
Sunderland	1-0	A	Third	1967-8	Division One
Stoke City	1-0	A	Third	1981-2	Division One

FA Cup Games where City have been beaten by teams from a Lower Division

As a First Division Side

Bradford City	1-2	H	Fifth	1975-6	Division Four
Orient	0-1	H	Third	1986-7	Division Two
Leicester City	0-3	A	Third	1978-9	Division Two
Derby County	1-2	A	Fifth	1983-4	Division Two
Wigan Athletic	0-1	A	Third	1986-7	Division Three
Swindon Town	0-2	A	Third	1987-8	Division Two
Sunderland	0-1	N	S/final	1991-2	Division Two
Brentford	1-2	H	Third	1995-6	Division Two
Grimsby Town	0-3	A	Third	1997-8	Division Two

As a Second Division Side

Opponents	Result	V	Round	Season	Status of Other Club
Bristol Rovers	1-2	A	Third	1963-4	Division Three
Wrexham	1-2	H	Third	1969-70	Division Four

As a Third Division Side

Corinthians	0-5	H	Third	1928-9	Non League
Folkestone Town	0-1	A	First	1932-3	Non League
Bedford Town	2-4	H	First	1956-7	Non League

GOAL SCORERS

Top Scorers for Each Season

Season	Top Scorer		Goals
1902-3	Bert	Playford	10
1903-4	Percy	Gooch	18
1904-5	Herbert	Vigar	12
1905-6	Davie	Ross	21
1906-7	Davie	Ross	28
1907-8	James	Bauchop	12
1908-9	John	Smith	24
1909-10	Walter	Rayner	13
1910-1	William	Ingham	15
1911-2	Dick	Birchall	8
1912-3	Henry	Woods	9
1913-4	Arhur	Wolstenholme	15
1914-5	Cecil	Potter	13
	Danny	Wilson	13
1919-20	John	Doran	18
1920-1	James	Travers	14
1921-2	Sam	Austin	12
1922-3	Bob	Dennison	13
1923-4	James	Jackson	15
1924-5	James	Jackson	14
	Frank	McCudden	14

GOAL SCORERS

Season	Top Scorer	Goals
1925-6	James Jackson	21
1926-7	Reg Cropper	15
1927-8	Percy Varco	32
1928-9	Francis McKenna	18
1929-30	Tommy Hunt	25
1930-1	Tom Williams	12
1931-2	Cecil Blakemore	16
1932-3	Oliver Brown	19
	Ken Burditt	19
1933-4	Jack Vinall	19
	Billy Warnes	19
1934-5	Jack Vinall	19
1935-6	Jack Vinall	24
1936-7	Frank Manders	17
1937-8	Tim Coleman	16
1938-9	Frank Manders	8
1946-7	Leslie Eyre	18
1947-8	Leslie Eyre	16
1948-9	Ron Ashman	13
1949-50	Noel Kinsey	17
1950-1	John Gavin	18
1951-2	Roy Hollis	22
1952-3	Alf Ackerman	22
1953-4	Tom Johnston	16
1954-5	Bobby Brennan	11
	Fred Kearns	11
1955-6	Ralph Hunt	33
1956-7	Ralph Hunt	21
1957-8	John Gavin	22
1958-9	Terry Bly	29
1959-60	Jimmy Hill	16
	Terry Allcock	16
1960-1	Terry Allcock	16
1961-2	Terry Allcock	21
1962-3	Terry Allcock	37
1963-4	Ron Davies	30
1964-5	Gordon Bolland	20
1965-6	Ron Davies	21
1966-7	Laurie Sheffield	16

Season	Top Scorer	Goals
1967-8	Hugh Curran	18
1968-9	Hugh Curran	22
1969-70	Ken Foggo	11
1970-1	Ken Foggo	17
1971-2	Ken Foggo	14
1972-3	David Cross	17
1973-4	Ted MacDougall	13
1974-5	Ted MacDougall	23
1975-6	Ted MacDougall	28
1976-7	Viv Busby	11
1977-8	John Ryan	16
1978-9	Kevin Reeves	13
1979-80	Justin Fashanu	13
1980-1	Justin Fashanu	22
1981-2	Ross Jack	14
1982-3	John Deehan	21
1983-4	John Deehan	17
1984-5	John Deehan	18
1985-6	Kevin Drinkell	24
1986-7	Kevin Drinkell	21
1987-8	Kevin Drinkell	12
1988-9	Robert Fleck	15
1989-90	Robert Fleck	12
1990-1	Robert Fleck	11
1991-2	Robert Fleck	19
1992-3	Mark Robins	16
1993-4	Chris Sutton	28
1994-5	Ashley Ward	8
1995-6	Ashley Ward	13
1996-7	Darren Eadie	17
1997-8	Craig Bellamy	13
1998-9	Iwan Roberts	23
1999-2000	Iwan Roberts	19
2000-1	Iwan Roberts	18
2001-2	Iwan Roberts	14
2002-3	Paul McVeigh	15
2003-4	Darren Huckerby	14

GOAL SCORERS

First Ever Goal Scorer

Jimmy Shields .... v... Harwich & Parkeston ...Friendly................ 06.09.02*

First Ever Goal Scorer in a Competitive Match

Bert   Playford .... v...Beccles Caxton ....A 27.09.02*

First Ever Football League Goal Scorer

Vic   Whitham ..... v...Plymouth Argyle ....A............................28.08.20

1902

Highest Goalscorers for City and Ratio per Game

Scorer	Total Goals	Seasons	Average	Top Average
John Gavin	132	1948-58	**0.40**	11
Terry Allcock	127	1958-69	0.33	
Iwan Roberts	96	1997-2004	0.32	
Robert Fleck	84	1987-92, 95-98	0.28	
Jack Vinall	80	1933-7	0.44	8
Ralph Hunt	72	1955-8	**0.54**	4
John Deehan	70	1981-5	0.36	
Leslie Eyre	69	1946-51	0.35	
Ron Davies	66	1963-6	**0.53**	5
Jimmy Hill	66	1957-63	0.34	
Ted MacDougall	66	1973-6	**0.47**	7
Noel Kinsey	65	1947-53	0.27	
Ken Burditt	61	1930-6	0.35	
Roy Hollis	59	1947-57	**0.55**	3
Ken Foggo	57	1967-72	0.28	
James Jackson	57	1923-8	**0.50**	6
Ron Ashman	56	1947-64	0.08	
Tommy Bryceland	55	1962-70	0.19	
Hugh Curran	53	1966-9	**0.43**	9
Bobby Brennan	52	1953-60	0.21	
Martin Peters	50	1975-80	0.21	
David Ross	49	1905-7	**0.69**	2
Willie Warnes	49	1927-30	**0.42**	10

Scorer	Total Goals	Seasons	Average	Top Average
Percy Varco	47	1927-30	**0.73**	**1**
Frank Manders	43	1935-9	0.31	
Dale Gordon	43	1984-91	0.16	
Chris Sutton	43	1990-4	0.34	
Kevin Reeves	42	1977-80	0.32	
Phil Boyer	40	1974-7	0.29	
Justin Fashanu	40	1979-81	**0.39**	**12**

Bold indicates top performers

Johnny Gavin, top scorer for City with 132 goals.

Percy Varco, highest scoring ratio for Norwich

Most Goals Scored in a Season

Top Scorer		Goals	Season	Division
Terry	Allcock	37	1962-3	Division Two
Ralph	Hunt	33	1955-6	Division Three South
Ted	MacDougall	28	1975-6	Division One
Chris	Sutton	28	1993-4	Premier

Most League Goals in a Season

Ralph	Hunt	31	1955-6	Division Three South
Ron	Davies	27	1963-4	Division Two
Ted	MacDougall	23	1975-6	Division One
Chris	Sutton	25	1993-4	Premier

Ted MacDougall was the First Division's leading league scorer in 1975-6

Least League Goals in a Season by Top Scorer

Frank	Manders	8	1938-9	Division Two
Ashley	Ward	8	1994-5	Premier

Most Goals in a Match

Scorer		Goals	Opponents	Date	Score
Fred	Chadwick	6	Brighton & HA	25.12.40	18-0
Thomas	Hunt	5	Coventry City	15.03.30	10-2
Leslie	Eyre	5	Brighton & HA	30.11.46	7-2
Roy	Hollis	5	Walsall	29.12.51	8-0

Fred Chadwick is listed above as the 18-0 win against Brighton is the highest ever City victory, although it was during wartime. Wally Taylor also scored five, six and seven goals in First World War matches.

Most League Goals Scored

John	Gavin	122
Terry	Allcock	106

Most FA Cup Goals Scored

Terry	Allcock	12
Leslie	Eyre	11
Robert	Fleck	11

Most League Cup Goals Scored

Robert	Fleck	12
Terry	Allcock	9
Ted	MacDougall	9
Graham	Paddon	9

Goal of the Season

City Players who have Scored one of the TV Goals of the Season

Justin	Fashanu	Liverpool	H	3-5	09.02.80
Robert	Rosario	Southampton	H	4-4	09.09.89

Scored in Successive Matches

Ross Jack scored in seven successive matches between 5 September and 7 October 1981.

Terry Allcock scored in six successive matches between 21 January and 4 March 1961, totalling eight goals.

GOALS SCORED

City scored 11 goals in successive matches. They beat Stoke City 6-0 in the league on 9 March, followed by Newcastle United in the FA Cup 5-0 on 13 March 1963, with both matches being at home.

Goals Conceded in Successive Matches

City conceded 14 goals in successive matches against Luton Town 0-4 and Swindon Town 2-10, on 2 and 5 September 1908. Both matches were away.

Goal Difference

City had a goal difference of plus 44 in 1952-3 having scored 99 goals and conceding 55.

When they were First Division champions in 2003-4 they scored 79 goals, but only conceded 39, to give them a goal difference of 40.

Amazingly, when City finished third in the Premier League, they did so with a negative goal difference of four having scored 61 and conceded 65 goals.

Most Goals Scored (per Division)

Goals	Season	Division
99	1952-3	Division Three South
84	1985-6	Division Two
79	2003-4	Division One
65	1993-4	Premier

Most Goals Conceded

100	1946-7	Division Three South
91	1938-9	Division Two
73	1980-1	Division One
65	1992-3	Premier

Least Goals Scored

44	1920-1	Division Three South
49	1966-7, 1969-70	Division Two
36	1972-3	Division One
37	1994-5	Premier

Least Goals Conceded

45........................... 1950-1 ....Division Three South
39 .... 2003-4 ....Division One
36 .... 1971-2 ....Division Two
54........................... 1994-5 ....Premier

Goal Milestones (League)

Goal	Opponents		Date	Scorer
1000........................	Bury...............	A	1935	John Friar
2000........................	Millwall..........	H	1957	Peter Gordon
3000........................	Man. City.	H	1972	Graham Paddon
4000........................	Nottm. Forest .	H	1992	Lee Power

Successive Scoring by Norwich

City scored in 31 successive games in 1963, toalling 49 goals with Ron Davies contributing 20 of them.

Date	Opponents	V	Result		League/ Cup
Aug.28	*Bury*	*H*	*0-1*	*L*	*League*
Aug.31	Orient	H	1-2	L	League
Sep.3	Bury	A	2-4	L	League
Sep.7	Scunthorpe United	H	2-1	W	League
Sep.11	Northampton Town	H	3-3	D	League
Sep.14	Portsmouth	A	1-1	D	League
Sep.16	Northampton Town	A	2-3	L	League
Sep.21	Rotherham United	H	2-2	D	League
Sep.25	Birmingham City	H	2-0	W	League Cup
Sep.28	Leeds United	A	2-4	L	League
Oct.2	Preston North End	H	2-1	W	League
Oct.5	Sunderland	H	2-3	L	League
Oct.15	Swansea Town	A	1-3	L	League

Date	Opponents	V	Result		League/ Cup
Oct.19	Southampton	H	1-1	D	League
Oct.26	Grimsby Town	A	1-3	L	League
Oct.30	Blackpool	H	1-0	W	League Cup
Nov.2	Newcastle United.	H	3-1	W	League
Nov.9	Huddersfield Town	A	1-1	D	League
Nov.16	Derby.County	H	3-0	W	League
Nov.23	Plymouth Argyle	A	2-1	W	League
Nov.27	Halifax Town	A	7-1	W	League Cup
Nov.30	Charlton Athletic	H	1-3	L	League
Dec.7	Middlesbrough	A	1-0	W	League
Dec.14	Cardiff City	H	5-1	W	League
Dec.18	Leicester City	H	1-1	D	League Cup
Dec.21	Orient	A	1-1	D	League
Dec.26	Swindon Town	H	3-2	W	League
Dec.28	Swindon Town	A	2-2	D	League
Jan.4	Bristol Rovers	A	1-2	L	FA Cup
Jan.11	Scunthorpe Utd.	A	2-2	D	League
Jan.15	Leicester City	A	1-2	L	League Cup
Jan.18	Portsmouth	H	3-1	W	League
Feb. 1	*Rotherham United*	A	*0-4*	L	*League*

Beginning and end of sequence.

GREAT ESCAPES

1972-73

City seemed to be doomed as mid April approached having gone 19 league games without a win. However, with a late spurt they managed to just jump clear of the relegation trap door.

Date	Opponents	V	Result		Position	Attendance
Apr.3	Everton	A	2-2	D	21	21,806
Apr.7	Manchester Utd.	A	0-1	L	22	48,593
Apr.14	Chelsea	H	1-0	W	22	24,763
Apr.21	W.B.A	A	1-0	W	20	23,431
Apr.23	Wolves	A	0-3	L	20	20,222
Apr.24	Crystal Palace	H	2-1	W	20	36,688
Apr.28	Stoke City	A	0-2	L	20	19,350

1987-8

After losing to Charlton Athletic on 7 November 1987, City were 19th and sacked manager Ken Brown. David Stringer was appointed and turned results around to achieve safety with comparative ease.

Date	Opponents	V	Result		Position	Attendance
Nov.7	Charlton Athletic	A	0-2	L	19	5,044
Nov.14	Arsenal	H	2-4	L	20	20,558
Nov.21	Liverpool	A	0-0	D	20	37,446
Nov.28	Portsmouth	H	0-1	L	20	13,099
Dec.5	Luton Town	A	2-1	W	20	7,002
Dec.18	Wimbledon	A	0-1	L	21	4,026
Dec.26	Derby County	A	2-1	W	20	15,452

Date	Opponents	V	Result		Position	Attendance
Dec.28	Chelsea	H	3-0	W	18	19,668
Jan.1	West Ham Utd	A	4-1	W	16	20,059
Jan.16	Everton	H	0-3	L	18	15,750
Jan.23	Southampton	A	0-0	D	16	12,002
Feb.6	Watford	H	0-0	D	16	13,316
Feb.13	Newcastle Utd.	A	3-1	W	16	21,068
Feb.20	Coventry City	A	0-0	D	16	15,577
Mar.5	Manchester Utd.	H	1-0	W	14	19,129
Mar.12	Tottenham H.	A	3-1	W	13	19,322
Mar.16	Oxford Utd.	H	4-2	W	9	12,260
Mar.19	Q.P.R	A	0-3	L	10	9,033
Mar.26	Sheffield Wed.	H	0-3	L	14	13,208
Apr.2	Charlton Athletic	H	2-0	W	12	15,015
Apr.4	Arsenal	A	0-2	L	13	19,341
Apr.20	Liverpool	H	0-0	D	13	22,509
Apr.23	Portsmouth	A	2-2	D	13	12,762
Apr.30	Luton Town	H	2-2	D	13	12,700
May 4	Nottm. Forest	A	0-2	L	13	11,610
May 7	Wimbledon	H	0-1	L	14	11,872

GROUND DEVELOPMENT

Year(s)	Development	Capacity
1902-08	Newmarket Road	11,500
1908-35	The Nest	25,000
1935	Carrow Road	35.000
1937	Barclay Covered	38,000
1956	Floodlights installed	38,000
1960	South Stand covered	44,000
1975	South Stand seated	32,000
1979	River Stand built	28,500
1984	Main Stand destroyed by fire	23,500
1986	Main Stand (City) replaced	26,812
1989	Disabled Stand	26,408
1992	Double tier new Barclay Stand	20,319
1992	River Stand (Norwich & Peterborough) all seated	20,319
1993	New Pitch laid with under-soil heating	
1993	Barclay / City infill	20,634
1994	Norwich & Peterborough / City infill	21,272
2004	New Jarrold Stand	24,369
2004	New pitch laid	
2004/5	Jarrold Stand/ Norwich & Peterborough corner infill 25,969 est.	

Pitch measurement ....114 yards by 74 yards

The number of season ticket holders set a new record of 18,750 in 2004. This was despite the figure being capped with a waiting list of nearly 2000. With the building of the infill the number will be increased to around 20,000.

The number of season tickets in 1946-7 was 376.

Training Ground

After many years at Trowse, City moved to Colney in 1994, where a new purpose built training ground was constructed. This had six pitches, administration offices, gymnasium, recovery pool, well equipped changing and games rooms. A hostel, able to accommodate up to 20 youth trainees under the supervision of a resident warden was also built on the complex enabling City to offer some of the bestfacilities in the land for attracting young players. With the advent of the

Premier League Academy, City were required to add a half pitch size indoor area. This was built in 2002 and provided much needed protection against the weather. The indoor pitch was made of the highest quality artificial turf to give the correct bounce and texture

The City Stand before corner infills were added

GROUP CUP

This pre-season competition, sometimes known as the League Group Cup was played on a regional basis and used for match practice in 1981.

Opponents	Venue	Result	Date	Attendance
Peterborough Utd.	H	2-2	15.08.81	2,707
Lincoln City	A	1-0	19.08.81	1,990
Notts County	H	3-0	22.08.81	4,038

HALL OF FAME

During City's Centenary celebrations a 'Hall of Fame' was produced for the top 100 Canaries of all time. Twenty five members were pre-selected (Allcock to Watling, as below), with 75 being voted for by fans. Each member has a banner in the concourse of the new Jarrold Stand and also features in the special display area of bricks in the wall, where fans can have their own inscriptions.

Member		Seasons	Appearances	Goals	Other	
Terry	Allcock	1958-69	389	127		
Ron	Ashman	1947-63	662	56	Manager	1962-66
Bobby	Brennan	1953-60	250	52		
Barry	Butler	1957-66	349	3		
Ron	Davies	1963-66	126	66		
John	Deehan	1981-85	199	70		
Duncan	Forbes	1968-80	357	12		
Johnny	Gavin	1949-58	338	132		
Bryan	Gunn	1986-98	477			
Joe	Hannah	1921-35	427	22		
Kevin	Keelan	1963-80	673			
Doug	Lochhead	1929-35	220	5	Manager	1947-50
Archie	Macaulay		n/a		Manager	1957-62
Ken	Nethercott	1947-59	416			
Joseph	Nutchey		n/a		Club Founder	1902
Martin	Peters	1975-80	232	50		
Stan	Ramsay	1932-34	83	1		
Iwan	Roberts	1997-2004	306	96		
Bernard	Robinson	1932-49	380	14		
Davie	Ross	1905-07	71	49		
Ron	Saunders		n/a		Manager	1969-73
Sir Arthur	South		n/a		Chairman	1973-85
David	Stringer	1965-76	499	22	Manager	1987-92
Percy	Varco	1927-29	65	47		
Geoffrey	Watling		n/a		Chairman	1957-73

HALL OF FAME

Long serving chairman Geoffrey Watling, with Norfolk born player and manager, David Stringer and manager Ron Saunders, who led City to the top Division for the first time.

Member		Seasons	Appearances	Goals	Other	
Neil	Adams	1994-99	206	30		
Craig	Bellamy	1997-2001	91	34		
Gordon	Bennett	n/a			Chief Exec	1996-99
Terry	Bly	1956-60	67	38		
John	Bond	n/a			Manager	1973-80
Jimmy	Bone	1972-73	51	15		
Mark	Bowen	1987-96	399	27		
Phil	Boyer	1974-77	140	40		
Ken	Brown	n/a			Manager	1980-87
Steve	Bruce	1984-87	180	21		
Tommy	Bryceland	1962-69	284	55		
Mick	Channon	1982-85	112	25		
Robert	Chase	n/a			Chairman	1986-96
Ian	Crook	1986-97	418	24		

126

Member		Seasons	Appearances	Goals	Other
David	Cross	1971-73	106	30	
Errol	Crossan	1958-60	116	32	
Matt	Crowe	1957-62	214	18	
Ian	Culverhouse	1985-94	369	2	
Hugh	Curran	1966-69	124	53	
Kevin	Drinkell	1985-88	150	57	
Darren	Eadie	1993-99	204	38	
Les	Eyre	1946-51	201	69	

Leslie Eyre in action at Carrow Road.

Justin	Fashanu	1979-81	103	40	
Robert	Fleck	1987-92			
		1995-98	299	84	
Craig	Fleming	1997-2004	289	10	
Kenny	Foggo	1967-72	201	57	
Reg	Foulkes	1950-56	238	8	
Ruel	Fox	1986-94	219	25	

HALL OF FAME

Member		Seasons	Appearances	Goals	Other	
Billy	Furness	1937-46	96	21		
Dale	Gordon	1984-91	261	43		
Jerry	Goss	1984-96	238	23		
Asa	Hartford	1984-5	40	5		
Jimmy	Hill	1958-63	195	66		
Roy	Hollis	1948-52	107	59		
Gary	Holt	2000- 2004	153	3		
Ralph	Hunt	1955 58	134	72		
Sandy	Kennon	1959-64	255	0		
Darren	Kenton	1997-2003	163	9		
Noel	Kinsey	1947-53	243	65		
Bill	Lewis	1949-55	256	1		
Doug	Livermore	1970-75	139	6	Asst Man	2001-
Norman	Low		n/a		Manager	1950-55
Ted	MacDougall	1973-76	138	66		
Malky	Mackay	1998-2004	232	17		
Andy	Marshall	1994-2001	219	0		
Roy	McCrohan	1951-62	426	23		
Paul	McVeigh	1999-2004	154	31		
Peter	Mendham	1978-86	267	29		
Gary	Megson	1992-95	54	1	Manager	1995-96
Denis	Morgan	1946-56	250	3		
Jimmy	Neighbour	1976-79	115	5		
Rob	Newman	1991-97	249	17		
Jon	Newsome	1994-96	76	8		
Maurice	Norman	1955	35	0		
Martin	O'Neill	1981-83	75	13		
Graham	Paddon	1969-73 1976-81	340	37		
Don	Pickwick	1947-56	244	11		
John	Polston	1990-98	263	12		
Tony	Powell	1974-81	275	5		
Bill	Punton	1959-66	256	29		
Kevin	Reeves	1977-80	133	42		
Tim	Sheppard		n/a		Physio	1990-2002
Delia	Smith		n/a		Director	1996-
Colin	Suggett	1973-78	243	29		
Daryl	Sutch	1989-2003	352	9		
Chris	Sutton	1990-94	126	43		

Member		Seasons	Appearances	Goals	Other	
Bryan	Thurlow	1955-64	224	1		
Andy	Townsend	1988-90	88	10		
Jack	Vinall	1933-37	181	80		
Mike	Walker	n/a			Manager	1992-94
		n/a			Manager	1996-98
Dave	Watson	1980-86	256	15		
Dave	Williams	1985-89	74	12	Coach	1988-92
Chris	Woods	1981-86	267			
Nigel	Worthington	n/a			Manager	2001-
Michael	Wyn Jones	n/a			Director	1996-

HALVES

The highest half time score in a Norwich match at Carrow Road was 5-2 in the Second Division game with Portsmouth on 16 April 1962, with the final result being 5-3.

Seven goals were also scored before half time during a Southern League match on 5 September 1908 at Swindon. Unfortunately it was City who were 1-6 down and eventually suffered their record defeat 2-10.

Against Brighton and Hove Albion in the FA Cup on 30 November 1946, Norwich were 1-2 down at half time, but came back scoring six goals to win 7-2.

HAT TRICKS

Last column denotes number of goals scored if more than three.

Scorer		Result	Opponents	League / Cup	Date	X
Bert Playford	A	4-5	Lynn Tn.	Norfolk & Suffolk	08.04.03	
Vic Whitham	H	8-1	Lynn Tn.	Norfolk & Suffolk	30.04.03	
Percy Gooch	H	4-1	Lowestoft	FA Cup	19.09.03	
Bob Collinson	A	4-2	Harwich	FA Cup	17.10.03	
Herbert Vigar	A	4-2	Kirkley	Norfolk & Suffolk	25.02.05	
David Ross	A	5-0	Tunbridge Wells Rang.	FA Cup	17.01.06	

Scorer		Result	Opponents	League / Cup	Date	X
Cyril Dunning	H	6-1	Brentford	Southern League	26.12.08	
Bill Silor	H	6-1	Leyton Orient	Southern League	10.04.09	
John Smith	H	3-2	Q P R	Southern League	12.04.09	
Percy Gooch	H	6-0	Luton Town	Southern League	09.09.09	
Percy Gooch	H	4-2	Reading	Southern League	23.10.09	
Bill Rayner	H	4-1	Millwall	Southern League	04.12.09	
Harry Woods	H	6-0	Walthamstow	FA Cup	29.11.13	
Arthur Wolstenholme	H	6-0	Southend United	Southern League	03.01.14	4
Danny Wilson	H	5-2	Merthyr Town	Southern League	14.03.14	
John Doran	H	5-1	Bristol Rovers	Southern League	01.11.19	
Bob Dennison	H	3-2	Millwall	Division Three South	14.04.23	
James Jackson	H	5-0	Aberdare	Division Three South	03.09.23	
Ernest North	H	4-3	Crystal Palace	Division Three South	25.12.25	
Eric Price	H	6-1	Northampton Town	Division Three South	20.09.26	
Joe Richmond	H	4-0	Watford	Division Three South	18.04.27	
Percy Varco	H	5-0	Poole	FA Cup	01.12.27	
Percy Varco	H	3-1	Q.P.R	Division Three South	21.04.28	
Percy Varco	H	6-0	Newport Co.	FA Cup	08.12.28	4
James Thompson	A	3-6	Brighton & Hove Albion	Division Three South	07.09.29	
Bernard McLaverty	H	5-2	Watford	Division Three South	02.05.29	
James Thompson	A	4-4	Newport County	Division Three South	23.11.29	
Thomas Hunt	H	10-2	Coventry City	Division Three South	15.03.30	5
George Anderson	H	5-1	Merthyr Town	Division Three South	12.04.30	
Thomas Williams	H	4-0	Gillingham	Division Three South	20.12.30	

Scorer		Result	Opponents	League / Cup	Date	X
Oliver Brown	H	4-1	Watford	Division Three South	26.12.31	
Thomas Scott	H	5-2	Swindon Town	Division Three South	22.10.32	
Cecil Blakemore	H	5-3	Coventry City	Division Three South	02.02.33	
Oliver Brown	H	6-0	Bournemouth	Division Three South	11.03.33	4
Jack Vinall	H	7-2	Bristol City	Division Three South	28.08.33	4
Jack Vinall	H	4-3	Exeter City	Division Three South	28.10.33	
Billy Warnes	H	3-0	Charlton Athletic	Division Three South	18.11.33	
Rod Williams	H	3-2	Northampton T	FA Cup	21.03.34	
Jack Vinall	H	4-1	Notts County	Division Three South	17.11.34	
Jack Vinall	A	3-4	Swansea Town	Division Three South	07.09.35	
Jack Vinall	H	5-1	Southampton	Division Three South	08.02.36	
Leslie Eyre	H	7-2	Brighton & Hove Albion	Division Three South	30.11.46	5
Harold Joy	A	4-4	Mansfield Town	Division Three South	22.03.47	
Roy Hollis	H	5-2	Q.P.R	Division Three South	21.04.48	
Noel Kinsey	A	6-1	Bristol City	Division Three South	15.01.49	
Terry Ryder	H	5-1	Hartlepools U	FA Cup	15.12.49	
Roy Hollis	H	3-0	Southend United	Division Three South	18.11.50	
Roy Hollis	A	5-0	Crystal Palace	Division Three South	18.04.51	
Roy Hollis	H	8-0	Walsall	Division Three South	29.12.51	5
John Gavin	A	5-2	Bristol City	Division Three South	16.02.52	

Scorer		Result	Opponents	League / Cup	Date	X
John Gavin	H	7-0	Torquay United	Division Three South	14.04.52	
John Gavin	H	5-0	Gillingham	Division Three South	26.04.52	
Tom Johnston	A	8-1	Shrewsbury Town	Division Three South	13.09.52	4
John Gavin	H	3-0	Reading	Division Three South	28.02.53	
Fred Kearns	H	4-2	Headington U	FA Cup	20.11.54	
Ralph Hunt	H	4-1	Millwall	Division Three South	24.09.55	
John Gavin	H	7-2	Southend United	Division Three South	17.12.55	4
Jimmy Moran	H	5-2	Newport County	Division Three South	16.04.58	
Terry Bly	H	5-1	Q.P.R	Division Three	31.01.59	
Terry Allcock	H	3-1	Bury	Division Two	19.08.61	
Terry Allcock	A	4-5	Liverpool	Division Two	13.01.62	
Terry Allcock	H	5-0	Carlisle Utd.	League Cup	24.10.62	
Jimmy Hill	H	4-2	Sunderland	Division Two	27.10.62	
Jimmy Hill	A	3-0	Bury	Division Two	19.01.63	
Terry Allcock	H	5-0	Newcastle Utd	FA Cup	13.03.63	4
Jim Oliver	H	6-0	Stoke City	Division Two	09.03.63	
Ron Davies	H	5-1	Cardiff City	Division Two	14.12.63	
Gordon Bolland	H	5-3	Chester	League Cup	21.10.64	
Ron Davies	A	3-0	Portsmouth	Division Two	04.12.65	
Laurie Sheffield	H	4-1	Derby County	Division Two	12.11.66	
Hugh Curran	H	4-2	Birmingham City	Division Two	21.10.67	
Hugh Curran	A	4-2	Ipswich Town	League Cup	03.09.68	
Albert Bennett	A	4-1	Portsmouth	Division Two	04.04.70	
Graham Paddon	A	3-0	Arsenal	League Cup	21.11.72	
Mel Machin	A	3-1	Nottingham Forest	Division Two	12.10.74	
Ted MacDougall	H	5-3	Aston Villa	Division One	23.08.75	
Ted MacDougall	H	4-2	Everton	Division One	06.09.75	

Scorer		Result	Opponents	League / Cup	Date	X
Viv Busby	H	3-2	Leicester City	Division One	01.01.77	
Justin Fashanu	H	5-1	Stoke City	Division One	16.08.80	
John Deehan	H	5-0	Charlton Ath	Division Two	10.04.82	
Mick Channon	H	3-0	Cardiff City	League Cup	26.10.83	
John Deehan	H	6-1	Watford	Division One	07.04.84	4
John Deehan	H	3-2	Watford	Division One	22.09.84	
Dave Hodgson	H	4-1	Millwall	League Cup	29.10.86	
Robert Fleck	H	8-0	Sutton Utd.	FA Cup	28.01.89	
Malcolm Allen	H	8-0	Sutton Utd.	FA Cup	28.01.89	4
Darren Beckford	H	4-3	Everton	Division One	21.03.92	
Mark Robins	A	3-2	Oldham Ath.	Premier	09.11.92	
Chris Sutton	H	4-2	Leeds United	Premier	14.04.93	
Efan Ekoku	A	5-1	Everton	Premier	25.09.93	4
Ashley Ward	A	5-3	Bradford City	League Cup	07.11.95	
Craig Bellamy	H	4-2	Q.P.R	Division One	22.08.98	
Iwan Roberts	H	4-0	Stockport Co	Division One	20.02.01	

Last column shows the number of goals scored if more than three.

Efan Ekoku sored four goals in 28 minutes on 25 September 1993 against Everton.

Most Hat Tricks

Jack Vinall............. 5.................... between 1933-6
John Gavin .... 5.................... between 1952-5

Jack Vinall, joint scorer of the most City hat tricks and the first at Carrow Road.

Most Hat Tricks in a Season

John Gavin .... 3..................... 1951-2 ....Division Three South

In Successive Home Games

John Gavin .... Torquay Utd. 14.04.52........Division Three South
John Gavin .... Gillingham ... 26.04.52........Division Three South

Ted MacDougall ..... Aston Villa ... 23.08.75........Division One
Ted MacDougall .... Everton .... 06.09.75........Division One

Ted MacDougall, scored hat tricks in successive home games in 1975.

Two in One Game

Malcolm Allen and Robert Fleck both scored hat tricks in the 8-0 victory against Sutton United during the FA Cup fourth round match on 28 January 1989.

First at Carrow Road

Jack Vinall.............. Southampton 08.02.36.......Division Two

HOME MATCHES

LEAGUE MATCHES

Note the record of either Division Three or Division Three South has been shown for the Divisional figures below.

Most Home Wins in a Season

18	1951-2	Division Three South
18	2003-4	Division One
16	1985-6	Division Two
13	1992-3	Premier

Least Home Wins in a Season

4	1993-4	Premier
6	1973-4	Division One
6	1946-7	Division Three South
7	1968-9	Division Two

Most Home Defeats in a Season

11	1956-7	Division Three South
8	1987-8	Division One
8	1968-9	Division Two
8	1993-4	Premier

Least Home Defeats in a Season

0	1971-2	Division Two
1	1933-4, 1950-1, 1952-3	Division Three South
2	1989-90, 2003-4	Division One
2	1992-3	Premier

Most Home Draws in a Season

10	1920-1	Division Three
10	1978-9, 1986-7, 1989-90	Division One
9	1993-4	Premier
8	1970-1, 1971-2	Division Two

Least Home Draws in a Season

1.............................. 1951-2 .... Division Three South
2.............................. 1935-6 .... Division Two
3.............................. 1990-1, 2003-4............................ Division One
6.............................. 1992-3 .... Premier

Best Home Records

Won	Drew	Lost	Season	Division
18	3	2	2003-4	Division One
18	1	4	1951-2	Division Three South
16	4	1	1933-4	Division Three South
16	4	1	1985-6	Division Two
13	8	0	1971-2	Division Two
13	6	2	1992-3	Premier

Worst Home Record

Won	Drew	Lost	Season	Division
4	9	8	1993-4	Premier
6	9	6	1973-4	Division One
7	6	8	1968-9	Division Two
6	3	12	1946-7	Division Three South

Most Home Goals Scored

56.............................. 1952-3, 1955-6............................ Division Three South
51.............................. 1985-6 .... Division Two
44.............................. 2003-4 .... Division One
31.............................. 1992-3 .... Premier

Least Home Goals Scored

22.............................. 1972-3 .... Division One
24.............................. 1968-9 .... Division Two
26.............................. 1993-4 .... Premier
27.............................. 1921-2 .... Division Three South

Most Home Goals Conceded

48	1946-7	Division Three South
33	1962-3	Division Two
32	1990-1	Division One
29	1993-4	Premier

Least Home Goals Conceded

14	1989-90	Division One
14	1969-70	Division Two
14	1950-1	Division Three South
19	1992-3	Premier

HOME SEQUENCES

Successive League Home Wins

12	1952	Division Three South

City went From 15 March, when they beat Reading 2-1, until 4 October 1952, when they were prevented from winning a thirteenth successive home win by a 2-2 draw with Millwall.

Successive League Home Wins from Start of Season

8	2003	Division One

City won all their first eight home games in the promotion season 2003-4. They scored 17 goals and conceded six. Surprisingly, they then lost 1-2 at home to lowly Watford on 15 November 2003.

Successive Home Defeats

4	1968	Division Two

City suffered three league home defeats in succession plus one in the League Cup between 21 September and 16 October 1968.

Portsmouth 0-1, Hull City 1-2, Crystal Palace 0-1 and Southampton 0-4 (Cup)

Although the sequence was broken by a draw in the next home game, City suffered a further two home defeats and a draw before finally winning 2-0 against Fulham on 14 December 1968. The total run yielded two draws from eight home games.

League Home Games without a Defeat

31............................1971-2 ....Division Two / One

Norwich lost the last home game of the 1970-1 season, but then remained **undefeated at home throughout the promotion season of 1971-2.** They also went the first ten matches in the following season, their first in Division One, until losing to Manchester United on 2 December 1972. During this run they won 18 and drew 13 and their only defeats were in the League Cup to Chelsea and the FA Cup to Hull City.

All Home Games without a Defeat

12............................1970...Division Two

From 14 February 1970, when they beat Aston Villa 3-1, until losing 0-2 to Hull City on 26 September 1970, City did not lose at home for 11 league games plus one cup tie.

Home Games without a Draw

27............................1951-2 ....Division Three South

After drawing with Exeter City on 12 September 1951, City went 24 league and three cup games before drawing with Millwall on 4 October 1952.

League Home Games Without a Win

13............................1956-7 ....Division Three South

Despite winning their first five home games, City then went 12 home league and one FA Cup game without a win before defeating Millwall 2-0 on 2 March 1957.

City also went ten home games without a win in the Premier League. From 13 December 1993, when they beat Leeds 2-1, they then went nine league and one FA Cup game before beating Everton 3-0 on 21 March 1994. City continued this unsuccessful run in the remaining four home games of the season, which included 3-4 and 4-5 defeats. Including a draw in the first game of the next season, this meant they had achieved a solitary home win in 16 games.

Best Home Wins (6+)

18-0 ....Brighton & H A ......25.12.40........War League
10-2 ....Coventry City.......... 15.03.30.......Division Three South
8-0 ....Walsall................... 29.12.51.......Division Three South
8-0 ....Sutton United.......... 28.01.89 ....FA Cup

NORWICH CITY'S AMAZING PERFORMANCE.

DOUBLE FIGURES SCORE AGAINST COVENTRY.

CUP-TIE DEFEAT AVENGED.

Norwich City broke all their records and supplied the sensation of the day in the Football League by defeating Coventry City at the Nest by 10 goals to 2.

Hunt scored five times, and over 8000 spectators experienced a great thrill in seeing Coventry's defence riddled and the cup defeat avenged in such a convincing manner.

TIME-TABLE OF THE MATCH.

-3.15.—Game started.
3.19.—Hunt scored No. 1.
3.24.—Scott scored No. 2.
3.29.—Porter scored No. 3.
3.51.—Hunt scored No. 4.
4.0.—Half-time: Norwich 4, Coventry 0.
4.5.—Second half started.
4.12.—Scott scored No. 5.
4.15.—Lochhead scored No. 6.
4.19.—Slicer scored No. 7.
4.22.—Pick scored No. 1 for Coventry.
4.24.—Hunt scored No. 8.
4.46.—Hunt scored No. 9.
4.49.—Pick scored No. 2 for Coventry.
4.50.—Hunt scored No. 10.
4.53.—Match ended. Norwich 10, Coventry 2.

The players were desperately keen to wipe out the stain of that Cup defeat, and jumping into their stride they secured the tonic of an early goal. They remembered that three goals had not been enough to beat Coventry in November, and every nerve was strained to put themselves in a position secure against all possible chance of a Coventry recovery. They succeeded beyond all expectations. As the time table of the match shows, Norwich scored their first three goals within fourteen minutes of the start, and upon this solid foundation was built the biggest victory in the history of the club. By dashing runs and skilful passing the Norwich forwards swept through the Coventry defence in irresistible fashion, and with his backs overrun Allen was helpless against the invaders, who were extremely quick in seizing their scoring opportunities.

BRILLIANT FORWARD PLAY.

The Norwich forwards may on some previous occasions have been as delightful to watch in their approach play, but they have never in

An extract from the press report, for the 10-2 win over Coventry

Score	Opponents	Date	Division / Cup
7-0	Torquay United	14.04.52	Division Three South
7-2	Bristol City	28.08.33	Division Three South
7-2	Southend United	17.12.55	Division Three South
6-0	Exeter City	11.11.22	Division Three South
6-0	Bristol Rovers	13.02.32	Division Three South
6-0	Bournemouth	11.03.33	Division Three South
6-1	Northampton T	20.09.26	Division Three South
6-1	Bournemouth	24.03.34	Division Three South
6-2	Coventry City	09.04.32	Division Three South
6-3	Bournemouth	09.10.24	Division Three South
7-2	Notts County	17.11.34	Division Two
6-0	Stoke City	09.03.63	Division Two
6-0	Birmingham City	15.04.70	Division Two
6-1	Bradford City	23.03.35	Division Two
6-1	Bradford City	23.03.35	Division Two
6-1	Millwall	21.12.85	Division Two
6-1	Watford	07.04.84	Division One
8-0	Sutton United	28.01.89	FA Cup

Score	Opponents	Date	Division / Cup
7-2	Brighton & HA	30.11.46	FA Cup
6-0	Newport County	08.12.28	FA Cup
6-0	Walthamstow G.	29.11.13	FA Cup
6-1	Chatham T	24.11.28	FA Cup
6-1	Redhill	16.11.57	FA Cup
6-1	Preston N E	10.10.84	League Cup
6-1	Torquay United	20.09.95	League Cup
6-2	Oldham Athletic	26.10.60	League Cup
6-2	Wrexham	10.10.73	League Cup
6-0	Luton Town	09.09.09	Southern
6-0	Southend United	03.01.14	Southern
6-1	Luton Town	21.04.08	Southern
6-1	Leyton	10.04.09	Southern
6-1	Brentford	26.12.08	Southern
6-3	West Ham United	12.12.08	Southern

Biggest Home Defeat (5+)

2-6	Nottingham Forest	02.01.91	Division One
3-5	Liverpool	02.02.80	Division One
2-6	West Ham United	17.11.38	Division Two
1-5	Newcastle United	28.12.36	Division Two
1-6	Bournemouth	26.12.46	Division Three South
1-5	Swindon Town	26.04.30	Division Three South
1-5	Swindon Town	12.09.46	Division Three South
1-5	Southend United	02.11.46	Division Three South
1-5	Ipswich Town	13.09.47	Division Three South
1-5	Bristol Rovers	20.09.47	Division Three South
2-5	Reading	02.02.57	Division Three South
4-5	Southampton	09.04.94	Premier
0-5	Corinthians.	12.01.29	FA Cup
0-5	Man City	12.01.39	FA Cup
0-5	Arsenal	12.01.52	FA Cup

Biggest Home Draw

4-4	Exeter City	18.09.26	Division Three South
4-4	Q P R	14.12.46	FA Cup
4-4	Southampton	09.09.89	Division One

INJURIES

Several players have suffered serious injuries that have sometimes ended their careers. With the improvement in modern medicine and treatment there are many injuries that can now be cured and playing carers resumed. Some Norwich players have spent long periods recovering and the following are those who returned after nearly two years.

Peter Silvester had three cartilage operations on his knee. This kept him sidelined from 22 January 1972 until 1 January 1974 although he did play four games on loan to Colchester in 1973. He only played six games for City after his return before moving to Southend.

Gerry Mannion broke his leg in November 1965 against Preston North End and did not play in the first team again until September 1967 and then for only two games. He was transferred to Chester in January 1968.

Mick McGuire damaged his achillies tendon in the summer of 1976 playing tennis and did not play for the first team again until Oct 1977 and then only for two games. It was not until February 1968 that he started playing regularly.

Zema Abbey had the misfortune to damage his cruciate ligament in both knees. He was out of action from September 2001 for over 18 months, returned for half a season and then did the same again to the other knee to miss the whole of season 2003-4.

David Jones was injured while on international duty in the close season of 1978. He was out for a season and a half, but fought his way back into the side before incredibly suffering a reoccurrence of the knee injury when playing for Wales again in 1980, which finished his career.

John O'Neill was most unfortunate when, having just signed from QPR for £100,000, he was badly injured after only 34 minutes in his first game at Wimbledon on 18 December 1987. The severely damaged knee ligaments forced him to retire from the game, never to play again, after one of the shortest ever Norwich careers. He later pursued legal action against John Fashanu, who had inflicted the injury, and received £70,000 in 1994 as an out of court settlement.

INTERNATIONALS

Three England representative matches have been played at Carrow Road.

These were two England under 23 Internationals and a Football League X1 match.

Team	Country	Score	Date	Attendance
England Under 23	Czechoslovakia	3-0	15.10.58	38,000
England Under 23	France	3-0	03.11.65	20,253
England Under 21	Greece	4-2	17.12.97	14,114
Football League	Irish League	3-1	31.10.62	14,522

Other matches featuring Ladies, Schoolboy / Youth Internationals

England Schoolboys	Ireland	1-1	03.04.56
England Schoolboys	Wales	2-3	11.04.81
England Under 19	Switzerland	1-1	19.03.91
England Ladies	Nigeria Ladies	0-1	23.07.02

KEEPERS

City have been fortunate to have a number of long serving goalkeepers, particularly since the war.

Bryan Gunn, long serving Scottish International goalkeeper.

Goalkeeper	Seasons	Appearances
Charlie Dennington	1922-29	209
Ken Nethercott	1947-59	416
Sandy Kennon	1959-64	255
Kevin Keelan	1963-80	673
Chris Woods	1981-86	267
Bryan Gunn	1986-96	477
Andy Marshall	1994-2001	219
Robert Green	2001-	155

Goalkeeper Chris Woods, holding the Milk Cup, was capped by England.

KIT

Until 9 June 1907, Norwich were known as the "Citizens" and played in blue and white halved shirts. The present colours were adopted from their mascot, the yellow canary, in 1907. The first canary kit had yellow shirts with green cuffs and collar.

The predominant colour has always been yellow with usually green included in some way, although green shorts were not introduced until 1965. One of the more contentious strips was in 1997, when an all yellow strip was used, but public opinion persuaded the club to revert back to the traditional yellow and green.

In the last twenty years the kits have been changed every other year and often the second and third strips are designed more flamboyantly or to incorporate sponsor's colours. This included one to mark the club's centenary in the original blue and white halves with supporters' names displayed discreetly all over the shirt.

How the colours have varied

Season	Shirts	Shorts
1902-05	Blue & white halves	White
1905-07	Blue & white halves	Blue
1907-09	Yellow, green collars & cuffs	White
1909-15	Yellow, green sleeves	White
1919-23	Yellow and green stripes	Black
1923-27	White with canary badge	Black
1927-47	Yellow & green halves	Black
1947-65	Yellow, green collar & cuffs	Black
1965-74	Yellow, green collar & cuffs	Green

From the mid seventies the kit started to become more stylish with shirt manufacturers and sponsors wishing to make their mark.

Season	Shirts	Shorts	Makers
1974-76	Yellow, green collar & cuffs	Green	Umbro
1976-81	Yellow, green emblems on sleeve	Green	Admiral
1981-84	Yellow, green pinstripe, green collar & cuffs	Green	Addidas
1984-86	Yellow shadow stripes, with green chevrons	Green	Hummell
1986-87	Yellow with green sleeves	Green	Hummell
1987-89	Yellow with green side stripes, collar & cuffs	Green	Scoreline
1989-92	Yellow with green diagonal shoulder stripes	Green	Asics
1992-4	Yellow with green fleck	Green	Ribero.
1994-97	Yellow, green collar & trim, baggy shorts	Green	Mitre
1997-99	All Yellow with green trim	Yellow	Pony
1999-2001	Yellow with one green side.	Green	Pony
2001-03	Yellow with yellow & green sleeves	Green	Xara
2003	Yellow, green sides, yellow & green sleeves	Green	Xara

See sponsors' section.

LEAGUE APPEARANCES

League	Seasons	Years
Division One	1972-74	2
	1975-81	6
	1982-85	3
	1986-92	6
Premier	1992-95	3
Top Flight		**20**
Division One since Premier	1995-2004	9
Division Two	1934-39	5
	1960-72	12
	1974-75	1
	1981-82	1
	1985-86	1
Division Three South	1921-34	13
	1946-58	12
Division Three	1920-21	1
	1958-60	2
Southern	1905-20	11
Norfolk & Suffolk	1902-05	3
United	1906-07, 1908-09	2

(Concurrent with Southern League)

There was no Football League competition during 1915-19 and 1939-46.

City have played in the Football League for 77 seasons, to 2004, of which over a quarter have been in the top division.

LEAGUE CUP

The League Cup has been sponsored by various companies: – The Milk Marketing Board, Littlewoods, Rumbelows, Coca Cola, Worthington Brewery and Carling. The Cup tends to be referred to by the sponsor's name although it is still classed as the Football League Cup, open to those League members only.

City's record is summarised below: -

Winners

Season	Opponents	Result			Attendance	Scorers
1961-2	Rochdale	3-0	A	1st Leg	11,123	Punton, Lythgoe
		1-0	H	2nd Leg	19,800	Hill
1984-5	Sunderland	1-0	N		100,000	Hartford

Chris Woods, Dave Watson, Louie Donowa and John Devine parade around Wembley with the Milk Cup in 1985.

LEAGUE CUP

Finalists

Season	Opponents	Result		Attendance
1972-3	Tottenham H	0-1	N	100,000
1974-5	Aston Villa	0-1	N	100,000

Semi – Finalists

Winning

Season	Opponents	Result		Attendance	Scorers
1961-2	Blackpool	4-1	H	19,296	Hill, Punton, Lythgoe, Scott
1961-2	Blackpool	0-2	A	9,142	
1972-3	Chelsea	2-0	A	31,775	Bone, Cross
1972-3	Chelsea	1-0	H	34,265	Govier
1974-5	Manchester Utd	2-2	A	58,010	Powell, MacDougall
1974-5	Manchester Utd	1-0	H	31,621	Suggett
1984-5	Ipswich Town	0-1	A	27,404	
1984-5	Ipswich Town	2-0	H	23,545	Deehan, Bruce

Losing

1973-4	Wolves	1-1	H	20,517	Mellor
1973-4	Wolves	0-1	A	32,605	

CITY'S PERFORMANCE IN THE LEAGUE CUP

Biggest Win

Result	Opponents	Venue	Round	Attendance	Date
7-1	Halifax Town	A	Fourth	4,822	27.11.63
6-1	Preston N.E	H	Second	13,506	10.10.84
6-1	Torquay United	H	Second	7,542	20.09.95
6-2	Oldham Ath.	H	Second	13,080	26.10 60
6-2	Wrexham	H	Second	10,937	10.10.73

The Preston tie was also City's highest aggregate of goals scored in this competition following a 3-3 draw in the first leg, making 13 in all for the tie.

Biggest Defeat

Result	Opponents	Venue	Round	Attendance	Date
1-6	Manchester City	N	Second	6,239	29.09.75
0-4	Southampton	H	Fourth	25,309	16.10.68
0-4	Fulham	H	Second	11,760	14.09.99
1-4	Aston Villa	A	Fifth	14,868	03.12.62

Longest Without Win

4 games

City have gone four games without winning on four separate occasions, but they have only lost all four in one sequence. (See consecutive defeats below).

Longest Without Home Win

6 games

After beating Chester 5-3 in the Third Round in 1964, City did not win another League Cup home game until 8 August 1971, beating Brighton & Hove Albion 2-0

Longest Without an Away Win

8 games

After beating Charlton Athletic 2-0 on 25 September 1991, City did not win away again until 4 October 1995 when they beat Torquay United 3-2 in the second round second leg.

Longest Without a Defeat

10 games

During the 1974-5 League Cup run between the second round and the final, where they lost to Aston Villa, City had gone ten matches without defeat.

Longest Without a Home Defeat

12 games

From their first home game in the competition on 26 October 1960, when they beat Oldham Athletic 6-2, City did not lose a League Cup home game until Brighton & Hove Albion defeated them on 14 September 1966, a run of 12 games.

Longest Without an Away Defeat

8 games

After losing 1-2 to Bristol Rovers on 7 October 1970, City didn't lose a League Cup game away for nine games. They were beaten 0-1 in the semi-final second leg by Wolves on 26 January 1974.

Successive Home Ties

4..**1995-6**

Torquay United. 6-1
Bradford City 0-0
Bolton Wanderers.....................................0-0
Birmingham City 1-1

Although most of these ties were drawn with City at home in each of them, they had to play away in a second leg or replay on all occasions.

Successive Away Ties

5................................**1976-8**	**5**...................................**1992-4**
Exeter City...................... 1976	Tottenham Hotspur............ 1992
Aston Villa...................... 1976	Carlisle United.................. 1993
Burnley 1977	Blackburn Rovers.............. 1993
Wrexham........................ 1978	Bradford City.................... 1994
Chester........................... 1978	Arsenal 1994

Best Period

From 1972-5, City reached two finals and one semi-final

Tottenham Hotspur....... 1972-3 ....Final
Wolves .... 1973-4 ....Semi-Final
Aston Villa................... 1974-5 ....Final

Worst Period

From 1 November 2000 to date (2004), City lost four successive matches and exited the competition at the first hurdle in the last three years.

Consecutive Wins

6............................... **1972-3**

On route to the League Cup Final in 1972-3, City won all their ties outright at the first attempt.

Round	Opponents	Result	Attendance
Second	Leicester City	H .. 2-1	22,498
Third	Hull City	A .. 2-1	11,524
Fourth	Stockport County	A .. 5-1	16,533
Fifth	Arsenal	A . 3-0	37,671
Semi-Final	Chelsea	A .. 2-0	34,316
Semi-Final	Chelsea	H .. 3-0	34,265

Consecutive Defeats

4...................... 2000-3

From 1 November 2000 to 2003 on going.

Round	Opponents	Result	Attendance	Year
Third	Derby County	A 0-3	11,273	2000
First	Brentford	A .. 0-1	4,111	2001
First	Cheltenham Town	H .. 0-3	13,285	2002
First	Northampton Town	A . 0-1	5,476	2003

Famous League Cup Semi-Final Victories

Opponents	Result		Date	Attendance
Chelsea	A 2-0	First Leg	13.12.72	34,316
	H 1-0	Second Leg	03.01.73	34,265

City had already beaten Arsenal in the previous round, but had lost a league match 1-3 at Chelsea, only four days prior to the first leg. Two goals in the 12th and 13th minutes by Bone and Cross gave City a cushion for the return at Carrow Road.

In the second leg, which had to be replayed after the aborted fogged off match,

Govier headed the winner in the 49th minute to see City safely through to their first Wembley final.

Team: Keelan. Butler, Black, Stringer, Govier, Briggs, Livermore, Bone, (Cheesley), Cross, Paddon, Anderson. Sub in 1st Leg - Howard

Man Utd   A   2-2 ....First Leg........... 15.01.75 58,010
               H   1-0 ....Second Leg........ 22.01.75 31,672

Both clubs were going for promotion from the Second Division and met in the semi-final. In the first leg in front of a massive crowd at Old Trafford, City went ahead through Powell in the 40th minute. However, United hit back to take the lead, but with only two minutes remaining, MacDougall seized on a defensive mix up to keep City on level terms for the second leg.

In the return leg, City fought bravely and Suggett snatched the vital goal in the 54th minute, leaving the Canaries to hold on doggedly to reach their second final in three years.

Team: Keelan, Machin, Sullivan, Stringer, Forbes, Peters, Powell, MacDougall, Boyer, Suggett, Benson (Miller).

Ipswich Town   A   0-1 ....First Leg........... 23.02.85 27,404
                    H   2-0 ....Second Leg........ 06.03.85 23,545

With such an important fixture against deadly rivals Ipswich Town, City had a battle on their hands, especially when they went behind after only six minutes in the first leg. They never came to grips with the game and were relieved to come away with only a one goal deficit.

In the second leg Ipswich started well, but after losing D'Avray the tide turned City's way. In the 35th minute Deehan pulled the tie level by a deflected shot from a free kick. Both sides had chances in the second half, but failed to score and extra time looked likely. City fans were ecstatic in the 88th minute when Bruce crashed a header into the net from a Barham corner. City's progress into the final was even sweeter being over their bitter rivals

Team: Woods, Devine (Haylock), Van Wyk, Bruce, Mendham, Watson, Barham, Channon, Deehan, Hartford, Clayton, (Donowa.

Steve Bruce celebrates after a last minute winner against Ipswich in the Milk Cup Semi- Final. Louie Donowa, Mick Channon and John Deehan join in.

LEAGUE TROPHY

Another pre-season competition that replaced the League Group Cup, but it only ran for one season.

Date	Opponents	Venue	Result	Attendance
14.08.82	Northampton Town	H	3-0	1,801
18.08.82	Peterborough Utd	H	6-2	2,192
21.08.82	Mansfield Town	A	3-1	1,985
08.12.82	Lincoln City	A	1-3	3,853

LOAN PLAYERS

LOAN PLAYERS

Norwich have used numerous loan players over the years, either as a short term measure or preceding a permanent transfer. For the short term loan players, the significant ones are shown below.

First Loan Player

Player	Club	Year	Appearances	Goals
Bobby Bell	Ipswich town	1972	3	

International Loan players

Peter Osgood	Southampton	1976	3	
Joe Corrigan	Brighton & H.A.	1984	4	
Jan Molby	Liverpool	1995-6	5	1
David Rocastle	Chelsea	1997	11	

Norwich used the loan system to their best advantage in 2003-4. The acquisition of Peter Crouch and Kevin Harper on loan for three months, as well as Darren Huckerby, who eventually joined permanently, enabled them to shoot up the table to top position before Christmas.

LONGEST CUP TIES

Birmingham City- FA Cup, four matches - Third Round 1985

Sat	5 January 5	A	0-0	12,041
Wed	23 January 23	H	1-1	11,883
Sat.	26 January 26	A	1-1	11,755
Mon.	28 January 28	H	1-0	12,396

The two 1-1 draws were after extra time, making the total time played to settle the tie as seven hours. There was little reward for this marathon as City lost 1-2 in the Fourth Round at West Ham United a week later.

LONGEST SERVING PLAYERS

Ron Ashman ready to start a match at Lincoln. He made the second highest appearances for City, was their longest serving captain, highest penalty scorer and manager.

The following players have played for the club for 10 years or more: -

Player		Seasons	Appearances
George	Martin	1913-27	337
Joe	Hannah	1921-35	427
Bernard	Robinson	1932-49	380
Harry	Proctor	1934-46	116
Dennis	Morgan	1946-56	250
Ken	Nethercott	1947-59	416
Ron	Ashman	1947-63	662
Roy	McCrohan	1951-62	426
Terry	Allcock	1958-69	389
Kevin	Keelan	1963-80	673
David	Stringer	1965-76	499
Duncan	Forbes	1968-80	357
Jeremy	Goss	1984-97	238
Ian	Crook	1986-97	418
Bryan	Gunn	1986-98	477
Daryl	Sutch	1990-2002	352

Manager		Seasons
Arthur	Turner	1902-05
James	Bowman	1905-07
James	McEwen	1907-08
Arthur	Turner	1908-10
James	Stansfield	1910-15
Major F	Buckley	1919-20
Charles	O'Hagan	1920-21
Albert	Gosnell	1921-26
Bert	Stansfield	1926
Cecil	Potter	1926-28
James	Kerr	1929-33
Tom	Parker	1933-37
Bob	Young	1937-39
Jimmy	Jewell	1939
Bob	Young	1939-46
Doug	Lochhead	1946
Cyril	Spiers	1946-47
Doug	Lochhead	1948-50
Norman	Low	1950-55
Tom	Parker	1955-57
Archie	Macaulay	1957-61
Willie	Reid	1961-62
George	Swindin	1962
Ron	Ashman	1962-66
Lol	Morgan	1966-69
Ron	Saunders	1969-73
John	Bond	1973-80
Ken	Brown	1980-87
Dave	Stringer	1987-92
Mike	Walker	1992-94
John	Deehan	1994-95
Martin	O'Neill	1995
Gary	Megson	1995-96
Mike	Walker	1996-98
Bruce	Rioch	1998-2000
Bryan	Hamilton	2000
Nigel	Worthington	2001-

Arthur Turner also served as secretary during his reign and was termed assistant manager in his first stint. He was assistant manager again during James McEwen's tenure in 1907-8

.

Longest Serving Manager

Ken Brown .... 7 years ....Oct 1980 - Oct 1987

Shortest Serving Managers

Apart from caretaker managers, the shortest reigning manager was Willie Reid. He was City's Scottish scout, appointed manager on 14 December 1961, but resigned on 9 May 1962 after just five months, not wishing to move from Scotland. During this time, however, City won the League Cup.

George Swindin, although manager from 23 May 1962 until he resigned to join Cardiff City on 10 November 1962 was only in charge for three months of the actual season, 20 games.

Martin O'Neill was appointed manager on 13 June 1995 and resigned six months later on 17 December 1995 after a fall out with chairman Robert Chase. This was also significant in that City were about to play a televised game at Leicester, which they lost 2-3 after leading 2-0. O'Neill had become Leicester City's manager immediately before the game and went on to not only gain promotion to the Premier Division, but also into Europe, before he moved to Celtic.

First Manager in Football League

Charles O'Hagan..Jul 1920 - Jan 1921

First Manager to Win a Trophy

Tom Parker.................. Division Three South 1933-4

MANAGERS

First Manager to reach First Division

Ron Saunders 1972

Most Successful Managers

Archie Macaulay took City from the brink of liquidation in 1956 to Semi Finalists as a Third Division club in 1959 during a wonderful Cup run and to promotion the following season.

City were managed by Ron Saunders when they were first promoted to Division One as Champions in 1972. They were also losing Finalists in the League Cup the following year.

Ken Brown took over the helm from John Bond in 1980 when City were already struggling and it was no surprise when they were relegated from the First Division.

Archie Macaulay

However, under Ken Brown and coach Mel Machin, City won promotion in the next season and also won the League (Milk) Cup in 1985, but suffered relegation in the same season before again returning to the top flight as champions.

Ken Brown, with one of the two trophies he won as manager, the Division Two Championship, held enthusiastically by some young supporters.

Mike Walker took City to their highest ever league position, finishing third in the Premier League, after being leaders with six games to go. They then successfully qualified for Europe and had a glorious run.

Managers Who Played for the Club

	Player	Manager
Doug Lochhead	1929-35	1948-50
Ron Ashman	1947-63	1963-66
David Stringer	1965-76	1987-92
John Deehan	1981-85	1994-95
Martin O'Neill	1981-83	1995
Gary Megson	1992-95	1995-96

James McEwen, played for City 1905-8, and was named manager in 1907-8, although he did not have a full management role and teams were often picked by assistant manager, Arthur Turner.

MASCOTS

Canary and Dumpling, mascots brought to life

The Norwich City mascots were for a long period, Canary and Dumpling, They were first depicted as cartoon caricatures in the 1950's by E H Banger. In 1981 the Norwich School of Art designed outfits, including heads. These brought the caricatures to life and for several seasons two fans wore the outfits to parade around the ground before matches. The outfits are currently (2004) on display in the Canary Centenary exhibition in the Bridewell Museum.

In 1995 new mascots appeared on the scene. These were Captain Canary and Splat the Cat, with the latter sponsored by Norwich & Peterborough Building Society. They were introduced to help promote reserve games as family fun evenings and attracted attendances up to 2,000.

MBE

Three players have been awarded an MBE whilst playing with Norwich: -

Martin Peters 1978
Kevin Keelan........................... 1980
Martin O'Neill........................... 1982

Martin O'Neill was later awarded an OBE whilst with Celtic.

MEDALS

City have won trophies with the attributable medals for players and management on six occasions. On two other occasions they have been runners up in League Cup finals.

The Football League stipulates that a player must compete in a third of the programme to qualify for a medal unless there are extenuating circumstances. The Club may have appealed for extra medals, but it is not clear how successful this was. In 2004, all players who had played any part in the championship campaign appeared to receive medals at the award ceremony at the City Hall.

The lists below show players who appeared for City on medal winning occasions, but in some cases may have not received them if their appearances were insufficient.

Champions Division Three 1933-4	App	Champions Division Two 1971-2	App	Champions Division Two 1985-6	App
Norman Wharton	42	Kevin Keelan	42	Steve Bruce	42
Jack Vinall	42	David Stringer	42	Chris Woods	42
Tom Halliday	40	Clive Payne	42	Dave Watson(Cap)	42
Lionel Murphy	39	Doug Livermore	41	Mike Phelan	42
Billy Warnes	39	Kenny Foggo	40	Kevin Drinkell	41
Stan Ramsay (Cap)	38	Graham Paddon	40	David Williams	39
Ken Burditt	37	Terry Anderson	34	Mark Barham	35
Bernard Robinson	33	David Cross	32	Peter Mendham	35

Championship medals (continued)

Division Three 1933-4	App	Division Two 1971-2	App	Division Two 1985-6	App
Doug Lochhead	31	Duncan Forbes(Cap)	27	Ian Culverhouse	30
Albert Thorpe	20	Max Briggs	27	Denis Van Wijk	29
Thomas Scott	17	Peter Silvester	26	Wayne Biggins	28
Joe Hannah	26	Geoff Butler	23	John Deehan	26
Harold Houghton	11	Alan Black	20	Garry Brooke	13
William Smith	11	Trevor Howard	20	Paul Haylock	12
Sam Bell	10	Jimmy Bone	13	Tony Spearing	8
Rod Williams	8	Phil Hubbard	8	Robert Rosario	8
Theo Pyke	8	Malcolm Darling	4	Dale Gordon	6
Robert Morris	6	Bobby Bell	3	Louie Donowa	2
Alf Kirchen	1	Steve Govier	3	Paul Clayton	1
Frank Perfect	1	Neil O'Donnell	2		
Tom Williamson	1	Steve Grapes	1		
Gordon Wilson	1	Gary Sargent	1		

Stan Ramsay holding City's first League trophy, the Division Three Shield in 1934.

MEDALS

Champions Division One 2003-4	App	Champions Division One 2003-4 (continued)	App
Craig Fleming	46	Clint Easton	10
Robert Green	46	Kevin Cooper	10
Gary Holt	46	Kevin Harper	9
Malky Mackay	45	Jason Shackell	6
Paul McVeigh	45	Elvis Hammond	4
Marc Edworthy	43	Keith Briggs	3
Adam Drury (Cap)	42	Zema Abbey	3
Damien Francis	41	David Nielsen	2
Iwan Roberts	41	Alex Notman	1
Darren Huckerby	36	Paul Crichton	0
Phil Mulryne	34		
Mathias Svensson	20		
Ian Henderson	18		
Leon McKenzie	18		
Jim Brennan	15		
Peter Crouch	15		
Mark Rivers	12		
Ryan Jarvis	12		

League Cup 1962	League (Milk) Cup 1985
Ron Ashman (Captain)	Mark Barham
Ollie Burton	Steve Bruce
Barry Butler	Mick Channon
Jimmy Hill	John Deehan
Sandy Kennon	John Devine (unused substitute)
Derrick Lythgoe	Louie Donowa
Gerry Mannion	Asa Hartford
Roy McCrohan	Paul Haylock
Joe Mullett	Peter Mendham
Bill Punton	Denis Van Wijk
Dick Scott	Dave Watson (Captain)
	Chris Woods

League Cup 1973 Runners Up	League Cup 1975 Runners Up
Duncan Forbes (Captain)	Duncan Forbes (Captain)
Kevin Keelan	Kevin Keelan
Geof Butler	Mel Machin
Clive Payne	Colin Sullivan
David Stringer	Peter Morris
Max Briggs	David Stringer
Doug Livermore	Ted MacDougall
Jim Blair	Phil Boyer
David Cross	John Miller
Graham Paddon	Colin Suggett
Terry Anderson	Tony Powell
Trevor Howard (substitute)	Billy Steele (unused substitute)

MINOR CUPS

City have played in several minor cup competitions, shown separately under their own sections. In order to understand how they fit in, they have been listed in order below: -

Cup   **Year**

Amateur Cup....................................1902-4
Norfolk Senior Cup 1902-4
Southern Charity Cup.........................1913-5
Division Three South Cup 1933-4
Texaco Cup......................................1972-5
Anglo Scottish Cup 1975-8
Willhire Cup 1978-80
Group Cup 1981
League Trophy.................................1982
Screen Sport Super Cup....................1985-6
Full Members Cup............................1986-7
Simod Cup 1987-9
Zenith Data Cup..............................1989-92

NEUTRAL GROUNDS

City have played the following games on neutral grounds: -

Year	Venue	Opposition	Score	Occasion
1909	Stamford Bridge ......Reading		0-0	FA Cup first round
	(Pitch not required size)			
1909	Villa Park ....Reading		3-2	FA Cup first round , second replay
1913	Stamford Bridge ......Bristol Rovers		0-1	FA Cup second round, second replay
1914	White Hart Lane ......Coventry City		0-3	Southern Charity Cup semi-final
1915	Sincil Bank..............Bradford City		0-2	FA Cup third round, second replay
1934	Highbury ....Torquay United		1-4 ...	Division Three South Cup semi- final
1959	White Hart Lane ......Luton Town		1-1	FA Cup semi-final
1959	St Andrews..............Luton Town		0-1	FA Cup semi-final replay
1975	Stamford Bridge ......Manchester City		1-6	League Cup second round, second replay
1973	Villa Park ....Leeds United.		0-5	FA Cup third round, second replay
1973	Wembley ....Tottenham H.		0-1	League Cup final
1975	Wembley ....Aston Villa		0-1	League Cup final
1985	Wembley ....Sunderland		1-0	Milk Cup final
1989	Villa Park ....Everton		0-1	FA Cup semi-final
1992	Hillsborough............Sunderland		0-1	FA Cup semi-final
2002	Millennium Stadium...Birmingham City		1-1	Play Off final
	(Lost 2-4 on penalties)			

Its noticeable that City have enjoyed very little success on neutral territory, having only won twice in 16 games.

NEWMARKET ROAD

Newmarket Road was City's first ground from 1902 until 1908. However, with the restricted capacity of around 11,000 and the conditions applied by the owners at the time, it soon proved to be too limiting, prompting the Club to move to bigger premises at The Nest. Some of the stands were moved to the new ground, but the original pavilion stood until the 1990's, on what is now the City of Norwich School playing field on the corner of the Norwich ring road.

A commemorative plaque was installed during the Centenary events in 2002, to denote the ground's part in City's history.

City's first ground at Newmarket Road

NICKNAME

Initially, Norwich were known as the 'Citizens', but soon switched to the 'Canaries' from 1907. This nickname was more appropriate as it identified with the popular bird extensively bred in the City at the time.

It also led to the change of colours from blue to yellow and City are one of the very few clubs to adopt that as their main colour.

Sections of the ground have had nicknames applied to them, usually for the more rowdy element. These have included the 'Chicken Run,' at The Nest and the 'Snakepit,' at Carrow Road.

NORFOLK BORN PLAYERS

There have been only a few Norfolk born players who have played over 100 games for City. These are: -

Player		Appearances	Years	Birthplace
David	Stringer	499	1965-76	Great Yarmouth
Joe	Hannah	427	1921-35	Sheringham
Peter	Mendham	267	1978-86	Kings Lynn
Dale	Gordon	261	1984-91	Caister
Bryan	Thurlow	224	1955-64	Loddon
Max	Briggs	170	1968-74	Bramerton
Trevor	Howard	156	1968-74	Kings Lynn
Clive	Payne	150	1968-73	Aylsham
Roy	Hollis	107	1948-52	Great Yarmouth
Reg	Wilkinson	107	1920-23	Norwich

Others, born just over the border, include: -

Darryl Sutch, Paul Haylock, John Church   Lowestoft
Charlie Dennington   Beccles

NORFOLK SENIOR CUP

City entered this competition for two seasons only, 1902-3 and 1903-4. On both occasions they lost away to Lynn Town in the first round.

OLDEST PLAYERS

Player	Age	Date	Opponents	Division
Albert Sturgess	42 yrs 116 days	14.02.25	H...Millwall	Division Three South
Duncan Forbes	39 yrs 114 days	11.10.80	H...Wolves	Division One
Kevin Keelan	39 yrs 35 days	09.02.80	H...Liverpool	Division One

Albert Sturgess was over 40 when he joined City from Sheffield United, but still made 52 appearances.

Duncan Forbes made three appearances in the early 1980-1 season of which the last was against Wolves, but he had not previously played in the first team for 18 months.

Kevin Keelan's last game was one of the most exciting games shown on 'Match of the Day.' It included Justin Fashanu's wonder goal, but ended up in a 3-5 defeat, with two late goals from Liverpool, ending Keelan's long career in disappointing style.

ON THE BALL

This was City's famous anthem written in the 1890's and adopted as the Club's song after their formation in the early 1900's. It has stood the test of time and been sung with fervour all over the country. More modern versions were produced from time to time, but these were never able to replace the original tune.

It was only the chorus, shown below, which was ever sung at matches.

Kick off, throw it in,
Have a little scrimmage,
Keep it low, a splendid rush,
Bravo, win or die ...

On the ball City,
Never mind the danger,
Steady on,
Now's your chance,
Hurrah! We've scored a goal.

OVERSEAS PLAYERS

Overseas players can cover many definitions. Certain City players were born abroad, often of British parents and were already living in England when they joined the club.

The list below is restricted to overseas players that had come to England from a foreign club, or who had no British parents.

Player	Country	Seasons	Apps	Goals
Antonio Gallego	Spain	1947	1	
Alf Ackerman	South Africa	1951-3	70	35
Errol Crossan	Canada	1958-60	116	32
Sandy Kennon	South Africa	1959-64	255	
Drazen Muzinic	Yugoslavia	1980-1	23	
Aage Hareide	Norway	1982-4	54	3
Dennis Van Wijk	Holland	1982-6	155	4
Henrik Mortensen	Denmark	1989-91	23	2
Jan Molby*	Denmark	1995-6	5	1
Ulf Ottosson	Sweden	1997	7	1
Victor Segura	Spain	1997-9	33	
Erik Fuglestad	Norway	1997-2000	82	2
Cedric Anselin	France	1998-2001	29	1
Pape Diop*	Senegal	1999-2000	10	
Jean Yves de Blasis	France	1999-2001	38	
Fernando Derveld	Holland	1999-2001	25	1
Raymond de Waard	Holland	1999-2001	13	
Gaetano Giallanza	Switzerland	1999-2003	18	5
Steen Nedergaard	Denmark	2000-3	97	5
Marc Libbra	France	2001-3	38	7
Paul Peschisolido*	Canada	2001	5	
David Nielsen	Denmark	2001-3	66	14
Elvis Hammond*	Ghana	2003	4	
Jim Brennan	Canada	2003-	16	2

Player	Country	Seasons	Apps	Goals
Mathias Svensson	Sweden	2003-	20	7
Youssef Safri	Morocco	2004-		
Thomas Helveg	Denmark	2004-		

Loan player

Several Norwich players were actually born abroad, but of British parents and include:-

Kevin Keelan - India, David Phillips – Germany, Jerry Goss - Cyprus.

Paddy Sloan, born in Ireland, was bought by Norwich from Italian Club Brescia in 1952. He made six appearances for City.

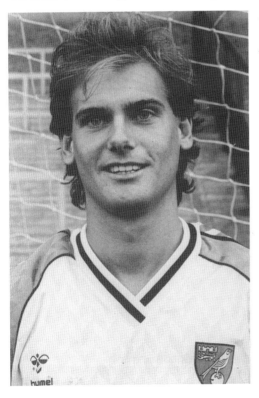

Dutchman Dennis Van Wijk, one of the most successful Overseas players with City. He won League (Milk) Cup and Division Two Championship medals.

OWN GOALS

All four goals scored in the Division One match at home to Everton on 17 November 1974, when City lost 1-3, were own goals.

Norwich led through an own goal by McLaughlin, before Forbes with two own goals and Stringer one, matched the feat to complete an embarrassing afternoon. This disastrous day was completed when Ron Saunders resigned as manager after the game.

Stan Ramsay, City versus Watford on 27 March 1932 and Steve Bruce, City versus Liverpool on 25 August 1984, both conceded own goals in the first minute of their City debuts.

Tony Spearing put through his own net on his League debut in the 78th minute at Tottenham Hotspur on 5 May 1984.

There have been some embarrassing gaffes by goalkeepers, resulting in unexpected goals.

One of the most bizarre instances was at Ipswich on 14 April 1996, when Bryan Gunn, trying to clear a simple back pass from Robert Ullathorne in the 86th minute, completely missed his kick as the ball took a wicked bounce and trickled into the net, causing City to lose 1-2 to their bitter rivals.

At Derby County on 5 April 2003, Robert Green conceded a goal from a long back pass by Darren Kenton, missing his kick badly, resulting in a 1-2 defeat.

At Nottingham Forest on 30 August 2003, Robert Green saved a shot and thinking all the players had run back up the pitch, threw the ball forward to kick out, when David Johnson, who had held back out of Green's sight, nipped out from behind him to knock the ball into an empty net to seal a 2-0 win. Although technically, not an own goal, this incident presented itself as a self inflicted act.

PENALTIES

First Ever

Scorer	Date	Opponents	Result	League
Bob Collinson .... 26.10.02* ..... Norwich CEYMS ....A ..4-2 .... Norfolk & Suffolk

First in Southern League

David Ross .... 14.10.05** ... Fulham .... A .1-2

First in FA Cup

Arthur Archer .... 12.01.07 .... Hastings & St Leonards .... H ..3-1

First in Football League

George Addy .... 27.11.20 ..... Luton Town .... H ..3-0

First in Second Division

Cecil Russell .... 23.11.35 .... Manchester United ..H ..3-5

First in First Division

Graham Paddon ...... 17.03.73 .... Leicester City ....H ..1-1

First in Premier League

Mark Bowen .... 17.10.92 .... Q.P.R .... H ..2-1

Two in Successive Days

Cecil Russell .... 25.12.35 .... Bury .... A ..1-0

26.12.35 .... Bury .... H ..5-3

Two in One Match

Bob Collinson   26.12.02* ..... CEYMS .... A ..4-2

Ron Ashman   30.04.52 .... Plymouth Argyle .....H ..3-0
21.03.53 .... Watford .... A ..2-3

* *1902*   ** *1905*

Two Penalties in One Match (continued)

John Gavin   16.11.57....... Redhill ....H ..6-1

John Deehan   20.11.82....... Stoke City...............H ..4-2
                   07.04.84....... Watford ....H ..6-1

Craig Bellamy.........22.08.98....... Q.P.R. ....H ..4-2

Most Penalties Scored

Ron Ashman 17

Although Ron played for the club from 1947-63, all his penalty conversions were made between 1951-54.

Most Penalties Converted in a Month

Ron Ashman ....6 .... April 1952

This included two in one game at home to Plymouth Argyle on 30 April and two in three days, against Southend United on 2 April and Bournemouth on the fifth.

Most Penalties Scored in a Season

Matt Crowe ....8 .... 1950-51 ....Division Three South

Neil Adams   ....8 .... 1996-7....................Division One and League
                                                            Cup

Most Costly Miss

Jack Milburn missed a penalty in the penultimate game of the 1938-9 season, in a game they lost 0-1 at Plymouth Argyle. Had they drawn, they would have saved themselves from relegation.

Most Successful Penalty Taker

Neil Adams 13 1994-99

Neil Adams was the most consistent penalty taker, scoring 13, including one in a penalty shoot out at Bolton. He only missed one for City, against Swansea in the League Cup on 11 August 1998.

Neil Adams, penalty taker supreme.

Penalty Shoot Out

City have been involved in five penalty shoot outs: -

On 8 November 1972, City beat Leicester City in a Texaco Cup-tie, 4-3 on penalties in the second leg after both ties had ended 2-0. Goalkeeper Kevin Keelan scored one of the penalties, along with Bone, Cross and Briggs, with only Paddon failing to convert.

On 19 December 1990, City beat Millwall in a Zenith Data Cup-tie 6-5 on penalties after the match had finished in a 1-1 draw. Mortensen, Gordon, Sherwood, Bowen, Butterworth and Polston were all successful, with only Phillips missing his attempt.

On 20 December 1995, City needed a penalty shoot out, to win the fourth round League Cup tie (Coca Cola) at Bolton Wanderers. The replay had ended 0-0 after extra time, but City won 3-2 on penalties from the 6 attempts made. Bryan Gunn brilliantly saved three and claimed the match ball for a hat trick of saves. Adams, Bowen and Newsome all scored for City, with Ward, Milligan and Sutch missing.

On 27 October 1998, City again needed a penalty shoot out against Bolton Wanderers in the Coca Cola Cup, but this time they tamely lost out 1-3.

The most vital penalty shoot out City were involved in, was against Birmingham in the First Division Play Offs. The final ended 1-1 after extra time. City lost out 2-4. Only Roberts and Easton were successful, with Mulryne and Sutch missing theirs.

PLAY OFFS

Play Offs were introduced in the late 1980's to keep interest going until the end of season. City did not feature in the Play Off tournament until 2002.

Following a tremendous run, they reached sixth place in Division One on the last game of the 2001-02 season.

They played Wolves in a two-legged tie, before meeting Birmingham City in the final, at the Millennium Stadium, Cardiff.

Opponents	Venue	Result	Date	Attendance
Wolves	H	3-1	28.04.02	20,127

City found themselves a goal down at half time, but came storming back through Rivers and McVeigh, to lead 2-1. In the last minute, Malky Mackay headed a third to set them up for the return leg.

Team: Green, Kenton, Drury, Mackay, Fleming, Holt, Rivers, (Roberts), Mulryne, McVeigh, (Notman), Nielsen, (Libbra), Easton.

Wolves	A	0-1	01.05.02	27,418

City made sure they were resolute in the face of an intimidating crowd at Molyneux. Despite going a goal down in the second half, they held on to secure their place in the final.

Team: Green, Kenton, Drury, Mackay, Fleming, Holt, Rivers, (Sutch), Mulryne, McVeigh, (Notman), Nielsen, (Roberts), Easton.

Birmingham City	N	1-1	12.05.02	71,597

City soon calmed their nerves, to play the better football, although Birmingham had more chances. With the game goal-less in normal time, the match went into extra time and within a minute City had taken a lead through Iwan Roberts. For 11 minutes City had one foot in the Premiership, but Horsfield equalised as the half drew to a close. With no further score in the final period, City found themselves in a penalty shoot out. After losing the toss and kicking into the end occupied by the baying Birmingham supporters, City faced a tense ten minutes. Iwan Roberts gave

City a perfect start by converting the first penalty, but with Mulryne and Sutch missing, City faced an uphill struggle. Despite Easton converting the fourth, it counted for little, as Birmingham had scored all four to end City's season on a terribly disappointing note.

Team: Green, Kenton, Drury, Mackay, Fleming, Holt, Rivers, (Notman), Mulryne, McVeigh, (Sutch), Nielsen, (Roberts), Easton.

PLAYER OF THE SEASON

Barry Butler

As a tribute to Norwich stalwart Barry Butler, who died tragically in a road accident in 1963, Chairman Geoffrey Watling presented a trophy to the club in his memory.

This was to be awarded to the 'Player of the Season' as voted by the supporters.

Six players have been honoured twice - Ken Foggo, Kevin Keelan, Martin Peters Kevin Drinkell, Bryan Gunn and Iwan Roberts.

Bryan Gunn regained the trophy five years after his first award.

Season	Winner	
1966-7	Terry	Allcock
1967-8	Hugh	Curran
1968-9	Ken	Foggo
1969-70	Duncan	Forbes
1970-1	Ken	Foggo
1971-2	David	Stringer
1972-3	Kevin	Keelan
1973-4	Kevin	Keelan
1974-5	Colin	Suggett
1975-6	Martin	Peters
1976-7	Martin	Peters
1977-8	John	Ryan
1978-9	Tony	Powell
1979-80	Kevin	Bond

Terry Allcock, the first winner of the Barry Butler 'Player of the Season' trophy, seen here receiving the cup from Geoffrey Watling who had donated the trophy. Allcock holds the record for most goals scored in a season.

Season	Winner
1980-1 ....Joe	Royle
1981-2 ....Greg	Downs
1982-3 ....Dave	Watson
1983-4...................Chris	Woods
1984-5...................Steve	Bruce
1985-6...................Kevin	Drinkell
1986-7...................Kevin	Drinkell
1987-8...................Bryan	Gunn
1988-9 ....Dale	Gordon
1989-90 ....Mark	Bowen
1990-1 ....Ian	Culverhouse
1991-2 ....Robert	Fleck
1992-3 ....Bryan	Gunn
1993-4...................Chris	Sutton

Season ・ Winner

Season	Winner	
1994-5	Jon	Newsome
1995-6	Spencer	Prior
1996-7	Darren	Eadie
1997-8	Matt	Jackson
1998-9	Iwan	Roberts
1999-00	Iwan	Roberts
2000-1	Andy	Marshall
2001-2	Gary	Holt
2002-3	Adam	Drury
2003-4	Craig	Fleming

POINTS

Most Points (Two points for a win)

Points	Division	Season	Games Played
64	Division Three South	1950-1	46
61	Division Three South	1933-4	42
57	Division Two	1971-2	42

Most Points (Three points for a win)

Points	Division	Season	Games Played
94	Division One	2003-4	46
84	Division Two	1985-6	42
72	Premier	1992-3	42

Least Points

Points	Division	Season	Games Played
31	Division Three South	1956-7	46
28	Division Three South	1930-1, 1946-7	42
31	Division Two	1938-9	42
29	Division One	1973-4	42
43	Premier	1993-4	42

POSITION

Highest Position

In 1992-3, City finished third in the Premier League after leading the table for more than half the season, at one time being eight points clear. They regained pole position six times during that momentous season and were top as late as the 36th game. They then lost 1-3 at home to title rivals Manchester United. This seemed to shake them and they were then thrashed 1-5 at Tottenham Hotspur. Although they beat Leeds United and Liverpool at home 4-2 and 1-0 respectively, another defeat to bitter rivals Ipswich Town 1-3 between these games, left them needing to draw the last match at Middlesbrough. This they did, in a dramatic game 3-3, to clinch the third spot and their highest ever position.

1992-3

Date	Opponents	V	Result		Position	Attendance
Aug.15	Arsenal	A	4-2	W	1	24,030
Aug.19	Chelsea	H	2-1	W	1	15,164
Aug.22	Everton	H	1-1	D	4	14,150
Aug.26	Manchester City	A	1-3	L	6	23,182
Aug.29	Crystal Palace	A	2-1	W	3	12,033
Aug.31	Nottm. Forest	H	3-1	W	1	14,104
Sep.5	Southampton	H	1-0	W	1	12,452
Sep.12	Chelsea	A	3-2	W	1	16,880
Sep.19	Sheffield Wed.	H	1-0	W	1	14,367
Sep.26	Coventry City	A	1-1	D	1	16,436
Oct.3	Blackburn Rovers	A	1-7	L	2	16,312
Oct.17	Q.P.R	H	2-1	W	1	16,009
Oct.25	Liverpool	A	1-4	L	2	36,318
Oct.31	Middlesbrough	H	1-1	D	2	14,499
Nov.9	Oldham Athletic	A	3-2	W	1	11,018
Nov.21	Sheffield United	H	2-1	W	1	14,874

Date	Opponents	V	Result		Position	Attendance
Nov.28	Aston Villa	A	3-2	W	1	28,837
Dec.5	Wimbledon	H	1-0	W	1	14,161
Dec.12	Manchester United	A	0-1	L	1	34,580
Dec.21	Ipswich Town	H	0-2	L	1	20,032
Dec.26	Tottenham Hotspur	H	0-0	D	1	19,413
Dec.28	Leeds United	A	0-0	D	1	30,282
Jan.10	Sheffield Wed.	A	0-1	L	3	23,360
Jan.16	Coventry City	H	1-1	D	3	13,613
Jan.22	Crystal Palace	H	4-2	W	3	13,543
Jan.30	Everton	A	1-0	W	1	20,301
Feb.9	Southampton	A	0-3	L	3	12,969
Feb.20	Manchester City	H	2-1	W	3	16,366
Feb.28	Blackburn Rovers	H	0-0	D	3	15,821
Mar.3	Arsenal	H	1-1	D	3	14,820
Mar.6	Q.P.R	A	1-3	L	3	13,892
Mar.10	Sheffield United	H	1-0	W	3	15,583
Mar.13	Oldham Athletic	H	1-0	W	3	19,597
Mar.17	Nottm. Forest	A	3-0	W	1	20,799
Mar.20	Wimbledon	A	0-3	L	3	10,875
Mar.24	Aston Villa	H	1-0	W	1	19,528
Apr.5	Manchester United	H	1-3	L	3	20,582
Apr.9	Tottenham Hotspur	A	1-5	L	3	31,425
Apr.14	Leeds United	H	4-2	W	3	18,613
Apr.19	Ipswich Town	A	1-3	L	3	21,087
May 1	Liverpool	H	1-0	W	3	20,610
May 8	Middlesbrough	A	3-3	D	3	15,155

On 27 March 1989, City were second in Division One, three points behind Arsenal who had played a game more, with nine games remaining. They were also in the semi-finals of the FA Cup. Sadly, a disastrous run saw them take only six more points, to finish fourth, and also lose their cup-tie 0-1 to Everton. This was the nearest City came to challenging for the coveted double.

The Closing Stages of the Near 'Double' Attempt

1989

Date	Opponents	V	Result		Position	Attendance
Mar.27	West Ham United	A	2-0	W	2	27,265
Apr.1	Liverpool	H	0-1	L	3	26,338
Apr.5	Nottm. Forest	A	0-2	L	3	19,872
Apr.8	Coventry City	A	1-2	L	3	12,740
Apr.15	Everton-FA Semi-Final	N	0-1	L	3	46,553
Apr.19	Southampton	A	0-0	D	3	14,403
Apr.22	Aston Villa	H	2-2	D	3	14,550
May 1	Arsenal	A	0-5	L	3	28,449
May 6	Everton	H	1-0	W	3	13,239
May 13	Luton Town	A	0-1	L	4	10,816
May 17	Sheffield Wednesday	A	2-2	D	4	16,238

Lowest Position

The lowest City have finished is in 24th position, bottom of Division Three South. This happened in 1956-7 when they gained only 31 points from 46 games, were five points from safety and had to apply for re-election to the Football League for the fourth time. It is more notable as the worst season ever, as they had been top with ten points after the first six games. They then fell away badly by going a record 26 games without a win, were dumped out of the FA Cup at home by non-league Bedford Town and were in the midst of a financial crisis which shook the foundations of the club.

City were successfully re-elected, no doubt boosted by having one of the highest average away gates in the division, nearly 11,000.

1956-7

Date	Opponents	V	Result		Position	Attendance
Aug.18	Crystal Palace	H	1-0	W		16,041
Aug.22	Exeter City	A	0-0	D		9,591
Aug.25	Southend United	A	0-0	D		10,022
Aug.29	Exeter City	H	1-0	W	3	12,054
Sep.1	Northampton Town	H	2-1	W	1	15,246
Sep.5	Coventry City	H	3-0	W	1	17,335
Sep.8	Q.P.R	A	1-3	L	3	12,631
Sep.10	Coventry City	A	2-3	L	3	18,394
Sep.15	Plymouth Argyle	H	3-0	W	2	15,880
Sep.22	Reading	A	1-2	L	12	9,897
Sep.29	Newport County	H	1-1	D	12	16,920
Oct.3	Southampton	A	0-2	L	12	18,986
Oct.6	Bournemouth	A	1-1	D	12	12,032
Oct.13	Torquay United	H	1-2	L	14	14,819
Oct.20	Millwall	A	1-5	L	17	14,191
Oct.27	Brighton & H A	H	1-1	D	19	11,526
Nov. 3	Gillingham	A	1-1	D	19	8,253

Lowest Position 1956-7 (continued)

Date	Opponents	V	Result		Position	Attendance
Nov.10	Swindon Town	H	2-4	L	19	10,966
Nov.24	Aldershot	H	1-1	D	19	7,437
Nov.28	Southampton	H	0-3	L	19	8,095
Dec.1	Watford	A	3-3	D	19	9,538
Dec.15	Crystal Palace	A	1-4	L	22	8,361
Dec.22	Southend United	H	1-2	L	23	8,948
Dec.25	Colchester United	A	1-1	D	24	6,376
Dec.26	Colchester United	H	1-2	L	24	8,481
Dec.29	Northampton Town	A	1-1	D	22	7,603
Jan.5	Walsall	H	2-2	D	21	9,789
Jan.12	Q.P.R	H	1-2	L	22	11,722
Jan.19	Plymouth Argyle	A	2-3	L	23	12,054
Jan.26	Walsall	A	3-6	L	23	16,169
Feb.2	Reading	H	2-5	L	24	12,344
Feb.9	Newport County	A	1-3	L	24	7,088
Feb.20	Bournemouth	H	1-3	L	24	14,079
Feb.23	Torquay United	A	1-7	L	24	6,,375
Mar.2	Millwall	H	2-0	W	24	11,921
Mar.9	Shrewsbury Town	A	5-4	W	23	7,206
Mar.16	Gillingham	H	1-3	L	23	13,764
Mar.23	Swindon Town	A	1-1	D	23	7,713
Mar.30	Brentford	H	1-1	D	22	11,685
Apr. 4	Aldershot	A	0-0	D	24	4,530
Apr.13	Watford	H	1-2	L	24	10,207
Apr.19	Ipswich Town	H	1-2	L	24	28,783

Date	Opponents	V	Result		Position	Attendance
Apr.20	Brighton & H A	A	0-3	L	24	12,807
Apr.22	Ipswich Town	A	1-3	L	24	21,755
Apr.27	Brentford	A	1-1	D	24	8,764
May 1	Shrewsbury Town	H	3-0	W	24	7,620

POSTPONEMENTS

City, like most clubs have had numerous matches postponed due to bad weather or international call ups. However, in 1963, the FA Cup third round tie against Blackpool was postponed 11 times due to continuous freezing conditions. When the game was finally played on 4 March, it ended in a 1-1 draw and City had to replay at Blackpool two days later, eventually winning the tie 3-1.

During the bad winter of 1963, City only played one game in January and did not play a home game at all from 29 December until 23 February, when they beat Rotherham 4-2.

PROMOTION

City have won promotion seven times since they were elected as founder members of Division Three in 1920.

City have a remarkable record in having regained their First Division status straightaway after each relegation to Division Two, being three times in all.

Division	Position	Season	Points
Division Three South	Champions	1933-4	61
Divison Three	Runners Up	1959-60	59
Division Two	Champions	1971-2	57
Division Two	Third	1974-5	53
Division Two	Third	1981-2	71
Division Two	Champions	1985-6	84
Division One	Champions	2003-4	94

The 1972 team who won promotion to the top flight for the first time.

The 1986 Division Two Champions

In many of their promotion seasons, City were consistent and were in a good position throughout. However, in 1981-2 when finishing third, they actually lost 15 games and only came through with a late run.

1981-2

Date	Opponents	V	Result		Pos	Attendance
Aug.29	Rotherham United	A	1-4	L		8,919
Sep.2	Crystal Palace	H	1-0	W		14,484
Sep.5	Barnsley	H	1-1	D	12	13,677
Sep.12	Wrexham	A	3-2	W	7	4,007
Sep.19	Newcastle United	H	2-1	W	5	14,384
Sep.22	Grimsby Town	A	2-1	W	3	10,185

Promotion 1981-2 (continued)

Date	Opponents	V	Result		Pos	Attendance
Sep.26	Chelsea	A	1-2	L	3	14,509
Oct.3	Oldham Athletic	H	1-2	L	7	13,710
Oct.10	Q.P.R	A	0-2	L	13	11,806
Oct.17	Shrewsbury Town	H	2-1	W	11	11,977
Oct.24	Watford	A	0-3	L	12	14,463
Oct.31	Bolton Wanderers	H	0-0	D	12	12,991
Nov.7	Cardiff City	A	0-1	L	13	5,704
Nov.14	Cambridge United	H	2-1	W	11	14,467
Nov.21	Derby County	H	4-1	W	7	13,457
Nov.24	Crystal Palace	A	1-2	L	8	9.010
Nov.28	Blackburn Rovers	A	0-3	L	12	8,153
Dec.5	Leicester City	H	0-0	D	12	13,367
Dec.28	Luton Town	H	1-3	L	13	19,348
Dec.30	Charlton Athletic	A	0-0	D	11	6,277
Jan.16	Rotherham United	H	2-0	W	10	12,750
Jan.30	Newcastle United	A	1-2	L	11	14,447
Feb.3	Sheffield Wed.	H	2-3	L	11	15,767
Feb.6	Wrexham	H	4-0	W	11	12,300
Feb.17	Oldham Athletic	A	0-2	L	13	5,283
Feb.20	Chelsea	H	2-1	W	12	16,018
Feb.24	Barnsley	A	1-0	W	12	15,360
Feb.27	Q.P.R.	H	0-1	L	12	15,928
Mar.13	Watford	H	4-2	W	12	15,534
Mar.16	Orient	A	1-1	D	13	2,933
Mar.20	Bolton Wanderers	A	1-0	W	12	6,199
Mar.27	Cardiff City	H	2-1	W	11	12,720
Apr.3	Cambridge United	A	2-1	W	10	7,035

Date	Opponents	V	Result		Position	Attendance
Apr.10	Charlton Athletic	H	5-0	W	9	14,908
Apr.12	Luton Town	A	0-2	L	10	15,601
Apr.17	Derby County	A	2-0	W	8	12,508
Apr.20	Shrewsbury Town	A	2-0	W	6	3,590
Apr.24	Blackburn Rovers	H	2-0	W	5	16,309
May 1	Leicester City	A	4-1	W	4	19,630
May 5	Grimsby Town	H	2-1	W	3	18,360
May 8	Orient	H	2-0	W	3	19,197
May 15	Sheffield Wed.	A	1-2	L	3	24,687

The 2003-4 Championship season is the best in the club's history for points gained and games won.

2003-4

Date	Opponents	V	Result		Position	Attendance
Aug.9	Bradford City	A	2-2	D	-	13,159
Aug.16	Rotherham United	H	2-0	W	6	16,263
Aug.23	Sheffield United	A	0-1	L	9	24,885
Aug.26	Wimbledon	H	3-2	W	7	16,082
Aug.30	Nottingham Forest	A	0-2	L	12	21,058
Sep.13	Burnley	H	2-0	W	10	16,407
Sep.16	Gillingham	A	2-1	W	7	9,022
Sep.20	Stoke City	A	1-1	D	7	10,672
Sep.27	Crystal Palace	H	2-1	W	5	16,425
Sep.30	Reading	H	2-1	W	3	16,387
Oct.4	Wigan Athletic	A	1-1	D	4	9,346

Promotion 2003-4 (continued)

Date	Opponents	V	Result		Position	Attendance
Oct.15	West Ham United	A	1-1	D	6	31,308
Oct.18	W.B.A	A	0-1	L	8	24,966
Oct.21	Derby County	H	2-1	W	7	16,346
Oct.25	Sunderland	H	1-0	W	3	16,427
Nov.1	Walsall	A	3-1	W	3	8,331
Nov.8	Millwall	H	3-1	W	3	16,423
Nov.15	Watford	H	1-2	L	3	16,420
Nov.22	Preston N.E.	A	0-0	D	2	14,775
Nov.25	Coventry City	H	1-1	D	2	16,414
Nov.29	Crewe Alexandra	H	1-0	W	2	16,367
Dec.6	Millwall	A	0-0	D	2	9,850
Dec.13	Cardiff City	H	4-1	W	2	16,428
Dec.21	Ipswich Town	A	2-0	W	1	30,152
Dec.26	Nottingham Forest	H	1-0	W	1	16,429
Dec.28	Derby County	A	4-0	W	1	23,783
Jan.10	Bradford City	H	0-1	L	1	16,360
Jan.17	Rotherham United	A	4-4	D	1	7,448
Jan.31	Sheffield United	H	1-0	W	1	18,977
Feb.7	Wimbledon	A	1-0	W	1	7,368
Feb.14	Coventry City	A	2-0	W	1	15,757
Feb.21	West Ham United	H	1-1	D	1	23,940
Mar.2	W.B.A	H	0-0	D	1	23,223
Mar.7	Ipswich Town	H	3-1	W	1	23,942
Mar.13	Cardiff City	A	1-2	L	1	16,370
Mar.16	Gillingham	H	3-0	W	1	23,198
Mar.20	Crystal Palace	A	0-1	L	1	23,798
Mar.27	Stoke City	H	1-0	W	1	23,565

Date	Opponents	V	Result		Position	Attendance
Apr.3	Burnley	A	5-3	W	1	12,417
Apr.9	Wigan Athletic	H	2-0	W	1	23,446
Apr.12	Reading	A	1-0	W	1	18,460
Apr.17	Walsall	H	5-0	W	1	23,558
Apr.24	Watford	A	2-1	W	1	19,290
May 1	Preston N.E.	H	3-2	W	1	23,673
May 4	Sunderland	A	0 -1	L	1	35,174
May 9	Crewe Alexandra	A	3-1	W	1	9,833

City's Championship team created several new club records in 2003-4.

Club Record

Highest points total..94

Most games won..28

Most away wins..10

Most home wins equalled 18

Most successive home wins from start 8

Most clean sheets..18

Most doubles over other clubs....................................8

The 2003-4 record breaking Championship team, parade the Division One
Trophy during the celebration tour of the City.

QUICKEST GOALS

The fastest goal scored at Carrow Road, was in 10 seconds by Ralph "Ginger" Johnson, against Leyton Orient on 19 October 1946 in Division Three South. He also scored a second goal in City's 5-0 win.

Keith O'Neill equalled this feat, in a 2-0 home victory over Stoke City on 12 April 1977, in a Division One game.

Jamie Cureton scored within 13 seconds of coming on as a **substitute** against Chelsea on 10 December 1994. On entering the pitch, he went straight up for a corner and headed in to clinch a 3-0 win in the Premiership.

Marc Libbra scored the quickest **debut** goal after coming on as a **substitute** in a Division One home fixture against Manchester City on 18 September 2001. He scored after 19 seconds, but this included the time coming on to the field when play was stopped and was actually nearer the 10 second record.

The quickest FA Cup goal was scored by Terry Allcock on 13 March 1963. He netted in the first minute, on his way to a four goal spree, in the 5-0 fourth round home win against Newcastle United.

Mike Kenning scored two goals in the first six minutes at home to Derby County, in the third round of the FA Cup on 28 January 1967. City went on to win 3-0.

The fastest goal scored by a visiting team at Carrow Road, was in 20 seconds by ex-Canary Nigel Cassidy, playing for Oxford United, on 18 September 1971 in Division Two. City recovered to win 3-2.

In the **opening game of the season** on 22 August 1964, Gordon Bolland scored in the first minute against Swansea. This was also the first goal of the season scored in the whole of the Football League.

In the Division One match against Queens Park Rangers on the 22 August 1998, City were 3-1 up after eight minutes, with two goals from Craig Bellamy and one by Matt Jackson. The game finished 4-2.

RECORDINGS

Norwich City players have made two recordings, both to celebrate promotion. The first was by the Division Two Championship squad in 1972. The record was called 'The Canaries', with the 'Norwich City Calypso' on the 'B' side. Both songs were written by Don Sheppard and Johnny Cleveland, members of a local band.

The second recording was 'Those Country Boys', written by one of the administration staff for the 1985-6 champions.

The 1971-2 Division Two Championship squad in the recording studio

RE-ELECTION

Before the automatic promotion from the current Conference League was established, there was a procedure where the bottom four clubs in the Football League had to apply for re-election. This meant that leading non-league clubs from the various regional leagues could also make their case to be considered in the voting.

City had to apply for re-election on four occasions after finishing in the bottom two of the Third Division South.

Season	Position	Points
1930-1	22nd	28
1946-7	21st	28
1947-8	21st	34
1956-7	24th	31

Remarkably, despite finishing bottom of the Football League in 1957, City were still the fourth most popular away side in their Division, as judged by the average attendances of nearly 11,000 they attracted.

Each time, City had no trouble gaining the necessary votes to be re-elected.

RELEGATION

City have suffered the indignity of relegation on five occasions.

1938-9......... Division Two   to   Division Three South.... 31 points

1973-4   .... Division One   to   Division Two............... 29 points

1980-1.......... Division One   to   Division Two............... 33 points

1984-5 .... Division One   to   Division Two............... 49 points (3 pts for win)

1994-5 .... Premier   to   Division One   .... 43 points

1984-5

The most agonising relegation City suffered was in 1985. They had already won the Milk Cup in March and were sitting comfortably in mid table. They then experienced a disastrous run and from April took only five points from 11 games, but won their last game of the season 2-1 at Chelsea to finish with 49 points, normally enough for safety. However, they had to wait for Coventry City, who were nine points behind, but still had three games to play and needed to win them all to overhaul Norwich. Surprisingly, Coventry beat Stoke City away and then Luton Town at home, leaving one remaining home game against champions Everton. This match didn't take place until three weeks after the season's end with

Everton having already been on a celebration holiday. The unlikely 4-1 win saw Coventry have a dramatic escape and relegate City. The Football League amended the rules as a result, stipulating all fixtures had to be completed on the last day.

1984-85 season - Results from January

Date	Opponents	V	Result		Position	Attendance
Jan.12	Southampton	H	1-0	W	8	13,735
Jan.19	Liverpool	A	0-4	L	10	30,627
Feb.2	Nottm. Forest	H	0-1	L	10	14,669
Mar.2	Q.P.R	A	2-2	D	11	12,975
Mar.9	Aston Villa	H	2-2	D	11	21,853
Mar.16	Sunderland	H	1-3	L	12	13,389
Mar.30	Coventry City	H	2-1	W	13	14,067
Apr.3	Sheffield Wed.	H	1-1	D	12	15,138
Apr.6	Arsenal	A	0-2	L	13	19,597
Apr. 8	Ipswich Town	H	0-2	L	14	18,227
Apr.13	Watford	A	0-2	L	15	15,372
Apr.16	Luton Town	A	1-3	L	16	8,794
Apr.20	Leicester City	H	1-3	L	16	13,395
Apr.24	Stoke City	A	3-2	W	14	4,597
Apr.27	Everton	A	0-3	L	16	32,085
May 4	Manchester Utd	H	0-1	L	17	16,006
May 6	West Ham Utd.	A	0-1	L	19	16,233
May 11	Newcastle Utd.	H	0-0	D	18	18,399
May 14	Chelsea	A	2-1	W	20	22,882

1994-5

The most costly relegation occurred in 1994-5, when City lost their Premiership status and all the television money with it. Football was starting to become more popular, with foreign stars coming to England as never before and attendances were rising in new all seater stadiums.

By Christmas, all thoughts of relegation were far away as City were pushing for a European place and standing seventh in the Premiership table. Unfortunately, they lost goalkeeper Bryan Gunn to injury on 27 December for the rest of the season. This seemed to unsettle the defence and the failure to replace him adequately, coupled with the sale of two strikers, Mark Robins and Efan Ekoku, in successive months, affected the team badly. City won only one game in the last 20, taking just ten points from 60, to finish in third from bottom place, two points from safety.

1994-95 season – Results from the New Year

Date	Opponents	V	Result		Position	Attendance
Dec.31	Newcastle United	H	2-1	W	7	21,172
Jan.2	Liverpool	A	0-4	L	8	34,709
Jan.14	Wimbledon	H	1-2	L	9	18,261
Jan.25	Coventry City	H	2-2	D	10	14,024
Feb.4	Everton	A	1-2	L	10	23,293
Feb.11	Southampton	H	2-2	D	10	18,261
Feb.22	Manchester United	H	0-2	L	12	21,824
Feb.25	Blackburn Rovers	A	0-0	D	14	25,579
Mar.4	Manchester City	H	1-1	D	14	16,266
Mar.8	Sheffield Wed.	H	0-0	D	15	13,530
Mar.11	West Ham United	A	2-2	D	14	21,464
Mar.15	Q.P.R	A	0-2	L	16	10,519
Mar.20	Ipswich Town	H	3-0	W	12	17,510
Apr.1	Arsenal	A	1-5	L	15	36,942
Apr.5	Leicester City	A	0-1	L	16	15,992
Apr.8	Newcastle United	A	0-3	L	16	35,518

Date	Opponents	V	Result		Position	Attendance
Apr.12	Nottm. Forest	H	0-1	L	18	19,005
Apr.17	Tottenham Hotspur	A	0-1	L	20	32,204
Apr.29	Liverpool	H	1-2	L	20	21,843
May 6	Leeds United	A	1-2	L	20	31,982
May 14	Aston Villa	H	1-1	D	20	19,374

1980-1

In 1980-1, City nearly escaped from the clutches of relegation from Division One after signing Martin O'Neill. With six games to go they were one off the bottom, but after an impressive sequence of four wins, seemed to have hauled themselves to safety, three positions clear of relegation. Unfortunately it was not to be. After losing at Manchester United in their penultimate game, City needed to beat already doomed Leicester City and rely on one of three other teams losing difficult matches. Although City disappointingly lost 2-3 at home in their last game, the other three threatened clubs all won anyway and City's fate was sealed.

1980-81 Season – Last eight games

Date	Opponents	V	Result		Position	Attendance
Mar.21	Arsenal	H	1-1	D	20	19,569
Mar.28	Nottm. Forest	A	1-2	L	21	22,353
Apr.4	Manchester City	H	2-0	W	20	17,957
Apr.11	Everton	A	2-0	W	19	16,254
Apr.18	Tottenham Hotspur	A	3-2	W	19	34,413
Apr.20	Ipswich Town	H	1-0	W	17	26,155
Apr.25	Manchester United	A	0-1	L	19	40,164
May 2	Leicester City	H	2-3	L	20	25,307

RESULTS

For all City's League and Cup results and performance summary against every club - see Appendix

RIVER END

The river end terrace was the last open side of the Carrow Road ground. In the late 1970's, as safety regulations became stricter, the City Board were faced with a decision on whether to re-create the terrace or build a new stand. They elected to build a new stand in 1979 at a cost of circa £1.7m, the first to be built at Carrow Road for 20 years. This provided covered accommodation around the whole ground. The River Stand was a double tier construction built by R G Carter Limited, with seating in the upper tier and standing terrace in the lower, holding a total of around 9,000 spectators. It was also the first Norwich stand to have executive boxes between the tiers. It contained a special area known as the '101 Club,' with its own lounge and central seats in the upper tier. There were also other purpose built function areas. A public house was built into the corner of the stand and was originally named 'The Nest.'

In 1992, the lower tier was converted to seats to conform to the recommendations set out in the Taylor Report, which endorsed all seater stadium by 1994. This reduced the capacity to around 6,000. The stand was renamed the 'Norwich & Peterborough Stand' in 1992 and connected to the main City Stand by an infill in 1994. Later, 'Delia's Restaurant' was located in this stand.

ROYALTY

There have been a number of connections with royalty over the years, assisted by the proximity of Sandringham, a royal residence.

King George VI was the first reigning monarch to attend a league match. This was on 29 October 1938, when he watched part of the Second Division game between Norwich and Millwall, a match City lost 0-2.

The Queen Mother sent a telegram of congratulations when City first won promotion to Division One in 1972.

A young Prince Andrew in the Director's Box at Carrow Road for the League Cup Semi-Final with Chelsea.

Prince Andrew attended the League Cup semi-final victory over Chelsea on 3 January 1973. He was still in his teens and was accompanied by the Bishop of Norwich, Maurice Wood.

The Duchess of Kent attended the Norwich versus Manchester City Division One match on 14 February 1987 and opened the new City Stand.

SCOREBOARD

Until the 1980's, City displayed half time scores from other games on two fixed boards in the corner at either end of the ground. Scores were displayed by numbers hung on hooks next to a letter, which depicted various other games, not dissimilar to a cricket scoreboard. Jackpot numbers or goal times were displayed on a board and carried around the pitch by two men.

City's first electronic scoreboard was bought from Chelsea at a cost of £40,000 in 1982. Sponsored by the Eastern Counties Newspapers, it was 90 feet long and placed on the roof of the old Barclay Stand. It was temperamental for a while, but a new part obtained from Canada in 1988 helped solve the problems.

When the new Barclay Stand was built in 1992, new scoreboards were erected between the two tiers of both that and the Norwich & Peterborough Stand.

SCOTTISH TEAMS

City have played a number of Scottish teams, both in 'friendlies' and minor cup competitions.

Texaco Cup

Team	Year	First leg	Second Leg
Dundee United	1972	A... 1-2	H . 2-0
Motherwell	1972	H .2-0	A .. 2-3
Motherwell	1973	H ..2-0	A .. 0-1
St Johnstone	1973	A ..2-0	H .. 1-0

Friendlies

Team	Date	Score
St Mirren	08.04.57	H .. 2-0
Heart of Midlothian	30.10.57	H .. 3-4
Aberdeen	06.11.57	H .. 1-0
Heart of Midlothian	12.10.59	A .. 0-0
Motherwell	17.04.61	H .. 2-0
St Mirren	04.08.62	A .. 1-1
St Mirren	01.08.64	A .. 0-0
Dundee	08.05.71	N .. 5-3-Batista tournament
St Mirren	05.06.72	H . 4-1

Team	Date	Score
Aberdeen	06.01.82	H .. 1-4
Dundee	23.03.84	H .. 3-2
Hibernian	16.07.94	A .. 2-0
St Mirren	19.07.97	A .. 2-2
Dumbarton	21.07.97	A .. 2-3
St Johnstone	15.07.00	A .. 1-2
Queen's Park	19.07.00	A .. 4-0
Dunfermline Athletic	22.07.00	A .. 0-1
Celtic	22.01.01	H . 2-4 -Testimonial
St Mirren	14.07.01	A .. 3-2
Queen's Park	17.07.01	A .. 1-0
Motherwell	21.07.01	A .. 0-0
St Mirren	13.07.02	A .. 1-0
Clyde	16.07.02	A .. 0-1
Livingston	20.07.02	A .. 0-0

The friendly against Celtic was a testimonial match for Tim Sheppard and attracted a crowd of 15,034, including 5,000 Celtic supporters.

SCREEN SPORT SUPER CUP

This cup was devised for the teams who had qualified for Europe in the 1985-6 season, but were denied appearing by the ban imposed after the violence and deaths at the previous year's final in Heysel, City had qualified through winning the Milk Cup.

The matches were televised on the Select Screen Sport medium.

Group Match	Date	Result	Attendance	Scorer
Everton	02.10.85...	A.. 0-1	10,329	
Everton	23.10.85...	H.. 1-0	12,021	Mendham
Manchester Utd.	06.11.85...	A.. 1-1	20,130	Biggins
Manchester Utd	11.12.85...	H.. 1-1	15,110	Williams

Semi-Final

Liverpool.	05.02.86...	H.. 1-1	15,313	Drinkell
Liverpool.	06.05.86...	H.. 1-3	26,696	Brooke

SHORTEST PLAYERS

The shortest City player is believed to have been Henry Howell at only five feet four inches tall. He played on the left wing and made four appearances at the end of the 1925-6 season.

Terry Ryder junior was also five feet four inches and made 51 appearances, scoring 12 goals, between 1946 and 1950.

James McEwen was five feet five inches tall. He played at left back and joined City at the age of 32 in 1905, making 121 appearances. He was the first player to play over 100 games for City.

SIMOD CUP

This cup was originally called the Full Members Cup. It was a supplementary competition for First and Second Division teams and was sponsored by Simod for two years.

Results were: -

Season	Opponents	Result	Attendance
1987-8	Millwall	A.. 3-2	4,654
	Swindon Town	A . 0-2	10,491
1988-9	Swindon Town	H.. 2-1	5,014
	Ipswich Town	A.. 0-1	18,024

SOUTH STAND

This stand was named after Arthur South, Lord Mayor of Norwich, in recognition of his leadership in overcoming the crisis of 1956.

It was first built to cover the existing terrace in 1960, at a cost of £15,000, although initially the roof only stretched as far as the penalty area at the Barclay end. In 1962, it was extended fully to join up with the Barclay Stand.

The capacity was originally around 18,000 as a terrace, before being reduced to less than 6,000 when fully converted to seats at a cost of £40,000 in 1975. Initially, a small standing area remained in front of the newly installed seats, but this proved impractical and was also converted to seats within the next two years.

The old South Stand, with terraces sweeping round from the River end and before being joined to the Barclay.

The change from terrace to seating was a very unpopular move at the time and the decision was criticised for several years, with claims being made that 5,000 supporters were lost as a result. Another criticism was the colour of seats being red and blue, but green and yellow were not available at the time.

It became the area for housing away supporters after the new Barclay Stand was built. As other stands were replaced, the South Stand became older and more decrepit, and was proving increasingly costly to pass the new safety regulations that were in place.

Finally in 2003, it was demolished to make way for a new larger modern structure, complete with executive boxes and a business centre. It was re-named the 'Jarrold Stand' after the new sponsors.

The Hall of Fame banners are hung in an area under the Stand and up to 3,000 bricks, sponsored by supporters with their own inscriptions on, form part of the outer wall. The capacity was the largest of the new stands at around 8,200. This was soon increased by the building of a two-tier corner infill in 2004/5 adding an extra 1,600 seats, as well as providing a specially designed area for disabled supporters with accommodation for wheel chairs between the two tiers.

SOUTHERN CHARITY CUP

This was a small cup competition for Southern League teams held for two seasons, before the First World War.

Season	Round	Opponents	Result	Attendance
1913-4	First	Gillingham... H..	1-0	
	Second	Q.P.R	H . 3-0	2,035
	Semi-Final	Coventry	N.. 0-3	
1914-5	First	Gillingham... A..	4-1	

City withdrew after the first round in 1914-5 as it was difficult to fit in with the FA Cup competition

SOUTHERN LEAGUE

When City became a professional club in 1905 they applied for election to the Southern League. After much lobbying and marketing, they were successful, being voted into second place ahead of Crystal Palace.

This was the first semi-professional league that Norwich played in from 1905 until 1920, before becoming founder members of the newly formed Third Division of the Football League, when the whole of the Southern League First Division were elected en bloc.

SPONSORS

During the 1980's, restrictions on sponsorship and shirt advertising were lifted, allowing a new revenue stream to be available to clubs.

Norwich's first shirt sponsors were Poll Withey, a local double glazing firm, with the first sponsored shirt worn on 19 October 1983 in the home match against Leicester City.

City's main sponsors have been as follows: -

Sponsor	Years
Poll Withey	1983-86
Fosters	1986-89
Asics	1989-92
Norwich & Peterborough Building Society	1992-97
Colmans	1997-01
Digital Phone Company	2001-03
Proton Cars	2003-

Other major sponsorships include: -

Jarrolds – 'Top of the Terrace' restaurant and the Jarrold Stand.

Norwich & Peterborough Building Society - Stand and a savings account, which donates a percentage of the interest earned to the Club.

Match balls, players individual kit, and matches are also sponsored on an individual basis.

STARTS TO SEASON

BEST

1904-5.......................Norfolk & Suffolk

City won their first **five** games and finished the season top.

Date	Opponents	V	Result		Attendance
Sept.24	Beccles Caxton	A	1-0	W	5,000
Oct 15	Cromer	A	1-0	W	
Nov.12	Kirkley	H	3-0	W	2,500
Nov.19	Beccles Caxton	H	3-0	W	2,000
Nov.26	Cromer	H	4-2	W	
Dec.17	*Lowestoft Town*	*H*	*1-1*	*D*	*3,500*

Sequence ended.

1971-2...............................Division Two

City went **13 league and two cup** games without defeat, before losing at second placed Millwall 1-2. They finished as champions.

Date	Opponents	V	Result		Attendance	League / Cup
Aug.14	Luton Town	A	1-1	D	12,428	League
Aug.21	Portsmouth	H	3-1	W	13,564	League
Aug.28	Fulham	A	0-0	D	10,668	League
Sep.1	Orient	H	0-0	D	13,940	League
Sep.4	Carlisle United	H	1-0	W	11.462	League
Sep.8	Brighton & H.A	H	2-0	W	11,610	League / Cup
Sep.11	Blackpool	A	2-1	W	15,960	League
Sep.18	Oxford United	H	3-2	W	14,239	League

1971-2 Good Start to Season (continued)

Date	Opponents	V	Result		Attendance	League/Cup
Sep.25	Bristol City	A	1-0	W	18,528	League
Sep.28	Preston N.E	A	2-0	W	15,644	League
Oct.2	Q.P.R	H	0-0	D	22,950	League
Oct.6	Carlisle United	H	4-1	W	17,726	League Cup
Oct.9	Sunderland	A	1-1	D	25,951	League
Oct.13	Burnley	H	3-0	W	24,707	League
Oct.16	Luton Town	H	3-1	W	22,558	League
Oct.23	*Millwall*	*A*	*1-2*	*L*	*22,763*	*League*

Sequence ended

1950-1................... Division Three South

City only suffered **one defeat in their first 26** games, to the eventual champions Nottingham Forest. Norwich finished second, but with only one club promoted, remained in the division.

Date	Opponents	V	Result		Attendance	League /Cup
Aug.19	Port Vale	H	2-0	W	27,288	League
Aug.23	Northampton T	H	0-0	D	27,300	League
Aug.26	*Nottingham Forest*	*A*	*2-4*	*L*	*28,250*	*League*
Aug.31	Northampton T	A	2-1	W	17,696	League
Sep.2	Torquay United	H	1-1	D	25,447	League
Sep.7	Walsall	A	1-0	W	10,831	League
Sep.9	Aldershot	A	1-1	D	8,238	League
Sep.13	Walsall	H	1-0	W	22,090	League
Sep.16	Swindon Town	H	2-0	W	23,289	League

Different to sequence

Date	Opponents	V	Result		Attendance	League / Cup
Sep.23	Colchester United	A	3-2	W	13,843	League
Sep.30	Bristol Rovers	H	2-0	W	23,965	League
Oct.7	Watford	H	3-1	W	24,507	League
Oct.14	Millwall	A	1-1	D	34,780	League
Oct.21	Bristol City	H	0-0	D	27,130	League
Oct.28	Gillingham	A	2-2	D	14,348	League
Nov.4	Bournemouth	H	3-0	W	23,160	League
Nov.11	Exeter City	A	2-1	W	12,595	League
Nov.8	Southend United	H	3-0	W	24,783	League
Nov.25	Watford	H	2-0	W	22,045	FA Cup
Dec.2	Plymouth Argyle	H	1-0	W	26,891	League
Dec. 9	Rhyl	A	1-0	W	7,448	FA Cup
Dec.23	Nottingham Forest	H	2-0	W	29,818	League
Dec.26	Brighton & H. A	A	1-1	D	14,134	League
Dec.27	Brighton & H. A	H	1-1	D	22,893	League
Dec.30	Torquay United	A	5-1	W	5,948	League
Jan.6	Liverpool	H	3-1	W	34,693	FA Cup
Jan.11	*Leyton Orient*	*A*	*1-3*	*L*	*4,475*	*League*

Sequence ended

1988-9................................Division One

City won their opening four games. They proceeded to drop only four points from their first nine games and also won all of their first five away games. As a result, they led the First Division until 27 December. However, they fell away at the end of the season, by only taking six points from the last 27, to eventually finish fourth.

Opening eleven games

Date	Opponents	V	Result		Attendance
Aug.27	Nottingham Forest	H	2-1	W	13,488
Sep.3	Middlesbrough	A	3-2	W	18,259
Sep.10	QPR	H	1-0	W	11,174
Sep.17	Newcastle United	A	2-0	W	22,801
Sep.24	*Millwall*	*H*	*2-2*	*D*	*16.616*
Oct.1	*Charlton Athletic*	*H*	*1-3*	*L*	*11,470*
Oct.8	Derby County	A	1-0	W	14,117
Oct.22	Totenham Hotspur	H	3-1	W	20,330
Oct.26	Manchester United.	A	2-1	W	36,998
Oct 29	*Southampton*	*H*	*1-1*	*D*	*14,808*
Nov. 5	Wimbledon	A	2-0	W	5,853

Different to sequence

1992-3.. Premier

In the inaugural Premier League season, City had gained 39 points from their first 18 games and led the Division by eight points. However, they only managed to finish in third place after just gaining seven points from the final six games.

Date	Opponents	V	Result		Attendance
Aug.15	Arsenal	A	4-2	W	24,030
Aug.19	Chelsea	H	2-1	W	15,164
Aug.22	Everton	H	1-1	D	14,150
Aug.26	*Manchester City*	*A*	*1-3*	*L*	*23,182*
Aug.29	Crystal Palace	A	2-1	W	12.033

Date	Opponents	V	Result		Attendance
Aug.31	Nottingham Forest	H	3-1	W	14,104
Sep.5	Southampton	H	1-0	W	12,452
Sep.12	Chelsea	A	3-2	W	16,680
Sep.19	Sheffield Wed.	H	1-0	W	14,367
Sep.26	Coventry City	A	1-1	D	16,436
Oct.3	*Blackburn Rovers*	*A*	*1-7*	*L*	*16,312*
Oct.17	QPR	H	2-1	W	16,009
Oct.25	Liverpool	A	1-4	L	36,318
Oct.31	Middlesbrough	H	1-1	D	14,499
Nov.9	Oldham Athletic	A	3-2	W	11,018
Nov.21	Sheffield United	H	2-1	W	14,874
Nov.28	Aston Villa	A	3-2	W	28,837
Dec.5	Wimbledon	H	2-1	W	14,161
Dec.12	*Manchester United.*	*A*	*0-1*	*L*	*34,580*

Defeats, different to sequence.

1993-4.. **Premier**

In 1993-4 in the Premiership, City were not defeated in their first eight away games; winning five, drawing three and scoring 21 goals, before losing at Oldham Athletic. This run was even more remarkable in that they were also performing away in Europe, drawing at Vitesse Arnhem on 29 September and beating Bayern Munich on 3 November.

Date	Opponents	V	Result		Attendance
Aug.18	Blackburn Rovers	A	3-2	W	14.236
Aug.21	Leeds United	A	4-0	W	32,008
Sep.1	Sheffield Wed.	A	3-3	D	25,175
Sep.18	Q.P.R	A	2-2	D	13,259
Sep.25	Everton.	A	5-1	W	20,531

1993-4 Opening away sequence (continued)

Oct.16	Chelsea	A	2-1	W	16,923
Oct.30	Arsenal	A	0-0	D	30,506
Nov.6	Sheffield United	A	2-1	W	18,254
Nov.27	*Oldham*	*A*	*1-2*	*L*	*10,198*

Sequence ended.

Conversely, at home, City only won two and drew three of their first eight league games.

WORST

1920-1 ....Division Three

City, in their inaugural season in the Football League, did not win until their 14th game. They finished 16th and failed to score at home until their sixth attempt, two months after the season started.

Date	Opponents	V	Result		Attendance
Aug.28	Plymouth Argyle	A	1-1	D	14,000
Sep.1	Exeter City	A	1-1	D	5.000
Sep.4	Plymouth Argyle	H	0-0	D	12,000
Sep. 8	Exeter City	H	0-0	D	7,000
Sep.11	Crystal Palace	H	0-1	L	11,000
Sep.16	Swansea Town	A	2-5	L	10,000
Sep.18	Crystal Palace	A	0-1	L	10,000
Sep.25	Southampton	H	0-1	L	9.000
Oct.2	Southampton	A	0-1	L	15,000
Oct.9	Brentford	H	0-0	D	9,000
Oct.16	Brentford	A	1-3	L	9,000
Oct.23	Bristol Rovers	A	2-2	D	12,000

Date	Opponents	V	Result		Attendance
Oct.30	Bristol Rovers	H	1-1	D	10,000
Nov.6	*Reading*	*A*	*1-0*	*W*	*8,000*

Sequence ended

1921-2 .... **Division Three South.**

City didn't win until their 12th game, which strangely enough, was against Reading, whom they beat to end the long winless sequence in the previous year.

City finished 15th.

Date	Opponents	V	Result		Attendance
Aug.27	Luton Town	H	0-1	L	11,000
Aug.29	Plymouth Argyle	A	1-1	D	12,000
Sep.3	Luton Town	A	1-2	L	11,000
Sep.8	Plymouth Argyle	H	1-1	D	7,000
Sep.10	Q.P.R	H	0-0	D	8,000
Sep.17	Q.P.R	A	0-2	L	10,000
Sep.24	Newport County	H	2-2	D	8,000
Oct. 1	Newport County	A	0-1	L	8,000
Oct.8	Southampton	H	2-2	D	8,000
Oct.15	Southampton	A	0-2	L	12,000
Oct.22	Reading	A	1-2	D	10,000
Oct.29	*Reading*	*H*	*4-1*	*W*	*7,500*

Sequence ended

1935-6 .... **Division Two.**

In their first ever season at Carrow Road, City won their opening game, but then lost seven matches in a row. They recovered to finish 11th.

Date	Opponents	V	Result		Attendance
Aug.31	West Ham United	H	4-3	W	29,779
Sep. 4	Blackpool	A	1-2	L	19,259
Sep. 7	Swansea Town	A	3-4	L	12,988
Sep.11	Blackpool	H	0-1	L	22,337
Sep.14	Leicester City	H	1-2	L	20,554
Sep.16	Doncaster Rovers	A	0-3	L	10,000
Sep.21	Bradford Park Avenue	A	0-1	L	10,719
Sep.28	Sheffield United	H	0-1	L	18,322
Oct.5	Southampton	A	1-1	D	15,073

Sequence start and finish.

1963-4 .... **Division Two.**

City lost their first four games and finished 17th. They signed Ron Davies before the Scunthorpe game and he went on to score 26 League goals that season.

Date	Opponents	V	Result		Attendance
Aug.24	Cardiff City	A	1-3	L	21,977
Aug.28	Bury	H	0-1	L	18,819
Aug.31	Leyton Orient	H	1-2	L	18,020
Sep.3	Bury	A	2-4	L	10,037
Sep.7	Scunthorpe United	H	2-1	W	16,888

Sequence ended

Ron Davies, who scored 26 League goals in 1963, pulled City round from a disastrous start.

1966-7.............................. **Division Two.**

City only won one of their first 12 league games and also went out of the League Cup in the first round at home to Brighton and Hove Albion.

Date	Opponents	V	Result		Attendance
Aug.20	Portsmouth	H	1-1	D	10,306
Aug.27	Birmingham City	A	1-2	L	26,846
Aug.31	Hull City	H	0-2	L	14,783
Sep.3	Ipswich Town	H	1-2	L	19,837
Sep.6	*Northampton Town*	*A*	*2-1*	*W*	*14,767*

1966-7 Poor start (continued)

Date	Opponents	V	Result		Attendance
Sep.10	Coventry City	H	1-1	D	13,454
Sep.17	Bury	A	0-2	L	5,761
Sep 20	Hull City	A	0-5	L	24,871
Sep.24	Preston N E	H	1-1	D	10,092
Sep.27	Carlisle United	A	0-1	L	10,329
Oct.1	Rotherham United	A	1-2	L	9,222
Oct.8	Bristol City	A	0-2	L	11,008
Oct.15	*Carlisle United*	*H*	*2-0*	*W*	*11,540*

Different to sequence

1973-4...............................Division One

In 1973-4, City only won one of their first 13 games before ending the season relegated.

Date	Opponents		Result		Attendance
Aug.25	Wolves	A	1-3	L	22,744
Aug.29	Q.P.R	H	0-0	D	24,660
Sep.1	West Ham United	H	2-2	D	25,706
Sep.4	Southampton	A	2-2	D	17,658
Sep.8	Manchester City	A	1-2	L	31,209
Sep.12	*Southampton*	*H*	*2-0*	*W*	*25,023*
Sep.15	Arsenal	A	0-4	L	29,278
Sep.22	Sheffield United	A	0-1	L	19,974
Sep.29	Leeds United	H	0-1	L	31,993
Oct.6	Derby County	A	1-1	D	25,984
Oct.13	Coventry City	H	0-0	D	22,841
Oct.20	Tottenham Hotspur	H	1-1	D	25,032

Date	Opponents		Result		Attendance
Oct.26	Chelsea	A	0-3	L	21,953
Nov.3	*Leicester City*	*H*	*1-0*	*W*	*20,929*

Different to sequence

STRIKERS

Norwich were the first club to have a public house attached to a football ground. It was situated in the River Stand and originally named 'The Nest'. It was open during normal licensing hours, but closed during match days. It was later named 'Strikers' and currently, 'Scores.' It ceased to be a public house, but remained as a bar area on match days to relieve the pressure on the concourse during half time. It was also used as an assembly point for junior members.

The River End stand in its early days. The 'Strikers' pub sign is displayed outside. It was previously called 'The Nest' and now 'Scores'

SUBSTITUTES

The first substitute appearance for Norwich was by Gordon Bolland, who on 31 August 1965 at Bristol City, came on for Terry Anderson in the 70th minute. At that time substitutes were only allowed to replace injured players.

City's most used substitute to the end of season 2003-4 has been Daryl Sutch, on 61 occasions out of a total 352 appearances between 1990-2003. However, this was during the time when up to three substitutes per game were allowed.

In the period up to 1987, when Clubs were restricted to just one substitute per game, the most used substitute was Trevor Howard, who made 45 such appearances. This was out of a total 156 appearances that he made for City between 1968 and 1974. Trevor was also the first scoring substitute at Hull City on 26 December 1968.

The earliest a substitute was used, occurred on 17 January 1984 in the League Cup (Milk) home tie against Aston Villa. Louie Donowa came on for the injured Dave Watson in the fourth minute.

The earliest League substitutes for City were both in the fifth minute. Steve Grapes replaced Trevor Howard at Newcastle United in a Division One match on 15 April 1974 and Don Heath came on for Terry Allcock in a Division Two home game against Ipswich Town on 3 September 1966.

The first time two substitutes both scored, was in the game against Manchester City on 18 September 2001. Marc Libbra scored within 19 seconds of coming on, in the 74th minute and Paul McVeigh added a second in the 90th minute.

In the game against Liverpool on 5 February 1994, Darren Eadie was substituted after only coming as a substitute himself a few minutes earlier. This was due to Bryan Gunn being sent off and the need to bring on the substitute goalkeeper.

There have been many instances where substitutions have been made tactically so late in the game to waste time that the player has not even touched the ball. However, these still count as appearances.

Gordon Bolland, City's first ever substitute in action

SUNDAY FOOTBALL

Sunday football was not made legal until the late 1980's. Gradually, Sunday matches became a normal match day to accommodate television needs.

Date	Opponents	Result	Occasion	Attendance

First game

24 March 1985 ....Sunderland.............. N.. 1-0..... Milk Cup Final 100,000

First League game

22.01.89 .... Millwall .... A . 3-2 .... Division One 13,687

First Home League game

21.01.90 ....Manchester United H.. 2-0 .... Division One 17,370

First FA Cup game

28.01.90 ....Liverpool .... H.. 0-0..... Fourth Round 23,152

SUSPENSIONS

Several City players have been suspended for sendings off or accumulation of bookings. The longest suspension was given to George "Pompey "Martin, for six weeks in 1922, after being sent off at Southend in the FA Cup on 2 December for striking an opponent.

George 'Pompey' Martin

Bryan Gunn was suspended on three occasions for sending off offences.

Coventry City .... A 08.04.89

Liverpool................ H 05.02.94

Sheffield United ...... A 09.09.95

Darren Eadie was suspended on three occasions in 18 months.

September 1995- March 1997 ...... See opposite page.

SUSPENSIONS

City had three players sent off in a five game spell during September 1995.

Bryan Gunn............A...................09.09.95 ......Sheffield United

Karl Simpson ....H...................20.09.95 ......Torquay United

Darren Eadie ....A...................23.09.95 ....Grimsby Town

Two players have been sent off on their debuts.

Mark Halsey............A...................26.04.78 ....Newcastle United

Karl Simpson ....H...................20.09.95 ....Torquay United

Two players sent off in one match

This occurred three times in just over a year.

Oxford United.........H...................04.09.96 ....Darren Eadie

04.09.96........Robert Fleck

City lost the League Cup match, 2-3 at home to Oxford United. Fleck was sent off for a straight red card and Eadie for a second bookable offence.

Huddersfield Town..H...................01.03.97 ....Keith Scott

01.03.97........Darren Eadie

The game ended with nine players on both sides. Huddersfield had already had one player sent off, followed by a second after a clash with Keith Scott in the 58th minute, which ended with both players departing. Then Eadie, who had scored both goals in the 2-0 win, was sent off in the 89th minute for a second bookable offence.

Tranmere Rovers.....A...................04.10.97 ....Rob Newman

04.10.97........Mike Milligan

City lost 0-2 at Tranmere, with Rob Newman sent off in the 30th minute for holding back Kelly as the Rovers striker headed for goal. Mike Milligan followed in the 62nd minute, after a horrendous head high tackle on Challinor, to earn himself a second booking and removal from the pitch.

TALLEST PLAYERS

The tallest players appearing for Norwich are believed to be: -

Player	Seasons	Height	Position	Appearances
Peter Crouch	2003	6 feet 7inches	Striker	15
George Ephgrave	1949-51	6 feet 4 inches	Goalkeeper	5
Joe Corrigan	1984	6 feet 4 inches	Goalkeeper	4
Andy Linighan	1988-90	6 feet 4 inches	Defender	106

Peter Crouch was acquired on loan from Aston Villa during the 2003-4 season. He was a catalyst to City's season, helping them progress to the top of the table. For one so tall he was exceptionally good with his feet.

Joe Corrigan was also a loan player who remained with City for one month.

Peter Crouch, in his first match on loan for City against Burnley.

TELEVISED MATCHES

Television, with the exposure and revenue it provides, has become more lucrative and essential to the economics of the game.

The first showing on television was by Anglia's 'Match of the Week,' which commenced in the early 1960's and showed recordings of regional matches only.

The BBC provided the main diet of recorded highlights in their popular 'Match of the Day' programme shown on Saturday evenings.

City were rarely shown until they reached the First Division and met the criteria of better floodlights and a gantry from the side of the pitch rather than from behind the River end terrace, as used by Anglia TV.

First Appearance on Match of the Day

11.03.67 .... Sheffield Wed .... H .. 1-3........FA Cup fifth round

First League Appearance on Match of the Day

26.08.67....................... Q.P.R................ A .. 0-2.......Division Two

First Win on Match of the Day

06.11.71 .... Hull City .... A .. 2-1.......Division Two

First Home League Appearance on Match of the Day

11.03.72..................... Sunderland .... H . 1-1.......Division Two

First Division One League Appearance on Match of the Day

26.08.72..................... Derby County ... H .. 1-0.......Division One

Biggest Win on Match of the Day

28.01.89..................... Sutton United .... H .. 8-0........FA Cup fourth round

07.02.84 .... Watford .... H . 6-1.......Division One

Biggest Defeat on Match of the Day

24.01.81 .... Manchester City A .. 0-6........FA Cup fourth round

04.10.80..................... Middlesbrough .. A .. 1-6 ....Division One

City fans with the Match of the Day flag during the filming of the opening sequence.

In August 1993, City fans were chosen to take part in the opening sequence of 'Match of the Day.' Fans were invited to fill the Norwich & Peterborough Stand to sing and cheer. A massive 'Match of the Day' flag was passed from one side of the stand to the other by the fans assembled there. Although filming lasted for much of the afternoon, only a few seconds were used in the actual sequence and it was shown on 'Match of the Day' for two years.

LIVE GAMES

A new era dawned when a contract was signed to show live matches. This tended to concentrate on the more famous teams, but as City became successful they started to appear more regularly. The terrestrial TV companies shared the showing between them, but when Sky Television came along in 1991, with a new format and razzamatazz, the image of football changed for ever. The massive payments enabled top world stars to be attracted to the Premiership and amazingly, attendances at the new all seater stadiums rocketed.

The first live match involving City was the Milk Cup final at Wembley when they beat Sunderland 1-0 on 24 March 1985.

The First Live League Game

Opponents	Date	Result	TV Company
West Ham Utd.	Dec. ... 1988	H ..2-1	BBC

The full list of live games is as follows: League, unless specified.

Opponents	Date	Result		TV Company
West Ham Utd.	Dec.... 1988	H ..2-1		BBC
Millwall	Jan. ... 1989	A...3-2		BBC
Arsenal	Apr.... 1989	A...0-5		BBC
Manchester Utd.	Jan. ... 1990	H ..2-0		BBC
Liverpool	Feb. ... 1990	H ..0-0	FA Cup	BBC
Tottenham Hotspur	Mar. .. 1990	A...0-4		BBC
Manchester Utd.	Mar. .. 1991	H ..2-1		SKY
Nottingham Forest	Mar. .. 1991	H ..0-1	FA Cup	BBC
Sunderland	Mar. .. 1992	A...0-1	FA Cup	BBC
Nottingham Forest	Aug. .. 1992	H ..3-1		SKY
Oldham Athletic	Nov. . 1992	A...3-2		SKY
Ipswich Town.	Dec.... 1992	H ..0-2		SKY
Sheffield Wed.	Jan 1993	A...0-1		SKY
Tottenham Hotspur	Jan. ... 1993	H ..0-2	FA Cup	BBC
Blackburn Rovers	Mar. . 1993	H ..0-0		SKY
Manchester Utd.	Apr. .. 1993	H ..1-3		SKY
Ipswich Town.	Apr. .. 1993	A...1-3		SKY
Manchester Utd.	Aug. . 1993	H ..0-2		SKY
Vitesse Arnhem	Sep. .. 1993	H ..3-0	UEFA	BBC
Bayern Munich	Oct. . 1993	A...2-1	UEFA	BBC
Bayern Munich	Oct. . 1993	H ..1-1	UEFA	BBC
Inter Milan.	Nov. . 1993	H ..0-1	UEFA	BBC
Inter Milan.	Nov. . 1993	A...0-1	UEFA	BBC
Leeds Utd.	Dec. .. 1993	H ..2-1		SKY
West Ham Utd.	Jan. ... 1994	A...3-3		SKY
Manchester Utd.	Jan. ... 1994	H ..0-2	FA Cup	BBC
Arsenal	Mar. . 1994	H ..1-1		SKY
Everton	Mar. . 1994	H ..3-0		SKY
Ipswich Town	Sep. .. 1994	A...2-1		SKY
Wimbledon.	Oct. .. 1994	A...0-1		SKY
Nottingham Forest	Dec. .. 1994	A...0-1		SKY

TELEVISED MATCHES

Opponents	Date	Result	TV Company
Ipswich Town	Mar. .. 1995	H .. 3-0	SKY
Luton Town	Aug. .. 1995	A... 3-1	ITV
Watford	Nov. .. 1995	A... 2-0	ITV
Leicester City	Dec. ... 1995	A... 2-3	ITV
Sunderland	Jan..... 1996	A... 1-0	ITV
Birmingham City	Feb .... 1996.	H .. 1-1	ITV
Ipswich Town	Apr. ... 1996	A... 1-2	ITV
Ipswich Town	Oct 1996	H .. 3-1	ITV
Sheffield United	Feb 1997	A... 3-2	ITV
Ipswich Town	Apr. ... 1997	A... 0-2	ITV
Manchester City	Apr. ... 1997	H .. 0-0	ITV
Ipswich Town	Sep 1997	H .. 2-1	ITV
Middlesbrough	Mar.. . 1998	A... 0-3	ITV
Bury	Sep. ... 1998	H .. 0-0	ITV
Oxford United	Nov. .. 1998	H .. 1-3	ITV
Ipswich Town	Apr. ... 1999	H .. 0-0	ITV
Bolton Wanderers	Oct. ... 1999	H .. 2-1	ITV
Grimsby Town	Nov. .. 1999	A... 1-2	ITV
Ipswich Town	Mar. .. 2000	A... 2-0	ITV
Wolves	Sep. ... 2000	A .. 0-4	SKY
W.B.A.	Oct. .. 2001	H .. 2-0	ITV digital
Crystal Palace	Oct. ... 2001	A... 2-3	ITV
Stockport County	Nov. . 2001	A... 1-2	ITV digital
Portsmouth	Dec. ... 2001	A... 2-1	ITV
Manchester City	Jan 2002	A... 1-3	ITV
Chelsea	Jan 2002	A... 0-4 ... FA Cup ... SKY	
Millwall	Jan..... 2002	H .. 0-0	ITV
WBA	Feb. ... 2002	A... 0-1	ITV
Preston N E	Feb. ... 2002	H .. 3-0	ITV digital
Birmingham	Mar . . 2002	H .. 0-1	ITV digital
Stockport County	Apr. ... 2002	H .. 2-0	ITV
Wolves	May .. 2002	A... 0-1	ITV digital
Birmingham City	May .. 2002	N .. 1-1	ITV
Ipswich Town	Sep. ... 2002	A... 1-1	SKY
Leicester City	Oct. ... 2002	H .. 0-0	SKY
Watford	Jan..... 2003	A... 1-2	SKY
Reading	Mar. .. 2003	H .. 0-1	SKY
Portsmouth	Mar. .. 2003	A... 2-3	SKY
Wolves	Apr. ... 2003	H .. 0-3	SKY

Opponents	Date	Result	TV Company
Leicester City	Apr.... 2003	A... 1-1	SKY
Nottingham Forest	Aug. .. 2003	A...0-2	SKY
Stoke City	Sep. ... 2003	A... 1-1	SKY
Nottingham Forest	Dec.... 2003	H . 1-0	SKY
W.B.A.	Feb. ... 2004	H ..0-0	SKY
Wigan	Apr.... 2004	H ..2-0	SKY
Reading	Apr.... 2004	A... 1-0	SKY

TESTIMONIALS

Player	Date	Opponents	Score
Pompey Martin	19.04.26	Hull City	2-5
Charlie Dennington	23.04.28	Tottenham Hotspur	3-0
Joe Hannah	25.04.32	Derby County	2-2
Bernard Robinson	25.04.49	Luton Town	1-2
Harry Proctor	20.01.54	All Star XI	2-4
Barry Staton	26.02.64	International X1	1-3
Ron Ashman	22.04.64	Ipswich Town	0-0
Barry Butler (In memory)	05.05.66	Ipswich Town	3-1
Phil Kelly	04.10.67	Select XI	6-3
Terry Allcock	30.04.69	Ipswich Town	3-1
Billy Furness	03.05.71	Select XI	6-1
Albert Bennett	03.05.72	All Star XI	0-1
Kevin Keelan	03.05.74	Ipswich Town	1-3
David Stringer	09.05.75	West Ham United	1-1
Duncan Forbes	11.04.78	Norwich 1971/2	0-3
Martin Peters	18.10.78	World Cup 1966	4-2
Billy Steele	11.12.79	England X1	0-5
Kevin Keelan	25.11.80	All star X1	4-3 Farewell
David Jones	16.11.82	All Star XI	3-2
Greg Downs	26.03.85	Norwich 1974/5	7-6
Peter Mendham	08.08.87	Real Sociedad	2-0
John O'Neill	16.05.89	All Star X1	2-8
Jerry Goss	09.05.94	Genoa	4-5
Ian Crook	10.08.96	Sparta Rotterdam	0-0
Bryan Gunn	04.11.96	Manchester United	0-3

Player	Date	Opponents	Score
Daryl Sutch	30.07.99	AZ Alkmaar	0-0
Tim Sheppard	22.01.01	Celtic	2-4

TEXACO CUP

This competition, sponsored by Texaco, commenced in 1972 and lasted for three seasons before being replaced by the Anglo Scottish Cup. It involved English and Scottish clubs and was played over two legs.

In 1973 Norwich reached the final, but lost to Ipswich Town 1-2 in both legs. A record crowd of 35,798 watched the second leg at Carrow Road.

Year	Opponents		Result	Attendance	
1972-3	First[t]	Dundee	A.... 1-2	8,000	
	First	Dundee ..	H.... 2-0	18,339	
	Second	Leicester City	A.... 0-2	9,721	
	Second	Leicester City	H.... 2-0	18,550	...4-3 on pens
	Third	Motherwell....	H.... 2-0	18,829	
	Third	Motherwell....	A.... 2-3	9,817	
	Final	Ipswich Town	A.... 1-2	29,698	
	Final	Ipswich Town	H.... 1-2	35,798	
1973-4	First	St Johnstone	A.... 2-0	3.700	
	First	St Johnstone	H.... 1-0	11.028	
	Second	Motherwell	H.... 2-0	10,721	
	Second	Motherwell	A.... 1-0	7,018	
	Third	Burnley ..	A.... 0-2	4,853	
	Third	Burnley ..	H.... 2-3	11,797	

1974-5

In 1974 the format was changed to a group basis.

	Opponents	Result	Attendance
	Peterborough Utd.	H.... 2-1	12.169
	W.B.A.	A.... 1-5	5,393
	Birmingham City	A.... 1-3	14,847

THE NEST

This was City's second ground, which they moved to in 1908 and stayed until 1935. It was an unusual location, built in a chalk pit in Rosary Road. It was very cramped and had a high retaining concrete wall some 50 feet tall behind one corner. Another concrete wall was positioned from the corner to the goal, which sloped down gradually from 20 feet to 10 feet as it reached the goal itself with spectators on top behind a small fence. This was a hazard to players, Jimmy Stoakes actually broke his leg when he crashed into the wall. The stands down the side were so close to the pitch the players could almost be touched. The ground was overhauled in 1910 with drainage installed and more terracing to increase capacity by 1,500. A cinder track was put round the pitch to assist with training and dressing rooms were expanded.

Against Northampton Town in April 1922, over fifty spectators fell on to the pitch when terrace fencing gave way at the top of the concrete wall, but fortunately there were few casualties

The record attendance at The Nest against Sheffield Wednesday in 1935.

For an FA Cup tie against Sheffield Wednesday, a crowd of 25,037 packed in, but it was becoming more unsuitable for big crowds and the pitch was liable to subsidence. Now that Norwich were in the Second Division the need to find a new ground became acute and in time for the start of the 1935-6 season the club moved to Carrow Road.

A public house was built in the River End Stand at Carrow Road in 1979 and was originally called 'The Nest.'

TOURS

Norwich have been on many end of and pre-season tours overseas.

Their first tour was in May 1952 when they played four games in Holland. This was followed by visits to several countries, including Iceland, Malta, Portugal, Kenya, Norway and Sweden. They went further a field in 1976 to play matches in Trinidad, to the USA in 1978 and Australia in 1979. However, their most ambitious tour was to China in 1980, being only the second League club to visit there. They played three games, winning two and drawing one before massive crowds of up to 80,000. The tour ended with a final match in Hong Kong.

In 2004 in conjunction with sponsors Proton, City had a pre season tour of Malaysia. This was very successful with victories over a local and the national side. City, together with Proton, used the opportunity to promote Norwich, in a country with incredible interest in the Premier League. This included coaching youngsters and setting up a supporters club.

TRANSFERS

The following transfer fees are those popularly quoted, but with VAT, add ons and other costs, may vary from other reportings.

Record Buys

Player		Transfer Fee	SellingClub	Year
Jon	Newsome	£1m	Leeds Utd.	1994
Darren	Beckford	£925,000	Port Vale	1991
Iwan	Roberts	£900,000	Wolves	1997
Mick	Milligan	£850,000	Oldham Athletic	1994
Mark	Robins	£800,000	Manchester Utd.	1992
Mike	Sheron	£800,000	Manchester City	1994
Darren	Huckerby	£750,000	Manchester City.	2003
Paul	Blades	£700,000	Derby County	1990
Mark	Rivers	£700,000	Crewe Alex.	2001
Efan	Ekoku	£665,000	Bournemouth	1993
Robert	Fleck	£650,000	Chelsea	1995
Rob	Newman	£600,00	Bristol City	1991
Robert	Fleck	£580,000	Rangers	1987
David	Phillips	£550,000	Coventry City	1989
Phil	Mulryne	£500,000	Manchester Utd.	1999
Adam	Drury	£500,000	Peterborough Utd.	2001
Neil	Emblem	£500,000	Wolves	2001
Youssef	Safri	£500,000	Coventry City	2004

Record Sales

Player		Transfer Fee	Buying Club	Year
Craig	Bellamy	£5.2m	Coventry City	2000
Chris	Sutton	£5m	Blackburn Rovers	1994
Darren	Eadie	£3m	Leicester City	1999
Ruel	Fox	£2,250,000	Newcastle Utd.	1994
Andy	Johnson	£2.200,000	Nottm. Forest	1997
Robert	Fleck	£2,100,000	Chelsea	1992
Jon	Newsome	£1,600,000	Sheffield Wed.	1996
Andy	Townsend	£1,200,000	Chelsea	1990
Andy	Linighan	£1,200,000	Arsenal	1990

Craig Bellamy, City's record sale.

Player		Transfer Fee	Buying Club	Year
Dale	Gordon	£1,200,000	Rangers	1991
Kevin	Reeves	£1m	Manchester City	1980
Dave	Watson	£1m	Everton	1986
Justin	Fashanu	£1m	Nottm. Forest	1981
Efan	Ekoku	£1m	Wimbledon	1994
Mark	Robins	£1m	Leicester City	1995
Ashley	Ward	£1m	Derby County	1996
Steve	Bruce	£825,000	Manchester.Utd.	1987
Mike	Phelan	£750,000	Manchester Utd.	1989
Keith	O'Neill	£700,000	Middlesbrough	1999
David	Phillips	£600,000	Nottm.Forest	1993
Kevin	Drinkell	£600,000	Rangers	1988
Chris	Woods	£600,000	Rangers	1988
Robert	Rosario	£600,000	Coventry City	1991
Lee	Marshall	£600,000	Leicester City	2001
Spencer	Prior	£600,000	Leicester City	1996
Tim	Sherwood	£500,000	Blackburn Rovers	1991

Craig Bellamy was originally sold for a potential £6.5m, but this depended on Coventry City staying in the Premiership. As they were relegated within 12 months the fee Norwich received reduced to £5.2m when he moved to Newcastle United.

Norwich, in some of their transfer deals, insisted on a sell on clause giving City a percentage of any further profit. These proved to be particularly lucrative, often netting much more than the original transfer fee, when the players moved on for higher fees.

Player		Fees	Buying Club
Danny	Mills	£50,000	Charlton Athletic
	Extra	£750,000	Leeds United
Tim	Sherwood	£500,000	Blackburn Rovers
	Extra	£500,000	Tottenham Hotspur
Ade	Akinbyi	£200,000	Gillingham
	Extra	£100,000	Bristol City
Mike	Sheron	£150,000	Stoke City
	Extra	£735,000	Q.P.R
Chris	Sutton	£5m	Blackburn Rovers
	Extra	£150,000	Chelsea

BUYS

First £2,000 Buy

Billy	Furness	£2,750	Leeds United	1937

First £10,000 Buy

John	Gavin	£10,500	Tottenham H.	1955

Johnny Gavin's fee, when he returned to City after a year with Tottenham Hotspur, was the value of the part exchange with Monty Norman.

First £20,000 Buy

Tommy	Bryceland	£20,000	St Mirren	1962

First £30,000 Buy

Ron	Davies	£35,000	Luton Town	1963

First £40,000 Buy

Ken	Mallender	£40,000	Sheffield United	1968

TRANSFERS

First £75.000 Buy

Colin   Suggett .... 75,000 .... W.B.A 1973

First £100,000 Buy

Ted   MacDougall .... £140,000 .... West Ham Utd 1973

Ted, was manager John Bond's first signing. He was a prolific scorer who had failed to make an impact at Manchester United and West Ham. Bond had always got the best out of him at Bournemouth, where they had previously been together, and soon restored his form.

He scored 64 goals in 144 appearances for Norwich including one season as top scorer of Division One.

First £300,000 Buy

Drazen   Muzinic .... £300,000 .... Hadjud Split 1980

The fashion at this time was to buy established internationals from other countries at a relatively cheap price. Drazen Muzinic, a Yugoslavian international, could hardly speak a word of English, but he possessed good ball skills. He only made 23 appearances, six of them as substitute, as he found it hard to adjust to the demands of English football. He was released at the end of the 1981-2 season having never found his form, although he had been asked to play in several different positions.

First £500,000 Buy

Robert   Fleck .... £580,000 .... Rangers 1987

In 1987 City were in desperate straits, being in a relegation position in the league and having just sacked manager Ken Brown. When Dave Stringer took over, his first purchases were Robert Fleck and Andy Linighan. It was a surprise when the fiery Scot came to Carrow Road, but he helped inspire the club to an improved position and immediately became a firm favourite with the fans. Robert moved to Chelsea for a massive fee of over £2m after scoring 66 goals in 181 appearances, but later returned for another stint with City for a £650,000 fee.

First £700,000 Buy

Paul   Blades .... £700,000 .... Derby County 1990

This was City's record buy for a defender until they bought John Newsome. However, Paul never looked worth the value and was sold to Wolves at a reduced fee of £325,000 after making only 62 appearances for City.

First £900,000 Buy

Darren   Beckford ....£925,000...........Port Vale................1991

Darren was top scorer with Vale, but never lived up to his fee and was beset with injury problems. The high points of his City career were scoring a hat trick against Everton and the winner against Coventry City in the FA Cup. He scored 13 goals in 49 appearances and was allowed to leave for Oldham Athletic at a reduced price of £300,000.

First £1m Buy

Jon   Newsome ....£1m ....Leeds Utd................1994

City at last broke the £1m barrier in securing this tall accomplished defender from Leeds and immediately made him captain of the team. He added quality to the defence and made 76 appearances, scoring eight goals, before being sold at a cut price £1.7m to ease the financial pressure on the club in 1996.

Jon Newsome, City's record £1m purchase from Leeds United in 1994.

TRANSFERS

SALES

First Sale

Davie   Ross .... £650 .... Manchester City 1907

First £2,000 Sale

Sam   Jennings .... £2,250 .... Middlesbrough 1920

First £20,000 Sale

Monty   Norman .... £28,000 .... Tottenham H. 1955

Including John Gavin as part exchange

First £30,000 Sale

Ollie   Burton .... £31,500 .... Newcastle Utd. 1963

A popular player, whose transfer caused outrage when he was sold, along with Jimmy Hill who went to Everton in the same period.

First £40,000 Sale

Ron   Davies .... £50,000 .... Southampton 1966

One of the best centre forwards in the country, Ron's controversial sale to Southampton for the paltry sum of £50,000 caused anger among the supporters. Ron scored over 40 goals in the First Division with his new club Southampton, who had just been promoted.

First £100,000 Sale

David   Cross .... £150,000 .... Coventry City 1973

Cross was a popular player who always gave his best. At the time, he was a record buy from Rochdale at £40,000 in 1971. He spearheaded the promotion drive in his first season and had scored 30 goals in 107 appearances before moving to Coventry City. He played for many clubs after this and was always a valuable player.

First £1m Sale

Kevin   Reeves....................£1m....................Manchester City...... 1980

Having been snapped up by manager John Bond from his former club Bournemouth for £50,000, this 19 year old, soon established himself as a quality player. He formed the youngest ever strike force for City when he teamed up with Justin Fashanu as 18 and 21 year olds. He made one England appearance and at the age of 22, having scored 42 goals in 133 appearances, joined Manchester City. He had limited success with them although he scored in the FA Cup final defeat against Tottenham Hotspur. A knee injury ended his career prematurely whilst at Manchester City.

Kevin Reeves was capped for England and then later sold for £1m to Manchester City in 1980.

First £2m Sale

Robert   Fleck......................£2.1m ....Chelsea 1992

Chelsea snapped up Robert Fleck on the eve of the 1992-3 season for £2.1m, much to the dismay of City fans. His successor, Mark Robins, made an immediate impact, which softened the blow, while Fleck had a disastrous time at Chelsea.

He scored only once in his first season and also missed out on selection for Chelsea's Cup final side in 1994. He returned to City in 1995.

First £2.250,000 Sale

Ruel   Fox.........................£2.250,000.........Newcastle United 1994

A firm favourite with the crowd as a dazzling winger, Ruel became disillusioned when Mike Walker departed and soon joined Newcastle United as City's record sale. He scored 25 goals, nine in his last season, in 219 appearances for Norwich.

First £5m Sale

Chris   Sutton ....£5m ....Blackburn Rovers.... 1994

The sale of Chris Sutton smashed the British transfer record. After a successful season in 1993-4, when he scored 28 goals, it was inevitable that he would leave Norwich for a bigger club, but it took £5m to prise him away to Blackburn Rovers. Here he teamed up with Alan Shearer to form a formidable strike force, won a Championship medal and was capped for England.

First £6m Sale

Craig   Bellamy..................£6.3m ....Coventry City.........2000

This sale, a record for City, was dependant on Coventry retaining their Premier status. When they were relegated the next year the fee was reduced to £5.2m. Craig was one of the best youth products and his pace and arrogant manner made him a handful on and off the pitch. Unfortunately, he suffered an horrendous injury by Muscatt of Wolves, which put paid to much of the 1998-9 season. This was followed by a pre-season cruciate injury to his knee, which put him out for the next season. As soon as he was fit he was sold after just one game in the new season.

Players Bought More Than Once

John	Gavin ....£1,500.........................Irish Free State 1948
	Player exchange............Tottenham H. 1955
Graham	Paddon...................£25,000.......................Coventry City.........1969
	£110,000.....................West Ham United 1976
Martin	O'Neill..................£300,000.....................Nottm. Forest. 1981
	£125,000.....................Manchester City. 1982
Robert	Fleck ....£580,000.....................Rangers.................1987
	£650,000.....................Chelsea 1995

TROPHIES

Norwich have won many trophies in their history. The 1984 fire destroyed some, but there are still several trophies (or replicas) on display at Carrow Road.

The major trophies won, include: -

Trophy	Year First Won
Milk Cup	1985
Football League Cup	1962
Division One Trophy	2004
Division Two Trophy	1972
Canon Second Division Trophy	1986
Division Three South Shield	1934
FA Youth Cup	1983

Other notable trophies are: -

South East Counties League Trophy	1980
The Batista Trophy (won in Portugal)	1971
Lowestoft Fishermans Widows & Orphans Cup	1959
Norwich Hospital Cup	1904 (original lost in fire)
	1991
The Friendship Cup	1986

One of the most magnificent trophies City have held is the Norwich Hospital Cup. Made in 1904, it stood over two feet tall and was made of hall marked silver. City competed against many famous sides for this cup, including FA Cup holders, in what was once an annual event. Tragically, it was destroyed in the Fire in 1984, but a new replacement cup was made in 1989 although not on the grandiose scale of the previous one. Between 1960 and 1989 the cup was not competed for, but after the new trophy was commissioned, the tradition was revived for two years with a pre- season fixture with Ipswich Town, both clubs winning once.

The Lowestoft Fisherman's Widows and Orphans Cup was made in 1922 and is one of the most valuable trophies held, but City did not compete for it until 1959. Most of the games were played at Lowestoft at the end of the season, although in 1972 the game was switched to Carrow Road to celebrate City's first promotion to Division One and 8,065 saw City win 6-0. With the demise of the fishing industry it has not been contested for several years.

The Division One trophy, won in 2004, dates back to the late 1880's and contains some illustrious names of clubs throughout the Football League history.

The Batista Trophy is the most unusual and was won in a summer tournament in Portugal. This trophy is large and ungainly, being two feet seven inches high with slender supports made from hollow alloy, holding a seven inch diameter football.

The Friendship Cup was presented by Piper Cars in recognition of the excellent atmosphere between supporters in the Milk Cup final. It is awarded to the winners of Norwich and Sunderland over the two league matches played each season .

Trophies won by Norwich in 1985-6.
From left to right: -
The Barry Butler Player of the Year
Trophy.
The Milk Cup.
The Canon Division Two Trophy.
The Football League Division Two
Champions Cup.

UNDEFEATED

The longest number of games in which City were undefeated was 23 in Division Three South. After losing 4-2 at Nottingham Forest in their third game of the season on 26 August 1950, City remained undefeated in a further 20 league and three FA Cup games before losing 1-3 at Leyton Orient on 11 January 1951. During this run they won 16 games and drew seven.

Their best undefeated start to a season was in 1971 when they went 13 league and two League Cup games before losing 1-2 at Millwall on 23 October.

UEFA CUP

City qualified initially in 1985, but the ban imposed on English clubs at the time, meant they missed out on three occasions (two league position qualifications), before playing in the UEFA Cup in 1993. A glorious campaign saw them defeat seeded teams Vitesse Arnhem and Bayern Munich, before going out narrowly and with a weakened team to Inter Milan, 0-1 in both legs.

UNITED LEAGUE

This was a mid week league held in parallel to the Southern League, but including some Northern and Midland teams. City only entered on two occasions, in 1906-7 and 1908-9, finishing fourth out of eight and third out of seven respectively, but interest was low and this league was soon abandoned.

UNUSUAL INCIDENTS

Having drawn with West Norwood in the Third Qualifying Round of the FA Cup in 1903, City then scratched from the competition, as they were more concerned with the Amateur Cup tie due the next week.

In 1910, Archie Livingstone played with a broken arm for 70 minutes of the FA Cup tie with Queens Park Rangers.

On 2 April 1910, in a match at Southampton, City had to play with ten men after Swann, based in London, failed to turn up. They managed to hold out for a goal-less draw.

Between 1908 and 1912, City suffered an incredible run of away defeats at Swindon Town, conceding 27 goals in four matches. The results were 2-10, 1-7, 1-5 and 3-5.

In March 1913 an early aeroplane was flown twice over The Nest in the match against Northampton Town.

In January 1939 Jimmy Jewell was appointed Norwich manager. He was the previous season's FA Cup final referee (Preston v Huddersfield).

Ken Nethercott suffered with a dislocated shoulder in the 63rd minute of the FA Cup game against Sheffield United in 1959, but he continued in goal and City managed to come from behind to equalise and earn a replay, by which time Sandy Kennon was able to take his place.

George Waites, when recently signed from Leyton Orient, married in the morning of the match at Brighton on 25 Feb 1961 and helped City to earn a 2-2 draw.

On 1 September 1962 in City's 2-0 win at Grimsby, a bottle was thrown on to the pitch. Norwich winger Gerry Mannion hurled it back into the crowd, unfortunately injuring a young City supporter. No action was taken in those days and an apology from Mannion saw the end of the matter.

On 3 September 1963 in a 2-4 defeat at Bury, Kevin Keelan was so incensed at the award of a penalty that he kicked the ball out of the stadium and was then booked for his trouble.

When Gerry Howshall was signed for £25,000 from West Bromwich Albion in January 1968, he did so in front of a live audience at the annual Supporters Club Dinner.

In their first match of the season on 25 August 1973 at Wolves, the cross bar broke and fell on to Keelan who was stretchered off, but he returned 15 minutes later after the goal was repaired. City lost 1-3.

A scantily clad girl ran across the pitch at Carrow Road during the game against Queens Park Rangers on 26 August 1989 and relieved some of the boredom of a 0-0 draw.

An amused Q.P.R player escorts a pitch invader from Carrow Road in 1989.

In two of the three League Cup finals City appeared in, they were not in the top Division, nor were their opponents, Rochdale and Aston Villa.

On 4 September 1976 in the Division One match at home to Birmingham City the referee blew the final whistle two minutes early. The Birmingham players pointed to the stadium clock as they were leaving the field and the referee had to then restart the game, leaving City to endure an extra couple of minutes protecting their 1-0 lead.

Mel Machin made 113 appearances for City and scored four goals. Surprisingly, most of these goals came in one match when he scored a hat trick away to Nottingham Forest.

In 1986, City's English international goalkeeper Chris Woods joined Scottish club Glasgow Rangers and was replaced by Scottish under 21 goalkeeper Bryan Gunn from Aberdeen.

When City clinched promotion from Division Two on 12 April 1986, they did so on a Rugby League ground at the Odsal stadium, where their opponents Bradford City were playing while their own ground was being rebuilt after a fire

In 1988, City received their biggest performance fine for a team violation against Arsenal at Highbury, where they lost 3-4 after conceding two disputed penalties. Although both teams were guilty, City were fined £50,000, but Arsenal only £25,000.

On 5 February 1994 in the home game against Liverpool, Darren Eadie was brought on as a second half substitute, but within minutes of coming on was himself substituted to make way for goalkeeper Scot Howie. This was necessary because Bryan Gunn had been sent off and a replacement goalkeeper was a more urgent need.

On 14 April 1996 in the derby game at Ipswich Town, some Norwich players had their hair dyed green, none more so than Jamie Cureton, who came on as substitute to score an equaliser in front of an incensed Ipswich crowd. Unfortunately Town had the last laugh when they won late in the game through a disastrous own goal past Bryan Gunn. He completely missed his kick as the ball bobbled past him from a tame back pass, to inflict a 1-2 defeat on City.

Against Reading on 12 April 2004, a ball was cleared by Reading defenders only to hit the referee and fall nicely to Phil Mulryne, who then scored an unlikely goal to give City an important 1-0 away victory in their quest for promotion.

It seems a strange quirk that City's three biggest FA Cup home defeats all occurred on the same day of the year; 12 January.

VICTORIES

Biggest Win Against Each Club in Terms of Goal Difference

Where biggest win was on more than two occasions these are not listed, but instead marked with the number of instances

Only League and Major Cup results included (see section- Minor Cups)

In some cases a club's full name has had to be abbreviated to fit table.

	Home			Away			Cup			
Aberdare	5-0	1923-4	D3	2-0	1922-3	D3				
Accrington	4-0	1959-0	D3	4-3	1959-0	D3				
Aldershot	5-0	1952-3	D3	3-1	1932-3	D3	4-0	A	1984-5	FL
Arsenal	3-1	1982-3	D1	4-2	1992-3	PR	3-0	A	1972-3	FL
Aston Villa	5-3	1975-6	D2	4-1	1986-7	D1	3-0	H	1983-4	FA
Barnsley	3-1	1935-6	D2	3-1	1998-9	D1	2-1	H	1953-4	FA
		1995-6	D1							
Barnet							2-1	H	1997-8	FL
Bath City							2-0	H	1934-5	FA
Birmingham	6-0	1969-0	D2	4-0	1982-3	D1	2-0	H	1963-4	FL
Blackburn R	4-0	1938-9	D2	3-2	1993-4	PR				
Blackpool	5-1	1971-2	D2	2-0	1936-7	D2	5-0	A	2000-1	FL
					1967-8	D2				
Bolton W.	3-0	1965-6	D2	1-0	1970-1	D2	4-0	H	1972-3	FL
					1981-2	D2				
Bourn'm'th	6-0	1932-3	D3	4-2	1933-4	D3	2-1	A	2000-1	FL
Bradford C.	6-1	1934-5	D2	2-0	1985-6	D2	5-3	A	1995-6	FL
					1996-7	D1				
Bradford PA	4-1	1925-6	D3							
Brentford	6-1	1908-9	SN	4-0	1958-9	D3	4-1	A	1991-2	FL
Brighton H	3-0	1985-6	D2	4-2	1979-0	D1	7-2	H	1946-7	FA
Bristol City	7-2	1933-4	D3	6-1	1948-9	D3	2-1	H	1990-1	FA
Bristol Rov.	6-0	1931-2	D3	2-0	1974-5	D2				
Burnley	4-0	1938-9	D2	5-3	2003-4	D1	1-0	H	1987-8	FL
Bury	4-0	1965-6	D2	5-2	1965-6	D2				
Cambridge	2-1	1981-2	D2	2-1	1981-2	D2	1-0	H	1980-1	FA
Cardiff City	5-1	1963-4	D2	4-2	1962-3	D2	3-0	H	1983-4	FL

	Home			Away			Cup			
Carlisle Utd.	2-0	1965-6 1966-7	D2 D2	4-0	1968-9 1985-6	D2 D2	5-0	H	1962-3	FL
Charlton A.	5-0	1981-2	D2	2-0	1962-3 1971-2	D2 D2	3-0	H	1991-2	FL
Chatham T.							6-1	H	1928-9	FA
Chelsea	4-1	1962-3	D2	3-0	1991-2	D1	2-0	A	1972-3	FL
Cheltenham							2-0	H	1999-0	FL
Chester							5-3	H	1964-5	FL
Chesterfield	3-0	1959-0	D3				3-1	H	1951-2	FA
Colchester	5-2	1951-2	D3	4-0	1952-3	D3				
Coventry C.	10-2	1929-0	D3	5-3	1932-3	D3	3-1	H	1994-5	FA
Crewe Alex.	2-1	1999-0	D1	3-1	2003-4	D1				
Croydon C	4-2	1909-0	SN							
Crystal Pal.	5-1	1952-3	D3	5-0	1950-1	D3	1-0	H	1926-7	FA
Dagenham &Redbridge							1-0	H	2002-3	FA
Derby Co.	5-2	1964-5	D2	4-0	2003-4	D1	4-1	A	1960-1	FL
Doncaster R	3-0	1958-9	D3	2-1	1936-7	D2	2-1	H	1924-5 1981-2	FA FA
Dorchester							4-0	H	1955-6	FA
Everton	3-0	1993-4	PR	5-1	1993-4	PR	1-0	A	1973-4	FL
Exeter City	6-0	1922-3	D3	4-2	1951-2	D3	3-1	A	1976-7	FL
Folkestone							2-0	H	1924-5	FA
Fulham	3-0	1936-7	D2	3-1	1934-5 1968-9	D2 D2	1-0	H	1962-3	FL
Gillingham	5-0	1951-2	D3	3-0	1952-3	D3	4-2	H	1979-0	FL
Gloucester							3-2	A	1949-0	FA
Grimsby T.	4-0	2002-3	D1	4-1	1996-7	D1	3-1	H	1971-2	FL
Halifax	3-0	1959-0	D3	1-0	1959-0	D3	7-1	A	1963-4	FL
Hartlepools							5-1	H	1949-0	FA
Harwich&P							4-2	A	1903-4	FA
Hastings & St Leonards							3-1	H	1906-7	FA
Hastings U							3-0	H	1953-4	FA
Headngtn U							4-2	H	1954-5	FA
Hudder'fi'ld	5-0	1997-8	D1	3-1	1997-8	D1	4-2	A	1986-7	FA
Hull City	3-0	1934-5 1935-6	D2 D2	2-0	1967-8	D2	2-1	A	1972-3	FL

	Home			Away			Cup			
Ilford							3-1	H	1958-9	FA
Ipswich T.	3-0	1994-5	PR	2-0	4 Occs		4-2	A	1968-9	FL
Leeds Utd.	4-0	1985-6	D2	4-0	1993-4	PR	2-1	A	1934-5	FA
Leicester C.	3-0	1969-0	D2	4-1	1981-2	D2	2-1	H	1972-3	FL
Leyton	6-1	1908-9	SN	2-0	1910-1	SN				
Leyton O.	5-0	1946-7	D3	3-0	1948-9	D3	3-1	A	1965-6	FA
Lincoln C.	5-1	1960-1	D2	4-1	1960-1	D2	3-2	H	1961-2	FL
Liverpool	3-0	1991-2	D1	3-1	1975-6	D1	3-0	H	1936-7	FA
Lowestoft T							4-1	H	1903-4	FA
Luton Town	6-0	1909-0	SN	3-1	1927-8	D3	2-0	A	1975-6	FA
Man. City	4-1	1964-5	D2	2-0	1964-5	D2	2-1	A	1962-3	FA
Man. Utd	2-0	1974-5 1989-0	D2 D1	2-0	1989-0	D1	4-1	H	1979-0	FL
Mansfield T	5-1	1959-0	D3							
Merthyr Tn	5-1	1929-0	D3	5-1	1929-0	D3				
Merthyr Tydfil							3-0	H	1947-8	FA
Metrogas							2-1	A	1921-2	FA
Middlesbro'	4-1	1960-1	D2	3-2	1988-9	D1	3-2	H	1961-2	FA
Millwall	6-1	1985-6	D2	3-1	1948-9	D3	4-1	H	1986-7	FL
Newcastle U	3-1	1963-4	D2	3-1	1987-8	D1	5-0	H	1962-3	FA
Newport Co	4-0	1949-0	D3	3-1	1922-3	D3	6-0	H	1928-9	FA
Northamptn	6-1	1926-7	D3	2-0	1905-6	SN	3-2	H	1951-2	FA
Nottm Forst	4-0	1935-6 1936-7	D2 D2	3-0	1992-3	PR	4-1	A	1914-5	FA
Notts Co	7-2	1934-5	D2	3-1	1958-9	D3	3-0 3-1	H H	1984-5 1991-2	FL FA
Oldham A.	2-0	1996-7	D1	3-1	1985-6	D2	6-2	H	1960-1	FL
Oxford City							3-0	H	1921-2	FA
Oxford Utd.	4-2	1987-8	D1	4-2	1998-9	D2				
Peterbro' U.							1-0	H	1986-7	FA
Plymouth A.	4-0	1937-8	SN	2-1	1963-4	D2				
Poole T.							5-0	H	1927-8	FA
Port Vale	5-1	1959-0	D3	3-1	1946-7	D3	3-1	A	1988-9	FA
Portsmouth	4-0	1907-8	SN	4-1	1969-0	D2				
Preston NE	3-0	2001-2	D1	3-1	1968-9	D2	6-1	H	1984-5	FL
Q.P.R	5-0	1923-4	D3	3-1	1990-1	D1				
Reading	4-1	1921-2	D3	5-2	1912-3	SN	3-2	N	1908-9	FA

	Home			Away			Cup			
Redhill							6-1	H	1957-8	FA
Rhyl							1-0	A	1950-1	FA
Rochdale	2-1	1958-9	D3	2-1	1958-9	D3	3-0	A	1961-2	FL
Rotherham United	4-2	1962-3	D2	3-0	1960-1	D2	2-0	A	1967-8	FL
									1989-0	FL
Scunthorpe	2-1	1963-4	D2				4-1	A	1960-1	FA
Sheff. Utd	4-0	1985-6	D2	5-2	1985-6	D2	2-0	H	1974-5	FL
Sheff. Wed	3-0	2002-3	D1	5-0	2001-2	D1	2-0	H	1907.8	FA
Sheppey U							2-0	A	1905-6	FA
Shrewsbury	3-0	1956-7	D3	8-1	1952-3	D3	2-0	H	1980-1	FL
Southmptn	5-0	1960-1	D2	5-2	1955-6	D3	2-1	H	1991-2	FA
Southend U	7-2	1955-6	D3	2-0	1950-1	D3	2-1	H	1922-3	FA
Stockport	4-0	2000-1	D1	3-1	2000-1	D1	5-1	A	1971-2	FL
Stoke City	6-0	1962-3	D2	2-0	1975-6	D1	1-0	A	1981-2	FA
Sunderland	3-0	1960-1 1983-4	D2 D1	3-0	1960-1	D2	4-1	A	1961-2	FL
Sutton Utd.							8-0	H	1988-9	FA
Swansea	5-0	1962-3	D2	3-0	1961-2	D2	3-0	H	1984-5	FL
Swindon T	5-2	1932-3	D3	4-2	1932-3	D3	3-1	H	1990-1	FA
Thames	7-0	1931-2	D3							
Tonbridge							1-0	H	1952-3	FA
Torquay U	7-0	1951-2	D3	5-1	1950-1	D3	6-1	H	1995-6	FL
Tottenham Hotspur	4-0	1979-0	D1	3-1	1987-8 1993-4	D1 PR	3-2	H	1913-4	FA
Tranmere R	3-0	1938-9 1959-0	D2 D3	3-1	1998-9	D1	4-2	H	1994-5	FL
Tunbridge							5-0	A	1905-6	FA
Walsall	8-0	1951-2	D3	4-1	1953-4	D3	3-2	H	1965-6	FA
Walthmst'w							6-0	H	1913-4	FA
Watford	6-1	1983-4	D1	4-1	1957-8	D3	3-0	A	1990-1	FL
Wellington							1-0	H	1948-9	FA
W.B.A	2-0	3 Occs	D1	4-1	1995-6	D1	3-0	H	1979-0	FA
West Ham	6-3	1908-9	SN	3-1	1977-8	D1	3-1	H	1988-9	FA
Wigan	2-0	2003-4	PR				3-2	A	1998-9	FL
Wimbledon	3-2	2003-4	D1	2-0	1988-9	D1	3-1	A	1931-2	FA
Wolves	3-0	1983-4	D1	2-0	1995-6	D1				
Wrexham	4-0	1981-2	D2	3-2	1981-2	D2	6-2	H	1973-4	FL

VICTORIES

	Home			Away			Cup			
Wycombe							2-0	A	1993-4	FA
Yarmouth							2-1	A	1903-4	FA
Yeovil							3-0	A	1979-0	FA
York City	1-0	1959-0	D3	2-1	1959-0	D3	1-0	H	1960-1	FA

PR = Premier, D1= Division One, D2 = Division Two, D3 = Division Three / Division Three South, SN = Southern League.

FA = FA Cup, FL = Football League Cup.

Other clubs not shown, have never been defeated by City.

Biggest Victories

City's biggest victories have been: -

Score	Opponents	Venue	Occasion	Date
18-0	Brighton & H.A.	H	Wartime League	25.12.40
10-2	Coventry City	H	Division Three South	15.03.30
8-1	Shrewsbury Town	A	Division Three South	13.09.52
8-0	Walsall	H	Division Three South	29.12.51
8-0	Sutton United	H	FA Cup Fourth Round	28.01.89
7-0	Thames	H	Division Three South	07.11.31
7-0	Torquay United	H	Division Three South	14.04.52
7-1	Halifax Town	A	League Cup	27.11.63
7-2	Brighton & H.A	H	FA Cup first round	30.11.46
7-2	Bristol City	H	Division Three South	28.08.33
7-2	Notts County	H	Division Two	17.11.34
7-2	Southend United	H	Division Three South	17.12.55

VITAL MATCHES

There have been several vital matches in City's history where so much was at stake. It can be argued that some of the later stages of cup competitions produced games which are critical to win, but it is in the league where it can suddenly be crucial to gain a result to achieve promotion or to avoid relegation.

Opponents	Result	Division	Date	Attendance
Coventry City	H .. 3-1	Division Three South	21.04.34	16,787

City needed to win over rivals Coventry City, the only side which could stop them from clinching promotion. Although City took an early lead through Bell, Coventry equalised and then chances were missed at both ends, before Burditt put City ahead again on the stroke of half time. A third goal, headed by Vinall, followed in the second half to clinch promotion to Division Two for the first time.

Team: Wharton, Thorpe, Ramsay, Morris, Halliday, Lochhead, Bell, Burditt, Vinall, Houghton, Murphy.

Plymouth Argyle	A .. 0-1	Division Two	03.05.39	7,747

Norwich were staring relegation in the face and with the last game to come against fellow strugglers Nottingham Forest, they needed to get at least a point at Plymouth. It was so disappointing when Jack Milburn missed a penalty, meaning City lost 0-1.They also failed to beat Forest by a sufficiently high score to save themselves.

Team: Wharton, Thorpe, Ramsay, Morris, Halliday, Lochhead, Bell, Burditt, Vinall, Houghton, Murphy.

Nottingham Forest	H .. 1-0	Division Two	06.05.39	19,715

City needed to win by four goals to relegate Forest and stay up themselves. They only achieved a solitary goal through Ware.

Team: Hall, Taylor, Milburn, Robinson, Reilly, Smalley, Church, Coleman, Ware, Acquroff, Furness.

Southend United	H .. 4-3	Division Three South	27.04.60	34,905

This ding-dong win clinched promotion to Division Two. City went behind after only three minutes, but soon hit back through Punton and Crossan, before Southend equalised. City's nerves were eased when Whitehouse scored to regain the lead just before half time. Although City pulled further ahead in the 49th minute through Crossan, another goal from Southend in the 78th minute could have rocked them. Instead City upped the tempo again and comfortably held on to win the coveted promotion place.

Team: Kennon, Thulow, Ashman, McCrohan, Butler, Crowe, Crossan, Whitehouse, Allcock, Hill, Punton.

Orient ....A .. 2-1.......... Division Two................24.04.72...... 15,530

Towards the end of their first promotion season to Division One, City needed two points from their last two matches. In the penultimate game, City won with goals from Foggo and Paddon (penalty) to achieve their long ambition. The Division Two Championship was clinched in the last game at Watford with a 1-1 draw.

Team: Keelan, Payne, Black, Stringer, Forbes, Briggs, Suggett, Livermore, Cross, Bone, Paddon, Foggo, Hubbard (Substitute).

David Cross celebrates City's first goal by Ken Foggo at Orient, which clinched promotion in 1972

Crystal Palace........H .. 2-1 .... Division One 24.04.73 36,922

Having appeared doomed for so long, City rallied near the end of the season and faced their relegation rivals Crystal Palace in their last home match. The situation was that the loser would be relegated. City fell behind to a first half penalty, but equalised by the interval through Suggett. With time running out and both sides pressing for the winner the game became very tense. Fortunately, it was City who secured the all important goal, through David Stringer in the last minute with a header from a corner. The game was watched by the second highest league gate at Carrow Road.

Team: Keelan, Payne, Black, Stringer, Forbes, Hockey, Suggett, Livermore, Cross, Briggs, Mellor

David Stringer is congratulated by Colin Suggett, after scoring with a late header against Crystal Palace to preserve City's First Division status.

Portsmouth............A .. 3-0 .... Division Two 26.04.75 18,977

This was City's penultimate game of the season and they desperately needed a win to keep clear of Sunderland. They were also mindful of the last game to come against fellow promotion candidates Aston Villa. Although City won 3-0 with goals from McGuire, Boyer and Peters, they still had some nervous moments. This win clinched promotion, as Sunderland failed to beat Villa, although Norwich did lose heavily 1-4 to Villa on the last game of the season.

Team: Keelan, Butler, Sullivan, Morris, Forbes, Powell, McGuire, MacDougall, Boyer, Suggett, Peters, (Steele).

Leicester City ....H.. 2-3......... Division One 02.05.81 25,307

Leicester were already relegated, but City had given themselves a chance after winning four of their previous five games. They had to win and were relying on one of the four other teams above them losing. 0-2 down early on, they drew level through Jack and Fashanu, only to lose eventually 2-3 to a hat trick by Melrose to confirm their relegation. None of the teams above them lost and so they would have been relegated anyway.

Team: Woods, McDowell, Downs, McGuire, Walford, Watson, O'Neill, Fashanu, Royle, Paddon, Barham, (Jack).

Leicester City ....A.. 4-1......... Division Two...............01.05.82 19,630

With four games to go, it was vital that City did not lose ground to their main rivals Leicester City. An emphatic win with goals from Barham, Bertshin, Deehan and an own goal, put them on course for promotion, although this was in the balance until the very last game of the season.

Team: Woods, Haylock, Symonds, McGuire, Walford, Watson, O'Neill, Deehans, Bertschin, Bennett, Barham.

Sheffield Wed. ....A.. 1-2......... Division Two...............15.05.82........24,687

Sheffield Wednesday, who had been one of City's rivals, had slipped away in the last few games leaving City needing one point to ensure promotion. After coming from behind to equalise through Keith Bertschin in the 86th minute and with 10,000 fans roaring them on, City seemed safe, but a last minute winner from Wednesday left them in suspense. Fortunately, rivals Leicester City could only manage a goalless home draw against lowly Shrewsbury Town meaning City were promoted after all.

Team: Woods, Haylock, Downs, McGuire, Walford, Watson, O'Neill, Deehans, Bertschin, Bennett, Barham, (Jack).

Wimbledon.............H .. 1-1......... Division One ....25.04.92.......11,061

Having suffered six successive defeats, City were in real danger of relegation. If they lost their last home match to Wimbledon, they would be very vulnerable. In front of a small crowd, due to the old Barclay stand being demolished, City took a first half lead through Fleck, but when Wimbledon equalised early in the second half a very nervous time followed as City hung on to draw to stave off relegation.

This game was more important considering City needed to retain their status to be founder members of the new Premier League starting the next season.

Team: Walton, Culverhouse, Bowen, Blades, Polston, Goss, Fox, Fleck, Newman, Beckford, Phillips, (Woodthorpe)

Aston Villa ....H .. 1-0......... Premier... ....24.03.93.......19,528

With only six games left, City needed to win to leap frog their rivals Villa and regain top spot. They duly obliged with a late winner from Polston to top the table for the sixth time.

Team: Gunn, Culverhouse, Bowen, Sutton, Polston, Megson, Crook, Goss, Robins, Fox, Phillips, (Power).

Manchester United H .. 1-3......... Premier... ....05.04.93.......20,582

City had to avoid defeat and preferably beat United to put them out of the championship race. Unfortunately it was United who rose to the occasion and gained a three goal lead in the first half hour. Despite pulling a goal back by Robins, it was beyond City and this effectively ended their dreams of a first ever championship.

Team: Gunn, Culverhouse, Bowen, Sutton, Polston, Megson, Crook, Goss, Robins, Fox, Phillips, (Ekoku).

Middlesbrough.......A .. 3-3......... Premier... ....08.05.93.......15,155

City were trying to claim a European place for the first time and needed to draw with already relegated Middlesbrough to ensure finishing in third place and above Blackburn Rovers. After leading and then going behind, City pulled level to gain a 3-3 draw. This proved to be enough to secure their European spot after Arsenal had won both FA and League Cups, to allow City to qualify through their league placing.

Team: Gunn, Culverhouse, Bowen, Newman, Polston, Johnson, Crook, Sutton, Fox, Phillips, (Ekoku).

Leeds United..........A.. 1-2.......... Premier... ....06.05.95........31,982

City had been trying to gain the six points they needed to stay up, for the last two months. This was their penultimate game and there was no room for manoeuvre. A game they had to win saw them take a first half lead through Ward. City managed to hold on until a disputed penalty was converted by Leeds in the 79th minute, followed by the winner deep into injury time, condemning City to relegation. Their last match was against Aston Villa and if City had only beaten Leeds, they could have saved themselves by then beating Villa and consigning them to the First Division instead in the final game.

Team: Marshall, Bradshaw, Bowen, Newsome, Polston, Goss, Newman, Crook, Ullathorne,Ward, Sutch, (Akinbyi),(Sheron).

Stockport County...H.. 2-0.......... Division One ....21.04.02........20,897

City had risen strongly up the league with 14 points from the last eight games. They needed to win by one goal more than Burnley to pip them to the Play offs . Incredibly the Stockport goalkeeper Andy Dibble was sent off for handling outside his area after only 40 seconds, leaving City to play against ten men. Despite this, it was a tense occasion against already relegated Stockport. Mulryne scored on the stroke of half time and Malky Mackay added a second midway through the second half. It was a tense final stage with news coming from Burnley that they were 1-0 ahead against Coventry City. The score remained as they were and City had qualified for the Play Offs, where they were to lose in the final.

Team: Green, Kenton, Drury, Mackay, Fleming, Holt, Mulryne, Rivers, McVeigh, Nielsen, Easton, (Notman).

Play Offs

All the Play off matches were tense affairs and are covered in the Play Off section.

WAR TIME FOOTBALL

The two World Wars had a dramatic affect on League Football. In the First World War football finished at the end of 1914-5 season and forced Norwich to go into voluntary liquidation.

When the Second World War commenced, three league games had been played. The League was immediately cancelled, but later various regional cup and league competitions were held with many players guesting for other clubs. Norwich enjoyed their highest ever win, 18-0 over Brighton & Hove Albion during this period, but football was in an unreal situation at the time and only provided some relief from the horrors and austerity of war time.

The FA Cup started in 1945-6 with two legs for each tie, but League football did not re-commence until the 1946-7 season. The Football League started with the same fixtures that had ceased in 1939 prior to the war.

WEMBLEY APPEARANCES

All Appearances have been in League Cup Finals

	Result	Date
Tottenham Hotspur	0-1	03.03.73
Aston Villa	0-1	01.03.75
Sunderland	1-0	24.03.85

WILLHIRE CUP

This was a regional pre-season tournament sponsored by Willhire and lasted for three seasons.

	Date	Venue	Result	Attendance
Cambridge United	29.07.78	A	3-1	3,420
Colchester United	01.08.78	A	2-1	2,223
Ipswich Town	08.08.78	A	1-2	7,000

Willhire Cup (continued)

	Date	Venue	Result	Attendance
Cambridge United	28.07.79	A	0-2	2,267
Colchester United	02.08.79	A	2-2	1,259
Ipswich Town	14.08.79	H	2-0	3,727
Cambridge United	29.07.80	H	4-0	2,600
Colchester United	31.07.80	H	1-1	1,744*
Ipswich Town	12.08.80	A	2-2	6,076

*This is City's lowest ever attendance for a non friendly match at Carrow Road.

WINS IN A SEASON

Note no records are shown for the three years City have played as a Division Three side as they are not better than those achieved in Division Three South.

Most by Division

Wins	Season	Division	Games
28	2003-4	Division One	46
26	1951-2	Division Three South	46
25	1985-6	Division Two	42
21	1992-3	Premier	42

Least by Division

Wins	Season	Division	Games
7	1973-4, 1978-9	Division One	42
8	1956-7	Division Three South	46
10	1994-5	Premier	42
11	1963-4	Division Two	42

YOUNGEST PLAYERS

Player	Age	Date	Opponents	Division
Ryan Jarvis...... 16 years	282 days	19.04.03..A..	Walsall........	Division One

Ryan made his first appearance as a substitute in an end of season game on 19 April 2003 at Walsall, coming on in the 73rd minute. He retained his place and started the next game at home to Wolves on 21 April. He also became the youngest ever scorer with his first goal against Watford at Carrow Road on 15 November 2003 at the age of 17 years 128 days.

Ryan Jarvis, City's youngest ever player with a commemorative mug

Ian Davies .... 17 years 29 days .....27.04.74..A.. Birmingham .Division One

Ian was a promising left back, but made only 37 appearances over five years before being signed by Newcastle for the surprisingly high fee of £175,000.

YOUNGEST PLAYERS

Player	Age	Date	Opponents	Division
Donald Edwards	17 years 46 days	17.09.47	Torquay Utd	Division Three South

Don was a goalkeeper and made his debut at Torquay United in a 1-1 draw on 17 September 1947. The next game, his second and last, saw him concede five at home to Bristol Rovers.

Mark Metcalf .. 17 years 49 days ......13.11.82..West Ham U.......Division One

Having played in the famous City Youth "Double" side, Mark made his only appearance as a substitute at West Ham in a 0-1 defeat on 13 November 1982.

Steve Goodwin. 17 years 67 days .....01.05.71..Hull City...........Division Two

Steve made his debut as a 67th minute substitute at Hull City in the last match of the season on 1 May 1971. His peak achievement, in the seven games he played, was scoring two goals against Sheffield United in the League Cup on 27 November 1974.

Mark Barham.. 17 years 135 days ....24.11.79..Man. Utd. ....Division One

Mark made his debut as a substitute on 24 November 1979 in a 0-5 drubbing at Manchester United. He did not appear again until the last three games of the season.

Dale Gordon .... 17 years 229 days ....25.08.74..Liverpool ....Division One

Dale, although not the youngest player to make his City debut, went on to make a record 24 appearances before his 18th birthday.

Justin Fashanu. 19 years 178 days ...16.08.80..Stoke City ....Division One

Justin Fashanu was the youngest City player to score a hat trick. He did this when he was 19 in the above 5-1 victory on the first day of the season. He had made his initial debut when he was a month short of 18.

For a year, he formed the youngest regular strike partnership in City's history. He was 18 and Kevin Reeves, his fellow striker, was 21.

YOUTH CAPS

Player		Season	Country
David	Stringer	1962-3	England
David	Evans	1974-5	Wales
John	Fashanu	1978-9	England
Mark	Barham	1979-80	England
Mark	Crowe	1982-3	England
Louie	Donowa	1982-3	England
Dale	Gordon	1982-3, 83-4, 84-5	England
Mark	Metcalf	1982-3	England
Tony	Spearing	1982-3	England
Derek	Johnstone	1984-5	Scotland
Paul	Kinnaird	1984-5	Scotland
Tony	Flanagan	1987-8	Eire
Mike	Magilton	1987-8	N. Ireland
Daryl	Sutch	1988-9	England
Lee	Power	1989-90	Eire
Robert	Ullathorne	1989/90	England
Sean	Collins	1990-1, 91-2	N. Ireland
Deryn	Brace	1992-3	Wales
Darren	Eadie	1992-3	England
Andy	Johnson	1992-3	England
Andy	Marshall	1992-3	England
Johnny	Wright	1993-4	N. Ireland
Jamie	Cureton	1993-4	England
Tom	Hansut	1994-5	Wales
Keith	O'Neill	1994-5	N. Ireland
Craig	Bellamy	1996-7	Wales
Chris	Llewellyn	1996-7	Wales
Adrian	Forbes	1996-7	England
Robert	Green	1997-8	England
Darrel	Russell	1998-9	England
Ian	Henderson	2002-3	England
Ryan	Jarvis	2003-4	England

YOUTH CUP

Winners   1983   6-5 on aggregate over three games

This win was the culmination of the best ever season for a Norwich Youth side. They had already won the **Championship of the South East Counties League**, without losing a game. In the FA Youth Cup they swept all before them to reach the final against Everton.

After winning the first leg 3-2 at Carrow Road in front of a record crowd of over 10,000, they lost the return leg by the same score. City lost the toss for the right to stage the decider, but before a huge crowd at Everton, City won the Cup to complete a coveted double when Paul Clayton headed home the winner.

Path to the Final

Round	Opponents	Result	Attendance
First	Southend	H.. 6-0	315
Second	Arsenal	A.. 2-2	
Second- replay	Arsenal	H.. 4-2	862
Third	Aston Villa	H.. 5-2	1,605
Fourth	Watford	H.. 3-1	3,823
Fifth	Man.Utd	A.. 1-0	1,234
Semi-Final first leg	Luton	A.. 3-1	2,270
Semi-Final second leg	Luton	H.. 0-0	8,312
Final first leg	Everton	H.. 3-2	10,559
Final second leg	Everton	A.. 2-3	15,540
Final decider	Everton	A.. 1-0	20,652

Team (Final): -

Pearce, Godbold, Spearing, Crowe, McIntyre, Goss, Donowa, Rigby, Clayton, O'Connor, Riley, Metcalf.

Interestingly, of those who played in this successful team, only three made it to the big time.

Jerry Goss eventually forced his way into the first team on a regular basis after a number of years as a fringe player. He completed over 13 years with the club as a player, also winning Welsh caps and earning himself European glory. He later moved to the commercial department.

Louie Donowa soon broke into the first team and won a Milk Cup medal and under 21 England Caps, before joining Spanish Club La Coruna for £50,000.

Tony Spearing, also captained England Youth, and played 82 times for Norwich before joining Leicester City for £100,000 in 1988.

Jon Rigby, Paul Clayton, Matt Crowe, Mark Metcalf and Darryl Godbold only made a handful of appearances before moving on to lower status clubs.

City also snapped up one of the Everton youth strikers Mark Farrington, after he was released. He was an aggressive striker, but he too played for only one season, making 18 appearances, before joining Cambridge United.

YOUTH TEAM

South East Counties Youth League

City Youth's had a glorious double winning season in 1982-3. They not only won the FA Youth Cup for the only time in City's history, but also were champions of the South East Counties League without losing a game.

Paul Clayton and Jon Rigby scored 32 and 31 goals respectively.

Played 28 Won 20 Drew 8 Lost 0

Goals For 80 Against 16 Points 68

Date	Opponents	V	Result	
Aug.28	Watford	A	4-1	W
Sep.4	Arsenal	H	4-0	W
Sep.11	Charlton Athletic	H	4-0	W
Sep.18	Chelsea	H	1-1	D
Oct.9	Fulham	A	4-1	W

Date	Opponents	V	Result	
Oct.16	Gillingham	H	6-0	W
Oct.23	Ipswich Town	A	3-0	W
Oct.30	Millwall	H	1-0	W
Nov.6	Arsenal	A	6-0	W
Nov.13	Southend Utd.	H	3-1	W
Nov.20	Tottenham Hotspur	A	2-1	W
Nov.27	Q.P.R.	H	3-1	W
Dec.4	Portsmouth	A	5-0	W
Dec.11	Orient	H	2-2	D
Dec.18	West Ham United	A	1-0	W
Jan.22	Chelsea	A	1-1	D
Jan.29	Orient	A	1-0	W
Feb.5	Fulham	H	6-0	W
Feb.21	Ipswich Town	H	3-0	W
Feb.26	Millwall	A	0-0	D
Mar.5	Charlton Athletic	A	1-1	D
Mar.19	Portsmouth	H	4-1	W
Mar.26	Q.P.R	A	3-3	D
Apr. 9	Southend United	A	1-0	W
Apr.16	Gillingham	A	0-0	D
Apr.23	Watford	H	6-1	W
May 7	West Ham United.	H	0-0	D
May 14	Tottenham Hotspur	H	5-1	W

The successful double winning Youth team of 1983, with League and Cup trophies

City Youth also won the South East Counties title in 1979-80 and again in 1996-97

1979-80

Team: -

Seward, Pownall, Budd, Webb, Hart, Lovett, Barham, Butcher, Harris,,Haylock, Fashanu John, Harrowing, Woolsey, Spooner, Foyster, Wilson, Reeve, Stanton, Sadd, Yaxley.

Keith Webb, who played in this championship team, went on to become youth team coach for a number of seasons and then reserve team manager.

1996-7

Team: -

Robert Green Kenton, Lewis Alexander, Joe Green, Allen, Russell, Walker Llewellyn, Wilson, Coote, Stuart, Andrews, Henderson, Forbes, Broughton, Bellamy, Davis, Roach, Marshall, Cropley, McCulloch

ZENITH DATA CUP

This cup replaced the Simod Trophy and had the incentive of a final at Wembley. The closest City came was in 1990-1, when they reached the semi-final.

1989-90

Round	Opponents	v	Result	Attendance	
2	Brighton & H.A	H	5-0	5,774	
3	Swindon Town	A	1-4	5,314	

1990-1

2	Millwall	H	1-1	4,741	won 6-5 on penalties
3	Southampton	H	2-1	5,920	
4	Ipswich Town	H	2-0	16,255	
Semi Final	Crystal Palace	H	1-1	7,554	
Semi Final	Crystal Palace	A	0-2	13,857	

1991-2

2	Q.P.R.	H	1-2	4,436

APPENDIX

RESULTS:

In this section the results are shown against every club City have played during their history. The Clubs are listed in alphabetical order.

All League results are included from 1905, when City turned professional, up to the end of season 2003-4. Results are shown in chronological order, commencing with the Southern League 1905-20.

The original Norfolk and Suffolk League, where City began their amateur existence 1902-5, and the United League (a mid week supplementary league 1906-1909) are excluded.

Cup games follow after the League results and feature every FA Cup and Football League Cup tie City have played, from 1902 up to the end of season 2003-4. Minor Cups are excluded.

The League Cup has been more recognisable by the sponsor's names since 1980 and these alternatives have been shown since then. Where more than one game took place these are shown in order. For some League Cup ties, where applicable, 1st and 2nd legs are shown. Any extra time played is shown as a.e.t with the score of any resultant penalty shoot out. Neutral venues are shown as N.

The summary for each club shows the analysis of all League games played against City, unless there has been fewer than six games.

City's score is shown first in each instance, with the summaries also shown from the Norwich viewpoint.

ABERDARE ATHLETIC

LEAGUE

1921-2	1922-3	1923-4	1924-5	1925-6	1926-7
H 0-0 D	H 1-4 L	H 5-0 W	H 1-1 D	H 2-3 L	H 2-2 D
A 2-1 W	A 2-0 W	A 0-0 D	A 1-2 L	A 1-3 L	A 2-1 W

SUMMARY	Played	Won	Drawn	Lost	For	Against
Home	6	1	3	2	11	10
Away	6	3	1	2	8	7
Total	12	4	4	4	19	17

ACCRINGTON STANLEY

LEAGUE

1958-9	1959-60
H 2-4 L	H 4-0 W
A 2-0 W	A 4-3 W

ALDERSHOT

LEAGUE

1932-3	1933-4	1946-7	1947-8	1948-9	1949-50
H 3-2 W	H 2-2 D	H 2-3 L	H 0-1 L	H 0-0 D	H 4-0 W
A 3-1 W	A 1-2 L	A 1-3 L	A 2-2 D	A 1-4 L	A 0-2 L

1950-1	1951-2	1952-3	1953-4	1954-5	1955-6
H 2-2 D	H 1-2 L	H 5-0 W	H 3-3 D	H 4-3 W	H 0-1 L
A 1-1 D	A 0-2 L	A 2-1 W	A 0-0 D	A 1-4 L	A 0-0 D

1956-7	1957-8
H 1-1 D	H 1-3 L
A 0-0 D	A 1-2 L

CUP

Milk
1984-5
H 0-0 D
A 4-0 W

SUMMARY	Played	Won	Drawn	Lost	For	Against
Home	14	4	5	5	28	23
Away	14	2	5	7	13	24
Total	28	6	10	12	41	47

ARSENAL

LEAGUE

1972-3	1973-4	1975-6	1976-7	1977-8	1978-9
H 3-2 W	H 0-4 L	H 3-1 W	H 1-3 L	H 1-0 W	H 0-0 D
A 0-2 L	A 0-2 L	A 1-2 L	A 0-1 L	A 0-0 D	A 1-1 D

1979-80	1980-1	1982-3	1983-4	1984-5	1986-7
H 2-1 W	H 1-1 D	H 3-1 W	H 1-1 D	H 1-0 W	H 1-1 D
A 1-1 D	A 1-3 L	A 1-1 D	A 0-3 L	A 0-2 L	A 2-1 W

1987-8	1988-9	1989-90	1990-1	1991-2	1992-3
H 2-4 L	H 0-0 D	H 2-2 D	H 0-0 D	H 1-3 L	H 1-1 D
A 0-2 L	A 0-5 L	A 3-4 L	A 0-2 L	A 1-1 D	A 4-2 W

1993-4	1994-5
H 1-1 D	H 0-0 D
A 0-0 D	A 1-5 L

CUP

FA	FA	FA	F League	F League	Coca-Cola
1951-2	1953-4	1973-4	1972-3	1981-2	1993-4
A 0-5 L	A 2-1 W	H 0-1 L	A 3-0 W	A 0-1 L	A 1-1 D
					H 0-3 L

RESULTS

SUMMARY	Played	Won	Drawn	Lost	For	Against
Home	20	6	10	4	24	26
Away	20	2	6	12	16	40
Total	40	8	16	16	40	66

ASTON VILLA

LEAGUE

1936-7	1937-8	1967-8	1968-9	1969-70	1974-5
H 5-1w	H 1-0 w	H 1-0 w	H 1-1 D	H 3-1 w	H 1-4 L
A 0-3 L	A 0-2 L	A 2-4 L	A 1-2 L	A 1-0 w	A 1-1 D

1975-6	1976-7	1977-8	1978-9	1979-80	1980-1
H 5-3 w	H 1-1 D	H 2-1 w	H 1-2 L	H 1-1 D	H 1-3 L
A 2-3 L	A 0-1 L	A 0-3 L	A 1-1 D	A 0-2 L	A 0-1 L

1982-3	1983-4	1984-5	1986-7	1988-9	1989-90
H 1-0 w	H 3-1 w	H 2-2 D	H 1-1 D	H 2-2 D	H 2-0 w
A 2-3 L	A 0-1 L	A 2-2 D	A 4-1 w	A 1-3 L	A 3-3 D

1990-1	1991-2	1992-3	1993-4	1994-5
H 2-0 w	H 2-1 w	H 1-0 w	H 1-2 L	H 1-1 D
A 1-2 L	A 0-1 L	A 3-2 w	A 0-0 D	A 1-1 D

CUP

FA 1937-8	FA 1983-4	F League 1962-3	F League 1974-5	F League 1976-7	Milk 1983-4
A 2-3 L	A 1-1 D H 3-0 w	A 1-4 L	N 0-1 L	A 1-2 L	H 0-2 L

SUMMARY	Played	Won	Drawn	Lost	For	Against
Home	23	12	7	4	41	28
Away	23	3	6	14	25	42
Total	46	15	13	18	66	70

BARNET

CUP

Coca-Cola 1997-8	
H 2-1 w	1st leg
A 1-3 l	2nd leg

BATH CITY

CUP

FA 1934-5
H 2-0 w

BEDFORD TOWN

CUP

FA 1956-7
H 2-4 l

BARNSLEY

LEAGUE

1934-5	1935-6	1936-7	1937-8	1959-60	1981-2
H 0-1 l	H 3-1 w	H 0-1 l	H 1-0 w	H 0-0 d	H 1-1 d
A 1-2 l	A 3-2 w	A 1-2 l	A 0-0 d	A 0-2 l	A 1-0 w

1985-6	1995-6	1996-7	1998-9	1999-00	2000-1
H 1-1 d	H 3-1 w	H 1-1 d	H 0-0 d	H 2-2 d	H 0-0 d
A 2-2 d	A 2-2 d	A 1-3 l	A 3-1 l	A 1-2 l	A 0-1 l

2001-2
H 2-1 w
A 2-0 w

CUP

FA 1921-2	FA 1953-4	FA 1991-2
A 1-1 d	H 2-1 w	H 1-0 w
H 1-2 l		

SUMMARY	Played	Won	Drawn	Lost	For	Against
Home	13	4	7	2	14	10
Away	13	4	3	6	17	19
Total	26	8	10	8	31	29

BIRMINGHAM CITY

LEAGUE

1965-6	1966-7	1967-8	1968-9	1969-70	1970-1
H 2-2 D	H 3-3 D	H 4-2 W	H 1-1 D	H 6-0 W	H 2-2 D
A 0-1 L	A 1-2 L	A 0-0 D	A 2-1 W	A 1-3 L	A 2-2 D

1971-2	1972-3	1973-4	1975-6	1976-7	1977-8
H 2-2 D	H 1-2 L	H 2-1 W	H 1-0 W	H 1-0 W	H 1-0 W
A 0-4 L	A 1-4 L	A 1-2 L	A 1-1 D	A 2-3 L	A 1-2 L

1978-9	1980-1	1982-3	1983-4	1995-6	1996-7
H 4-0 W	H 2-2 D	H 5-1 W	H 1-1 D	H 1-1 D	H 0-1 L
A 0-1 L	A 0-4 L	A 4-0 W	A 1-0 W	A 1-3 L	A 3-2 W

1997-8	1998-9	1999-00	2000-1	2001-2	
H 3-3 D	H 2-0 W	H 0-1 L	H 1-0 W	H 0-1 L	
A 2-1 W	A 0-0 D	A 0-2 L	A 1-2 L	A 0-4 L	

CUP

FA	FA	F League	Coca-Cola
1984-5	1984-5	1963-4	1995-6
H 1-0 W	H 0-0 D	H 2-0 W	H 1-1 D
A 1-1 D	A 1-1 D		A 1-2 L

Play Offs

2002-3	
N 1-1 D aet	2-4 L Pen

SUMMARY	Played	Won	Drawn	Lost	For	Against
Home	23	10	9	4	45	26
Away	23	5	4	14	24	44
Total	46	15	13	18	69	70

BLACKBURN ROVERS

LEAGUE

1936-7	1937-8	1938-9	1966-7	1967-8	1968-9
H 0-0 D	H 3-2 W	H 4-0 W	H 0-1 L	H 1-0 W	H 3-1 W
A 0-1 L	A 3-5 L	A 0-6 L	A 0-0 D	A 0-0 D	A 0-3 L

1969-70	1970-1	1981-2	1985-6	1992-3	1993-4
H 0-1 L	H 2-1 W	H 2-0 W	H 3-0 W	H 0-0 D	H 2-2 D
A 1-3 L	A 1-2 L	A 0-3 L	A 1-2 L	A 1-7 L	A 3-2 W

1994-5	1999-00	2000-1
H 2-1 W	H 0-2 L	H 1-1 D
A 0-0 D	A 1-1 D	A 2-3 L

CUP

FA	FA	Coco-Cola
1911-2	1965-6	1992-3
A 1-4 L	H 2-2 D	A 0-2 L
	A 2-3 L	

SUMMARY	Played	Won	Drawn	Lost	For	Against
Home	15	8	4	3	23	12
Away	15	1	4	10	13	38
Total	30	9	8	13	36	50

BLACKPOOL

LEAGUE

1934-5	1935-6	1936-7	1967-8	1968-9	1969-70
H 1-1 D	H 0-1 L	H 1-2 L	H 1-2 L	H 0-1 L	H 3-1 W
A 1-2 L	A 1-2 L	A 2-0 W	A 2-0 W	A 1-2 L	A 0-0 D

1971-2	1974-5
H 5-1 W	H 2-1 W
A 2-1 W	A 1-2 L

CUP

FA	F League		F League	Worthington	
1962-3	1961-2		1963-4	2000-1	
H 1-1 D	H 4-1 W	1st leg S/F	H 1-0 W	H 3-3 D	1st leg
A 3-1 W	A 0-2 L	2nd leg S/F		A 5-0 W	2nd leg

SUMMARY	Played	Won	Drawn	Lost	For	Against
Home	8	3	1	4	13	10
Away	8	3	1	4	10	9
Total	16	6	2	8	23	19

BOLTON WANDERERS

LEAGUE

1934-5	1964-5	1965-6	1966-7	1967-8	1968-9
H 2-3 L	H 3-2 W	H 3-0 W	H 1-0 W	H 3-1 W	H 2-0 W
A 0-4 L	A 2-5 L	A 1-1 D	A 1-1 D	A 0-2 L	A 1-1 D

1969-70	1970-1	1974-5	1978-9	1979-80	1981-2
H 1-0 W	H 2-1 W	H 2-0 W	H 0-0 D	H 2-1 W	H 0-0 D
A 0-0 D	A 1-0 W	A 0-0 D	A 2-3 L	A 0-1 L	A 1-0 W

1996-7	1998-9	1999-00	2000-1
H 0-1 L	H 2-2 D	H 2-1 W	H 0-2 L
A 1-3 L	A 0-2 L	A 0-1 L	A 0-1 L

CUP

FA	FA
1922-3	1936-7
H 0-2 L	A 1-1 D
	H 1-2 L

F League	F League	Coca-Cola	Coca-Cola		Worthington	
1962-3	1974-5	1994-5	1995-6		1998-9	
H 4-0 W	A 0-0 D	A 0-1 L	H 0-0 D		H 1-1 D aet	
	H 3-1 W		A 0-0 D aet	w 3-2 Pen	L 1-3 Pen	

SUMMARY	Played	Won	Drawn	Lost	For	Against
Home	16	10	3	3	25	14
Away	16	2	5	9	10	25
Total	28	12	8	12	35	39

BOURNEMOUTH

LEAGUE

1923-4	1924-5	1925-6	1926-7	1927-8	1928-9
H 1-1 D	H 6-3 W	H 3-1 W	H 4-1 W	H 3-3 D	H 5-1 W
A 2-1 W	A 0-0 D	A 2-2 D	A 1-0 W	A 1-2 L	A 0-2 L

1929-30	1930-1	1931-2	1932-3	1933-4	1946-7
H 1-0 W	H 2-1 W	H 1-2 L	H 6-0 W	H 6-1 W	H 1-6 L
A 3-2 W	A 1-4 L	A 0-1 L	A 1-1 D	A 4-2 W	A 1-0 W

1947-8	1948-9	1949-50	1950-1	1951-2	1952-3
H 0-1 L	H 1-1 D	H 0-1 L	H 3-0 W	H 2-0 W	H 1-1 D
A 3-1 W	A 2-1 W	A 0-2 L	A 0-0 D	A 2-1 W	A 0-0 D

1953-4	1954-5	1955-6	1956-7	1957-8	1958-9
H 1-3 L	H 0-1 L	H 0-2 L	H 1-3 L	H 2-2 D	H 2-2 D
A 0-2 L	A 3-1 W	A 1-0 W	A 0-2 L	A 1-3 L	A 0-2 L

1959-60
H 2-3 L
A 0-0 D

CUP

Worthington 2000-1	
H 0-0 D	1st leg
A 2-1 W	2nd leg

SUMMARY	Played	Won	Drawn	Lost	For	Against
Home	25	10	6	9	54	40
Away	25	10	7	8	29	31
Total	50	20	13	17	83	71

BRADFORD CITY

LEAGUE

1934-5	1935-6	1936-7	1958-9	1959-60	1985-6
H 6-1 w	H 1-1 D	H 0-0 D	H 4-2 w	H 0-0 D	H 0-0 D
A 1-1 D	A 1-0 w	A 0-2 L	A 2-2 D	A 1-1 D	A 2-0 w

1996-7	1997-8	1998-9	2001-02	2002-3	2003-4
H 2-0 w	H 2-3 L	H 2-2 D	H 1-4 L	H 3-2 w	H 0-1 L
A 2-0 w	A 1-2 L	A 1-4 L	A 1-0 w	A 1-2 L	A 2-2 D

CUP

FA	FA	FA	Coca-Cola	Coca-Cola
1910-1	1914-5	1975-6	1993-4	1995-6
A 1-2 L	H 0-0 D	H 1-2 L	H 3-0 w	H 0-0 D
	A 1-1 D		A 1-2 L	A 5-3 w
	N 0-2 L			

SUMMARY	Played	Won	Drawn	Lost	For	Against
Home	12	4	5	3	21	16
Away	12	4	4	4	15	16
Total	24	8	9	7	36	32

BRADFORD PARK AVENUE

LEAGUE

1907-8	1934-5	1935-6	1936-7	1937-8	1938-9
H 2-0 w	H 3-0 w	H 4-1 w	H 3-1 w	H 1-1 D	H 1-3 L
A 1-1 D	A 1-1 D	A 0-1 L	A 0-1 L	A 0-3 L	A 0-3 L

;UMMARY	Played	Won	Drawn	Lost	For	Against
Home	6	4	1	1	14	6
Away	6	0	2	4	2	10
Total	12	4	3	5	16	16

BRENTFORD

LEAGUE

1905-6	1906-7	1907-8	1908-9	1909-10	1910-1
H 1-1 D	H 1-1 D	H 3-2 W	H 6-1 W	H 5-1 W	H 1-0 W
A 2-0 W	A 1-2 L	A 1-2 L	A 1-3 L	A 1-0 W	A 0-2 L

1911-2	1912-3	1919-20	1920-1	1921-2	1922-3
H 2-0 W	H 2-0 W	H 1-1 D	H 0-0 D	H 0-0 D	H 0-2 L
A 0-3 L	A 0-1 L	A 1-1 D	A 1-3 L	A 1-2 L	A 4-1 W

1923-4	1924-5	1925-6	1926-7	1927-8	1928-9
H 2-3 L	H 3-0 W	H 1-0 W	H 2-1 W	H 1-1 D	H 2-4 L
A 0-3 L	A 1-1 D	A 1-5 L	A 0-3 L	A 1-3 L	A 0-4 L

1929-30	1930-1	1931-2	1932-3	1934-5	1954-5
H 2-2 D	H 3-0 W	H 1-0 W	H 3-0 W	H 2-1 W	H 1-0 W
A 0-3 L	A 1-3 L	A 1-0 W	A 2-2 D	A 1-2 L	A 0-1 L

1955-6	1956-7	1957-8	1958-9	1959-60
H 1-0 W	H 1-1 D	H 3-2 W	H 4-1 W	H 2-1 W
A 2-1 W	A 1-1 D	A 1-7 L	A 4-0 W	A 4-3 W

CUP

FA	FA	FA	F League	Rumbelows	Worthington
1930-1	1931-2	1995-6	1968-9	1991-2	2001-2
A 0-1 L	A 1-4 L	H 1-2 L	A 2-0 W	A 4-1 W	H 0-1 L

;UMMARY	Played	Won	Drawn	Lost	For	Against
Home	29	18	8	3	56	26
Away	29	7	4	18	33	62
Total	58	25	12	21	89	88

BRIGHTON & HOVE ALBION

LEAGUE

1905-6	1906-7	1907-8	1908-9	1909-10	1910-1
H 2-0 w	H 1-2 L	H 1-2 L	H 1-1 D	H 1-1 D	H 1-1 D
A 1-2 L	A 2-0 w	A 0-1 L	A 0-3 L	A 0-5 L	A 0-2 L

1911-2	1912-3	1913-4	1914-5	1919-20	1920-1
H 2-0 w	H 0-1 L	H 1-1 D	H 2-1 w	H 2-0 w	H 3-0 w
A 1-1 D	A 2-2 D	A 2-4 L	A 2-2 D	A 2-2 D	A 0-2 L

1921-2	1922-3	1923-4	1924-5	1925-6	1926-7
H 1-1 D	H 1-0 w	H 1-0 w	H 2-2 D	H 1-2 L	H 0-2 L
A 2-0 w	A 0-0 D	A 0-3 L	A 1-3 L	A 1-1 D	A 2-3 L

1927-8	1928-9	1929-30	1930-1	1931-2	1932-3
H 0-0 D	H 3-1 w	H 2-0 w	H 2-2 D	H 2-1 w	H 1-0 w
A 0-1 L	A 0-3 L	A 3-6 L	A 0-1 L	A 1-2 L	A 1-1 D

1933-4	1946-7	1947-8	1948-9	1949-50	1950-1
H 4-3 w	H 2-3 L	H 2-2 D	H 2-1w	H 1-2 L	H 1-1 D
A 1-1 D	A 3-3 D	A 0-2 L	A 0-1 L	A 3-1 w	A 1-1 D

1951-2	1952-3	1953-4	1954-5	1955-6	1956-7
H 0-1 L	H 3-2 w	H 1-0 w	H 0-0 D	H 3-3 D	H 1-1 D
A 0-2 L	A 3-2 w	A 0-0 D	A 1-0 w	A 0-6 L	A 0-3 L

1957-8	1960-1	1961-2	1979-80	1980-1	1982-3
H 0-0 D	H 2-2 D	H 3-0 w	H 2-2 D	H 3-1 w	H 2-1 w
A 1-0 w	A 2-2 D	A 1-2 L	A 4-2 w	A 0-2 L	A 0-3 L

1985-6	2002-3
H 3-0 w	H 0-1 L
A 1-1 D	A 2-0 w

CUP

FA 1945-6	FA 1946-7	FA 1952-3	FA 1954-5	FA 1955-6	FA 1957-8
H 1-2 L	H 7-2 W	A 0-2 L	H 0-0 D	A 2-1 W	H 1-1 D
A 1-4 L			A 1-5 L		A 2-1 W

FA 1982-3	FA 2002-3	F League 1966-7	F League 1971-2
A 0-1 L	H 3-1 W	H 0-1 L	H 2-0 W

SUMMARY	Played	Won	Drawn	Lost	For	Against
Home	44	19	16	9	68	47
Away	44	8	13	23	46	84
Total	88	27	29	32	114	131

BRISTOL CITY

LEAGUE

1922-3	1924-5	1925-6	1926-7	1932-3	1933-4
H 2-2 D	H 0-0 D	H 1-3 L	H 1-1 D	H 3-0 W	H 7-2 W
A 0-4 L	A 0-2 L	A 1-0 W	A 1-1 D	A 1-1 D	A 1-0 W

1946-7	1947-8	1948-9	1949-50	1950-1	1951-2
H 2-2 D	H 2-3 L	H 4-0 W	H 3-0 W	H 0-0 D	H 1-0 W
A 1-2 L	A 0-6 L	A 6-1 W	A 2-1 W	A 2-2 D	A 5-2 W

1952-3	1953-4	1954-5	1965-6	1966-7	1967-8
H 0-0 D	H 1-1 D	H 0-1 L	H 0-0 D	H 1-0 W	H 3-2 W
A 1-0 W	A 1-3 L	A 1-0 W	A 0-0 D	A 0-1 L	A 2-0 W

1968-9	1969-70	1970-1	1971-2	1974-5	1976-7
H 1-1 D	H 4-1 W	H 3-2 W	H 2-2 D	H 3-2 W	H 2-1 W
A 1-0 W	A 0-4 L	A 1-0 W	A 1-0 W	A 1-0 W	A 1-3 L

1977-8	1978-9	1979-80	1998-9
H 1-0 W	H 3-0 W	H 2-0 W	H 2-1 W
A 0-3 L	A 1-1 D	A 3-2 W	A 0-1 L

CUP

FA 1908-9 A 0-2 L	FA 1923-4 H 0-1 L	FA 1990-1 H 2-1 W

SUMMARY	Played	Won	Drawn	Lost	For	Against
Home	28	15	10	3	54	27
Away	28	13	5	10	34	40
Total	56	28	15	13	88	67

BRISTOL ROVERS

LEAGUE

1905-6 H 0-0 D A 1-0 W	1906-7 H 1-0 W A 1-3 L	1907-8 H 0-0 D A 2-2 D	1908-9 H 4-1 W A 0-2 L	1909-10 H 1-1 D A 0-1 L	1910-1 H 1-0 W A 1-0 W

1911-2 H 0-0 D A 1-4 L	1912-3 H 1-1 D A 1-2 L	1913-4 H 1-1 D A 1-2 L	1914-5 H 5-1 W A 2-4 L	1919-20 H 5-1 W A 3-5 L	1920-1 H 1-1 D A 2-2 D

1921-2 H 0-1 L A 2-4 L	1922-3 H 0-0 D A2-3 L	1923-4 H 3-1 W A 1-3 L	1924-5 H 1-1 D A 0-3 L	1925-6 H 1-0 W A 2-2 D	1926-7 H 2-0 W A 0-1 L

1927-8 H 4-2 W A 0-3 L	1928-9 H 2-1 W A 0-2 L	1929-30 H 4-2 W A 1-0 W	1930-1 H 1-3 L A 0-3 L	1931-2 H 6-0 W A 1-0 W	1932-3 H 1-1 D A 1-1 D

1933-4 H 0-0 D A 0-3 L	1946-7 H 3-3 D A 2-1 W	1947-8 H 1-5 L A 3-2 W	1948-9 H 3-0 W A 2-2 D	1949-50 H 4-0 W A 1-5 L	1950-1 H 2-0 W A 3-3 D

1951-2 H 1-0 W A 1-1 D	1952-3 H 0-0 D A 1-3 L	1960-1 H 2-1 W A 1-3 L	1961-2 H 2-2 D A 1-2 L	1974-5 H 0-1 L A 2-0 W	

RESULTS

CUP

FA 1912-3	FA 1963-4	F League 1970-1
H 2-2 D	A 1-2 L	H 1-1 D
A 1-1 D		A 1-3 L
N 0-1 L		

SUMMARY	Played	Won	Drawn	Lost	For	Against
Home	35	17	14	4	63	31
Away	35	7	7	21	42	77
Total	70	24	21	25	105	108

BURNLEY

LEAGUE

1934-5	1935-6	1936-7	1937-8	1938-9	1971-2
H 0-1 L	H 2-0 W	H 2-2 D	H 1-0 W	H 4-0 W	H 3-0 W
A 2-3 L	A 1-1 D	A 0-3 L	A 0-3 L	A 0-3 L	A 0-1 L

1973-4	1975-6	2000-1	2001-2	2002-3	2003-4
H 1-0 W	H 3-1 W	H 2-3 L	H 2-1 W	H 2-0 W	H 2-0 W
A 0-1 L	A 4-4 D	A 0-2 L	A 1-1 D	A 0-2 L	A 5-3 W

CUP

F League 1977-8	Littlewoods 1987-8	
A 1-3 L	A 1-1 D	1st leg
	H 1-0 W	2nd leg

SUMMARY	Played	Won	Drawn	Lost	For	Against
Home	12	9	1	2	24	8
Away	12	1	3	8	13	27
Total	24	10	4	10	37	35

BURY

LEAGUE

1934-5	1935-6	1936-7	1937-8	1938-9	1958-9
H 4-1 w	H 5-3 w	H 0-0 D	H 1-2 L	H 3-1 w	H 3-2 w
A 0-1 L	A 1-0 w	A 2-3 L	A 1-3 L	A 3-2 w	A 2-3 L

1959-60	1961-2	1962-3	1963-4	1964-5	1965-6
H 2-0 w	H 3-1 w	H 1-1 D	H 0-1 L	H 1-1 D	H 4-0 w
A 0-1 L	A 3-2 w	A 3-0 w	A 2-4 L	A 0-1 L	A 5-2 w

1966-7	1968-9	1997-8	1998-9
H 2-0 w	H 2-2 D	H 2-2 D	H 0-0 D
A 0-2 L	A 2-1 w	A 0-1 L	A 2-0 w

SUMMARY	Played	Won	Drawn	Lost	For	Against
Home	16	8	6	2	33	17
Away	16	7	0	9	26	26
Total	32	15	6	11	59	43

CAMBRIDGE UNITED

LEAGUE

FA CUP

1981-2
H 2-1 w
A 2-1 w

1980-1
H 1-0 w

CARDIFF CITY

LEAGUE

1913-4	1914-5	1919-20	1931-2	1932-3	1933-4
H 2-2 D	H 2-1 W	H 1-1 D	H 2-0 W	H 3-1 W	H 2-0 W
A 0-3 L	A 0-1 L	A 0-1 L	A 2-0 W	A 2-4 L	A 2-0 L

1946-7	1962-3	1963-4	1964-5	1965-6	1966-7
H 2-1 W	H 0-0 D	H 5-1 W	H 2-1 W	H 3-2 W	H 3-2 W
A 1-6 L	A 4-2 W	A 1-3 L	A 3-1 W	A 2-0 W	A 0-2 L

1967-8	1968-9	1969-70	1970-1	1971-2	1974-5
H 1-0 W	H 3-1 W	H 1-1 D	H 1-2 L	H 2-1 W	H 1-1 D
A 1-3 L	A 1-3 L	A 1-0 W	A 1-1 D	A 0-0 D	A 1-2 L

1981-2	2003-4
H 2-1 W	H 4-1 W
A 0-1 L	A 1-2 L

CUP

FA	Milk	
1959	1983-4	
H 3-2 W	A 0-0 D	1st leg
	H 3-0 W	2nd leg

SUMMARY	Played	Won	Drawn	Lost	For	Against
Home	20	14	5	1	42	20
Away	20	6	2	12	23	35
Total	40	20	7	13	65	55

CARLISLE UNITED

LEAGUE

1965-6	1966-7	1967-8	1968-9	1969-70	1970-1
H 2-0 w	H 2-0 w	H 2-1 w	H 2-1 w	H 1-0 w	H 1-1 D
A 1-4 L	A 0-1 L	A 2-2 D	A 4-0 w	A 1-2 L	A 2-4 L

1971-2	1985-6
H 1-0 w	H 2-1 w
A 0-3 L	A 4-0 w

CUP

F League 1962-3	F League 1971-2	Coca-Cola 1992-3	
A 1-1 D	H 4-1 w	A 2-2 D	1st leg
H 5-0 w		H 2-0 w	2nd leg

SUMMARY	Played	Won	Drawn	Lost	For	Against
Home	8	7	1	0	13	4
Away	8	2	1	5	14	16
Total	16	9	2	5	27	20

CHARLTON ATHLETIC

LEAGUE

1921-2	1922-3	1923-4	1924-5	1925-6	1926-7
H 2-0 w	H 2-3 L	H 2-2 D	H 2-1 w	H 3-0 w	H 2-3 L
A 1-2 L	A 0-3 L	A 0-0 D	A 2-3 L	A 0-3 L	A 0-2 L

1927-8	1928-9	1933-4	1935-6	1960-1	1961-2
H 0-0 D	H 0-1 L	H 3-0 w	H 3-1 w	H 4-0 w	H 2-2 D
A 2-3 L	A 0-1 L	A 3-3 D	A 1-4 L	A 1-0 w	A 2-2 D

1962-3	1963-4	1964-5	1965-6	1966-7	1967-8
H 1-4 L	H 1-3 L	H 2-0 w	H 2-0 w	H 1-1 D	H 1-1 D
A 2-0 w	A 1-3 L	A 1-2 L	A 1-2 L	A 0-0 D	A 3-3 D

1968-9	1969-70	1970-1	1971-2	1981-2	1985-6
H 0-1 L	H 1-1 D	H 2-0 W	H 3-0 W	H 5-0 W	H 3-1 W
A 1-2 L	A 0-3 L	A 1-2 L	A 2-0 W	A 0-0 D	A 0-1 L

1986-7	1987-8	1988-9	1989-90	1995-6	1996-7
H 1-1 D	H 2-0 W	H 1-3 L	H 0-0 D	H 0-1 L	H 1-2 L
A 2-1 W	A 0-2 L	A 2-1 W	A 1-0 W	A 1-1 D	A 4-4 D

1997-8	1999-00
H 0-4 L	H 0-3 L
A 1-2 L	A 0-1 L

CUP

F League	Rumbelows
1981-2	1991-2
H 1-0 W	H 3-0 W
A 1-0 W	A 2-0 W

SUMMARY	Played	Won	Drawn	Lost	For	Against
Home	32	13	8	11	52	39
Away	32	6	8	18	35	56
Total	64	19	16	29	87	95

CHATHAM TOWN

CUP

FA	FA
1926-7	1927-8
H 5-0 W	H 6-1 W

CHELSEA

LEAGUE

1962-3	1972-3	1973-4	1977-8	1978-9	1981-2
H 4-1 w	H 1-0 w	H 2-2 D	H 0-0 D	H 2-0 w	H 2-1 w
A 0-2 L	A 1-3 L	A 0-3 L	A 1-1 D	A 3-3 D	A 1-2 L

1984-5	1986-7	1987-8	1989-90	1990-1	1991-2
H 0-0 D	H 2-2 D	H 3-0 w	H 2-0 w	H 1-3 L	H 0-1 L
A 2-1 w	A 0-0 D	A 0-1 L	A 0-0 D	A 1-1 D	A 3-0 w

1992-3	1993-4	1994-5
H 2-1 w	H 1-1 D	H 3-0 w
A 3-2 w	A 2-1 w	A 0-2 L

CUP

FA	FA	FA	F League	Milk	
1935-6	1967-8	2001-2	1971-2	1972-3	
H 1-1 D	A 0-1 L	H 0-0 D	H 0-1 L	A 2-0 w	1st leg S/F
A 1-3 L		A 0-4 L		H 1-0 w	2nd leg S/F

SUMMARY	Played	Won	Drawn	Lost	For	Against
Home	15	8	5	2	25	12
Away	15	4	5	6	17	22
Total	30	12	10	8	42	34

CHELTENHAM TOWN

CUP

Worthington		Worthington
1999-00		2002-3
H 2-0 w	1st leg	H 0-3 L
A 1-2 L	2nd leg	

CHESTER

CUP

F League 1964-5	F League 1970-1	F League 1978-9
H 5-3 w	H 0-0 d	A 2-0 w
	A 2-1 w	

CHESTERFIELD

LEAGUE

1936-7	1937-8	1938-9	1958-9	1959-60
H 2-0 w	H 2-1 w	H 2-0 w	H 2-1 w	H 3-0 w
A 1-3 L	A 2-6 L	A 0-2 L	A 1-1 D	A 1-2 L

CUP

FA 1951-2	F League 1961-2
H 3-1 w	A 3-2 w

SUMMARY	Played	Won	Drawn	Lost	For	Against
Home	5	5	0	0	11	2
Away	5	0	1	4	5	14
Total	10	5	1	4	16	16

CLAPTON

CUP

FA 1925-6
A 1-3 L

COLCHESTER UNITED

LEAGUE

1950-1	1951-2	1952-3	1953-4	1954-5	1955-6
H 1-1 D	H 5-2 W	H 3-0 W	H 2-1 W	H 0-2 L	H 1-1 D
A 3-2 W	A 1-1 D	A 4-0 W	A 1-0 W	A 0-1 L	A 2-3 L

1956-7	1957-8	1958-9	1959-60
H 1-2 L	H 1-1 D	H 1-2 L	H 3-2 W
A 1-1 D	A 2-1 W	A 1-2 L	A 0-3 L

SUMMARY	Played	Won	Drawn	Lost	For	Against
Home	10	4	3	3	18	14
Away	10	4	2	4	15	14
Total	20	8	5	7	33	28

CORINTHIANS

CUP

FA
1928-9
H 0-5 L

COVENTRY CITY

LEAGUE

1908-9	1909-10	1910-1	1911-2	1912-3	1913-4
H 2-0 W	H 0-1 L	H 5-2 W	H 1-1 D	H 0-3 L	H 1-1 D
A 0-2 L	A 1-2 L	A 1-3 L	A 0-3 L	A 0-3 L	A 2-1 W

1926-7	1927-8	1928-9	1929-30	1930-1	1931-2
H 3-0 W	H 0-2 L	H 3-0 W	H 10-2 W	H 2-2 D	H 6-2 W
A 0-1 L	A 2-2 D	A 0-3 L	A 1-3 L	A 0-3 L	A 0-3 L

RESULTS

1932-3	1933-4	1936-7	1937-8	1938-9	1952-3
H 2-1 W	H 3-1 W	H 0-3 L	H 0-2 L	H 1-1 D	H 1-1 D
A 5-3 W	A 0-0 D	A 1-1 D	A 0-2 L	A 0-2 L	A 1-2 L

1953-4	1954-5	1955-6	1956-7	1957-8	1959-60
H 2-1 W	H 1-1 D	H 1-0 W	H 3-0 W	H 1-1 D	H 1-4 L
A 0-1 L	A 0-4 L	A 3-5 L	A 2-3 L	A 1-2 L	A 1-2 L

1964-5	1965-6	1966-7	1972-3	1973-4	1975-6
H 1-0 W	H 1-1 D	H 1-1 D	H 1-1 D	H 0-0 D	H 0-3 L
A 0-3 L	A 0-2 L	A 1-2 L	A 1-3 L	A 0-1 L	A 0-1 L

1976-7	1977-9	1978-9	1979-80	1980-1	1982-3
H 3-0 W	H 1-2 L	H 1-0 W	H 1-0 W	H 2-0 W	H 1-1 D
A 0-2 L	A 4-5 L	A 1-4 L	A 0-2 L	A 1-0 W	A 0-2 L

1983-4	1984-5	1986-7	1987-8	1988-9	1989-90
H 0-0 D	H 2-1 W	H 1-1 D	H 3-1 W	H 1-2 L	H 0-0 D
A 1-2 L	A 0-0 D	A 1-2 L	A 0-0 D	A 1-2 L	A 0-1 L

1990-1	1991-2	1992-3	1993-4	1994-5	2001-2
H 2-2 D	H 3-2 W	H 1-1 D	H 1-0 W	H 2-2 D	H 2-0 W
A 0-2 L	A 0-0 D	A 1-1 D	A 1-2 L	A 0-1 L	A 1-2 L

2002-3	2003-4
H 2-0 W	H 1-1 D
A 1-1 D	A 2-0 W

CUP

FA 1929-30	FA 1974-5	FA 1982-3	FA 1992-3	FA 1994-5	FA 1999-00
H 3-3 D	A 0-2 L	A 2-2 D	H 1-0 W	A 0-0 D	H 1-3 L
A 0-2 L		H 2-1 W		H 3-1 W	

SUMMARY	Played	Won	Drawn	Lost	For	Against
Home	50	22	19	9	83	54
Away	50	4	8	38	38	99
Total	100	26	27	47	121	153

CREWE ALEXANDRA

LEAGUE

1997-8	1998-9	1999-00	2000-1	2001-2	2003-4
H 0-2 L	H 2-1 w	H 2-1 w	H 1-1 D	H 2-2 D	H 1-0 w
A 0-1 L	A 2-3 L	A 0-1 L	A 0-0 D	A 0-1 L	A 3-1 w

SUMMARY	Played	Won	Drawn	Lost	For	Against
Home	6	3	2	1	8	7
Away	6	1	1	4	5	7
Total	12	4	3	5	13	14

CROYDON COMMON

LEAGUE

1909-10	1914-5
H 4-2 w	H 1-1 D
A 0-2 L	A 1-4 L

CRYSTAL PALACE

LEAGUE

1906-7	1907-8	1908-9	1909-10	1910-1	1911-2
H 4-2 w	H 0-1 L	H 2-0 w	H 1-0 w	H 0-1 L	H 1-1 D
A 1-0 w	A 1-2 L	A 0-4 L	A 0-4 L	A 3-0 w	A 0-6 L

1912-3	1913-4	1914-5	1919-20	1920-1	1925-6
H 2-2 D	H 0-0 D	H 2-1 w	H 2-0 w	H 0-1 L	H 4-3 w
A 0-1 L	A 0-3 L	A 1-2 L	A 1-3 L	A 0-1 L	A 0-2 L

1926-7	1927-8	1928-9	1929-30	1930-1	1931-2
H 0-1 L	H 4-1 w	H 0-1 L	H 2-2 D	H 2-1 w	H 3-2 w
A 1-7 L	A 1-2 L	A 1-2 L	A 2-3 L	A 1-2 L	A 1-3 L

RESULTS

1932-3	1933-4	1946-7	1947-8	1948-9	1949-50
H 3-0 w	H 2-0 w	H 2-3 L	H 3-1 w	H 3-0 w	H 2-0 w
A 0-4 L	A 1-0 w	A 1-0 w	A 0-2 L	A 1-1 D	A 0-2 L

1950-1	1951-2	1952-3	1953-4	1954-5	1955-6
H 3-1 w	H 1-0 w	H 5-1 w	H 2-1 w	H 2-0 w	H 3-1 w
A 5-0 w	A 0-2 L	A 1-1 D	A 0-1 L	A 0-2 L	A 0-2 L

1956-7	1957-8	1964-5	1965-6	1966-7	1967-8
H 1-0 w	H 3-2 w	H 1-2 L	H 2-1 w	H 4-3 w	H 2-1 w
A 1-4 L	A 3-0 w	A 0-2 L	A 0-0 D	A 0-0 D	A 0-6 L

1968-9	1972-3	1979-80	1980-1	1981-2	1985-6
H 0-1 L	H 2-1 w	H 2-1 w	H 1-1 D	H 1-0 w	H 4-3 w
A 0-2 L	A 2-0 w	A 0-0 D	A 1-4 L	A 1-2 L	A 2-1 w

1989-90	1990-1	1991-2	1992-3	1994-5	1995-6
H 2-0 w	H 0-3 L	H 3-3 D	H 4-2 w	H 0-0 D	H 1-0 w
A 0-1 L	A 3-1 w	A 4-3 w	A 2-1 w	A 1-0 w	A 1-0 w

1996-7	1998-9	1999-00	2000-1	2001-2	2002-3
H 1-1 D	H 0-1 L	H 0-1 L	H 0-0 D	H 2-1 w	H 2-0 w
A 0-2 L	A 1-5 L	A 0-1 L	A 1-1 D	A 2-3 L	A 0-2 L

2003-4
H 2-1 w
A 0-1 L

CUP

FA	FA	FA
1913-4	1926-7	1933-4
A 1-2 L	A 0-0 D	A 0-3 L
	H 1-0 w	

SUMMARY	Played	Won	Drawn	Lost	For	Against
Home	55	35	9	11	100	57
Away	55	13	6	36	48	106
Total	110	48	15	47	148	163

DAGENHAM & REDBRIDGE

CUP

FA
2002-3
H 1-0 w

DARLINGTON

CUP

FA	FA
1919-20	1957-8
A 0-5 L	H 1-2 L

DERBY COUNTY

LEAGUE

1960-1	1961-2	1962-3	1963-4	1964-5	1965-6
H 0-2 L	H 3-2 w	H 2-0 w	H 3-0 w	H 5-2 w	H 0-1 L
A 0-0 D	A 1-1 D	A 0-3 L	A 1-2 L	A 1-0 w	A 1-3 L

1966-7	1967-8	1968-9	1972-3	1973-4	1975-6
H 4-1 w	H 3-2 w	H 1-4 L	H 1-0 w	H 2-4 L	H 0-0 D
A 1-1 D	A 1-1 D	A 1-1 D	A 0-1 L	A 1-1 D	A 1-3 L

1976-7	1977-8	1978-9	1979-80	1981-2	1987-8
H 0-0 D	H 0-0 D	H 3-0 w	H 4-2 w	H 4-1 w	H 1-2 L
A 2-2 D	A 2-2 D	A 1-1 D	A 0-0 D	A 2-0 w	A 2-1 w

1988-9	1989-90	1990-1	1995-6	2002-3	2003-4
H 1-0 w	H 1-0 w	H 2-1 w	H 1-0 w	H 1-0 w	H 2-1 w
A 1-0 w	A 2-0 w	A 0-0 D	A 1-2 L	A 1-2 L	A 4-0 w

CUP

FA	FA	F League	Worthington
1966-7	1983-4	1960-1	2000-1
H 3-0 w	A 1-2 L	A 4-1 w	A 0-3 L

SUMMARY	Played	Won	Drawn	Lost	For	Against
Home	24	16	3	5	44	25
Away	24	6	11	7	27	27
Total	48	22	14	12	71	52

RESULTS

DONCASTER ROVERS

LEAGUE

1935-6	1936-7	1958-9
H 2-1 w	H 2-1 w	H 3-0 w
A 0-3 L	A 2-1 w	A 1-0 w

CUP

FA	FA
1924-5	1981-2
A 2-1 w	H 2-1 w

SUMMARY	Played	Won	Drawn	Lost	For	Against
Home	3	3	0	0	7	2
Away	3	2	0	1	3	4
Total	6	5	0	1	10	6

DORCHESTER TOWN

CUP

FA
1955-6
H 4-0 w

EVERTON

LEAGUE

1972-3	1973-4	1975-6	1976-7	1977-8	1978-9
H 1-1 D	H 1-3 L	H 4-2 w	H 2-1 w	H 0-0 D	H 0-1 L
A 2-2 D	A 1-4 L	A 1-1 D	A 1-3 L	A 0-3 L	A 2-2 D

1979-80	1980-1	1982-3	1983-4	1984-5	1986-7
H 0-0 D	H 2-1 w	H 0-1 L	H 1-1 D	H 4-2 w	H 0-1 L
A 4-2 w	A 2-0 w	A 1-1 D	A 2-0 w	A 0-3 L	A 0-4 L

1987-8	1988-9	1989-90	1990-1	1991-2	1992-3
H 0-3 L	H 1-0 w	H 1-1 D	H 1-0 w	H 4-3 w	H 1-1 D
A 0-1 L	A 1-1 D	A 1-3 L	A 0-1 L	A 1-1 D	A 1-0 w

1993-4	1994-5
H 3-0 w	H 0-0 D
A 5-1 w	A 1-2 L

CUP

FA	FA	FA	F League	Littlewoods
1988-9	1994-5	2003-4	1973-4	1986-7
N 0-1 L	A 0-5 L	A 1-3 L	A 1-0 w	H 1-4 L

SUMMARY	Played	Won	Drawn	Lost	For	Against
Home	20	8	7	5	26	22
Away	20	5	6	9	26	35
Total	40	13	13	14	52	57

EXETER CITY

LEAGUE

1908-9	1909-10	1910-1	1911-2	1912-3	1913-4
H 2-0 w	H 1-0 w	H 0-0 D	H 1-1 D	H 1-1 D	H 3-1 w
A 2-3 L	A 2-2 D	A 1-3 L	A 0-1 L	A 0-1 L	A 1-0 w

1914-5	1919-20	1920-1	1921-2	1922-3	1923-4
H 3-1 w	H 0-0 D	H 0-0 D	H 0-0 D	H 6-0 w	H 4-0 w
A 0-2 L	A 1-2 L	A 1-1 D	A 0-2 L	A 0-2 L	A 2-1 w

1924-5	1925-6	1926-7	1927-8	1928-9	1929-30
H 0-1 L	H 3-1 w	H 4-4 D	H 2-2 D	H 5-0 w	H 3-1 w
A 0-1 L	A 1-0 w	A 0-1 L	A 2-2 D	A 1-3 L	A 0-3 L

1930-1	1931-2	1932-3	1933-4	1946-7	1947-8
H 1-2 L	H 0-1 L	H 0-0 D	H 1-1 D	H 1-3 L	H 3-0 w
A 0-1 L	A 0-3 L	A 1-2 L	A 4-3 w	A 0-3 L	A 0-2 L

1948-9	1949-50	1950-1	1951-2	1952-3	1953-4
H 3-0 w	H 1-2 L	H 3-0 w	H 1-1 D	H 2-0 w	H 1-2 L
A 1-4 L	A 1-3 L	A 2-1 w	A 4-2 w	A 0-1 L	A 2-0 w

1954-5	1955-6	1956-7	1957-8
H 3-0 w	H 2-1 w	H 1-0 w	H 3-2 w
A 1-0 w	A 1-1 D	A 0-0 D	A 2-2 D

CUP

FA	F League
1989-90	1976-7
A 1-1 D	
H 2-0 w	A 3-1 w

SUMMARY	Played	Won	Drawn	Lost	For	Against
Home	34	17	11	6	64	28
Away	34	8	6	20	33	58
Total	68	25	17	26	97	86

FOLKESTONE TOWN

CUP

FA	FA	FA
1923-4	1924-5	1932-3
A 3-2 w	H 2-0 w	A 0-1 L

FULHAM

LEAGUE

1928-9	1929-30	1930-1	1931-2	1934-5	1935-6
H 2-2 D	H 0-4 L	H 1-1 D	H 2-2 D	H 0-0 D	H 1-0 w
A 1-2 L	A 3-3 D	A 0-1 L	A 0-4 L	A 3-1 w	A 1-1 D

1936-7	1937-8	1938-9	1968-9	1971-2	1974-5
H 3-0 w	H 1-2 l	H 3-3 d	H 2-0 w	H 2-1 w	H 1-2 l
A 3-2 w	A 4-3 w	A 0-2 l	A 3-1 w	A 0-0 d	A 0-4 l

1985-6	1999-00	2000-1
H 2-1 w	H 1-2 l	H 0-1 l
A 1-0 w	A 1-1 d	A 0-2 l

CUP

FA	F League	Worthington		
1907-08	1962-3	1999-00		
A 1-2 l	H 1-0 w	H 0-4 l	1st leg	
		A 0-2 l	2nd leg	

SUMMARY	Played	Won	Drawn	Lost	For	Against
Home	15	5	5	5	21	21
Away	15	5	4	6	20	27
Total	30	10	9	11	41	48

GILLINGHAM (as NEW BROMPTON 1905-12)

LEAGUE

1905-6	1906-7	1907-8	1908-9	1909-10	1910-1
H 4-1 w	H 2-2 d	H 2-1 w	H 0-0 d	H 1-0 w	H 2-1 w
A 0-0 d	A 1-0 w	A 1-2 l	A 0-2 l	A 2-5 l	A 1-1 d

1911-2	1912-3	1913-4	1914-5	1919-20	1920-1
H 1-0 w	H 4-0 w	H 2-0 w	H 4-0 w	H 5-0 w	H 2-1 w
A 1-3 l	A 0-1 l	A 0-0 d	A 3-3 d	A 0-1 l	A 0-0 d

1921-2	1922-3	1923-4	1924-5	1925-6	1926-7
H 2-0 w	H 1-1 d	H 1-0 w	H 0-0 d	H 1-0 w	H 0-0 d
A 2-5 l	A 0-5 l	A 1-3 l	A 1-3 l	A 0-2 l	A 0-1 l

1927-8	1928-9	1929-30	1930-1	1931-2	1932-3
H 0-0 d	H 1-2 l	H 2-0 w	H 4-0 w	H 1-1 d	H 2-0 w
A 0-3 l	A 0-4 l	A 2-1 w	A 1-2 l	A 3-3 d	A 2-0 w

RESULTS

H 4-1 w	H 2-0 w	H 5-0 w	H 3-2 w	H 1-0 w	H 0-0 d
A 2-1 w	A 2-2 d	A 2-1 w	A 3-0 w	A 1-2 l	A 1-3 l

1954-5	1955-6	1956-7	1957-8	2000-1	2001-2
H 1-2 l	H 5-1 w	H 1-3 l	H 2-0 w	H 1-0 w	H 2-1 w
A 1-2 l	A 1-3 l	A 1-1 d	A 0-1 l	A 3-4 l	A 2-0 w

2002-3	2003-4
H 1-0 w	H 2-1 w
A 3-4 l	A 2-0 w

Cup

F League
1979-80
A 1-1 d   1st leg
H 4-2 w   2nd leg

SUMMARY	Played	Won	Drawn	Lost	For	Against
Home	37	26	8	3	74	20
Away	37	8	8	21	40	67
Total	74	34	16	24	114	87

GLOUCS
CITY

GRAYS
UNITED

CUP

CUP

FA
1949-50
A 3-2 w

FA
1904-5
H 0-0 d
A 2-3 l

GRIMSBY TOWN

LEAGUE

1920-1	1959-60	1962-3	1963-4	1981-2	1985-6
H 0-0 D	H 1-1 D	H 0-0 D	H 2-0 w	H 2-1 w	H 3-2 w
A 1-1 D	A 1-1 D	A 2-0 w	A 1-3 L	A 2-1 w	A 0-1 L

1995-6	1996-7	1998-9	1999-00	2000-1	2001-2
H 2-2 D	H 2-1 w	H 3-1 w	H 3-0 w	H 2-1 w	H 1-1 D
A 2-2 D	A 4-1 w	A 1-0 w	A 1-2 L	A 0-2 L	A 2-0 w

2002-3
H 4-0 w
A 1-1 D

CUP

FA	FA	FA	F League	Milk
1920-1	1994-5	1997-8	1971-2	1984-5
A 0-1 L	A 1-0 w	A 0-3 L	A 1-1 D	A 1-0 w
			H 3-1 w	

SUMMARY	Played	Won	Drawn	Lost	For	Against
Home	13	8	5	0	25	10
Away	13	5	4	4	18	15
Total	26	13	9	4	43	25

HALIFAX TOWN

LEAGUE

1958-9	1959-60
H 3-1 w	H 3-0 w
A 1-1 D	A 1-0 w

RESULTS

CUP

FA	League
1913-4	1963-4
H 2-0 w	A 7-1 w

SUMMARY	Played	Won	Drawn	Lost	For	Against
Home	2	2	0	0	6	1
Away	2	1	1	0	2	1
Total	4	3	1	0	8	2

HARTLEPOOL UNITED

CUP

FA
1949-50
A 1-1 D
H 5-1 w

HARWICH & PARKESTON

CUP

FA
1903-4
A 4-2 w

HASTINGS & ST LEONARDS

CUP

FA
1906-7
H 3-1 w

HASTINGS UTD

CUP

FA
1953-4
H 3-0 w
A 3-3 D

HEADINGTON UTD

CUP

FA
1954-5
H 4-2 w

HUDDERSFIELD TOWN

LEAGUE

1960-1	1961-2	1962-3	1963-4	1964-5	1965-6
H 2-0 w	H 1-2 L	H 2-3 L	H 2-2 D	H 0-2 L	H 1-1 D
A 1-1 D	A 1-1 D	A 0-0 D	A 1-1 D	A 0-0 D	A 0-0 D

1966-7	1967-8	1968-9	1969-70	1985-6	1995-6
H 0-0 D	H 0-1 L	H 1-0 w	H 1-2 L	H 4-1 w	H 2-0 w
A 1-0 w	A 0-2 L	A 2-2 D	A 1-1 D	A 0-0 D	A 2-3 L

1996-7	1997-8	1998-9	1999-00	2000-1
H 2-0 w	H 5-0 w	H 4-1 w	H 1-1 D	H 1-1 D
A 0-2 L	A 3-1 w	A 1-1 D	A 0-1 L	A 0-2 L

CUP

FA	F League
1986-7	1967-8
H 1-1 D	H 0-1 L
A 4-2 w	

SUMMARY	Played	Won	Drawn	Lost	For	Against
Home	17	7	5	5	29	17
Away	17	2	10	5	13	18
Total	34	9	15	10	42	35

HULL CITY

LEAGUE

1934-5	1935-6	1958-9	1966-7	1967-8	1968-9
H 3-0 w	H 3-0 w	H 0-1 L	H 0-2 L	H 2-2 D	H 1-2 L
A 0-1 L	A 0-0 D	A 3-3 D	A 0-5 L	A 2-0 w	A 1-0 w

1969-70	1970-1	1971-2	1974-5	1985-6
H 2-1 w	H 0-2 L	H 2-0 w	H 1-0 w	H 2-0 w
A 0-1 L	A 0-1 L	A 2-1 w	A 0-0 D	A 0-1 L

RESULTS

CUP

FA	F League	F League
1971-2	1969-70	1972-3
H 0-3 L	A 0-1 L	A 2-1 W

SUMMARY	Played	Won	Drawn	Lost	For	Against
Home	11	6	1	4	16	10
Away	11	3	3	5	8	13
Total	22	9	4	9	24	23

ILFORD

CUP

FA	FA
1922-3	1958-9
H 5-1 W	H 3-1 W

IPSWICH TOWN

LEAGUE

1946-7	1947-8	1948-9	1949-50	1950-1	1951-2
H 0-1 L	H 1-5 L	H 2-0 W	H 1-1 D	H 1-3 L	H 2-0 W
A 0-5 L	A 2-1 W	A 2-1 W	A 0-3 L	A 1-0 W	A 2-0 W

1952-3	1953-4	1955-6	1956-7	1960-1	1964-5
H 1-0 W	H 1-2 L	H 3-2 W	H 1-2 L	H 0-3 L	H 2-1 W
A 1-2 L	A 1-1 D	A 1-4 L	A 1-3 L	A 1-4 L	A 0-3 L

1965-6	1966-7	1967-8	1972-3	1973-4	1975-6
H 1-0 W	H 1-2 L	H 3-4 L	H 0-0 D	H 1-2 L	H 1-0 W
A 0-2 L	A 2-0 W	A 0-0 D	A 2-1 W	A 1-1 D	A 0-2 L

1976-7	1977-8	1978-9	1979-80	1980-1	1982-3
H 0-1 L	H 1-0 W	H 0-1 L	H 3-3 D	H 1-0 W	H 0-0 D
A 0-5 L	A 0-4 L	A 1-1 D	A 2-4 L	A 0-2 L	A 3-2 W

1983-4	1984-5	1992-3	1993-4	1994-5	1995-6
H 0-0 D	H 0-2 L	H 0-2 L	H 1-0 W	H 3-0 W	H 2-1 W
A 0-2 L	A 0-2 L	A 1-3 L	A 1-2 L	A 2-1 W	A 1-2 L

1996-7	1997-8	1998-9	1999-00	2002-3	2003-4
H 3-1 W	H 2-1 W	H 0-0 D	H 0-0 D	H 0-2 L	H 3-1 W
A 0-2 L	A 0-5 L	A 1-0 W	A 2-0 W	A 1-1 D	A 2-0 W

CUP

FA 1961-2	FA 1982-3
H 1-1 D	H 1-0 W
A 2-1 W	

F League 1968-9	F League 1974-5	F League 1980-1	Milk 1983-4	Milk 1984-5	
A 4-2 W	H 1-1 D	A 1-1 D	A 1-0 W	A 0-1 L	1st leg S/F
	A 2-1 W	H 1-3 L		H 2-0 W	2nd leg S/F

SUMMARY	Played	Won	Drawn	Lost	For	Against
Home	36	15	7	14	41	43
Away	36	11	5	20	34	71
Total	72	26	12	34	75	114

LEEDS UNITED

LEAGUE

1960-1	1961-2	1962-3	1963-4	1972-3	1973-4
H 3-2 W	H 2-0 W	H 3-2 W	H 2-2 D	H 1-2 L	H 0-1 L
A 0-1 L	A 1-0 W	A 0-3 L	A 2-4 L	A 0-2 L	A 0-1 L

1974-5	1976-7	1977-8	1978-9	1979-80	1980-1
H 1-1 D	H 1-2 L	H 3-0 W	H 2-2 D	H 2-1 W	H 2-3 L
A 3-0 W	A 2-3 L	A 2-2 D	A 2-2 D	A 2-2 D	A 0-1 L

1985-6	1990-1	1991-2	1992-3	1993-4	1994-5
H 4-0 W	H 2-0 W	H 2-2 D	H 4 2 W	H 2-1 W	H 2-1 W
A 2-0 W	A 0-3 L	A 0-1 L	A 0-0 D	A 4-0 W	A 1-2 L

CUP

FA	FA	FA
1934-5	1972-3	1976-7
H 3-3 D	H 1-1 D	A 2-5 L
A 2-1 W	A 1-1 D	
	N 0-5 L	

SUMMARY	Played	Won	Drawn	Lost	For	Against
Home	18	10	4	4	38	24
Away	18	4	4	10	21	27
Total	36	14	8	14	59	51

LEICESTER CITY

LEAGUE

1935-6	1936-7	1969-70	1970-1	1972-3	1973-4
H 1-2 L	H 1-2 L	H 3-0 W	H 2-2 D	H 1-1 D	H 1-0 W
A 1-1 D	A 2-2 D	A 0-3 L	A 1-2 L	A 2-1 W	A 0-3 L

1975-6	1976-7	1977-8	1980-1	1981-2	1983-4
H 2-0 W	H 3-2 W	H 2-0 W	H 2-3 L	H 0-0 D	H 3-1 W
A 0-0 D	A 1-1 D	A 2-2 D	A 2-1 W	A 4-1 W	A 1-2 L

1984-5	1986-7	1994-5	1995-6	2002-3
H 1-3 L	H 2-1 w	H 2-1 w	H 0-1 L	H 0-0 D
A 0-2 L	A 2-0 w	A 0-1 L	A 2-3 L	A 1-1 D

CUP

FA 1912-3	FA 1953-4	FA 1962-3	FA 1978-9	FA 1996-7
A 4-1 w	H 1-2 L	H 0-2 L	A 0-3 L	A 1-2 L

F League 1963-4	F League 1972-3	Littlewoods 1988-9
H 1-1 D	H 2-1 w	A 0-2 L
A 1-2 L		

SUMMARY	Played	Won	Drawn	Lost	For	Against
Home	17	8	4	5	26	19
Away	17	4	6	7	21	26
Total	34	12	10	12	47	45

LEYTON

LEAGUE

1906-7	1907-8	1908-9	1909-10	1910-1	1911-2
H 1-1 D	H 1-1 D	H 6-1 w	H 1-1 D	H 0-0 D	H 2-0 w
A 1-1 D	A 0-2 L	A 1-2 L	A 1-2 L	A 2-0 w	A 0-1 L

SUMMARY	Played	Won	Drawn	Lost	For	Against
Home	6	2	4	0	11	4
Away	6	1	1	4	5	8
Total	12	3	5	4	16	12

LEYTON ORIENT (as Clapton Orient 1929-34,Orient 1970-82)

LEAGUE

1929-30	1930-1	1931-2	1932-3	1933-4	1946-7
H 1-0 w	H 2-0 w	H 3-2 w	H 2-0 w	H 3-0 w	H 5-0 w
A 0-0 D	A 0-2 L	A 3-1 w	A 0-0 D	A 2-3 L	A 0-3 L

1947-8	1948-9	1949-50	1950-1	1951-2	1952-3
H 3-0 w	H 0-0 D	H 4-0 w	H 3-1 w	H 1-0 w	H 5-1 w
A 1-2 L	A 3-0 w	A 2-1 w	A 1-3 L	A 3-3 D	A 1-3 L

1953-4	1954-5	1955-6	1960-1	1961-2	1963-4
H 3-1 w	H 1-1 D	H 2-2 D	H 3-2 w	H 0-0 D	H 1-2 L
A 1-3 L	A 2-1 w	A 2-2 D	A 0-1 L	A 0-2 L	A 1-1 D

1964-5	1965-6	1970-1	1971-2	1974-5	1981-2
H 2-0 w	H 2-1 w	H 4-2 w	H 0-0 D	H 2-0 w	H 2-0 w
A 3-2 w	A 0-0 D	A 0-1 L	A 2-1 w	A 3-0 w	A 1-1 D

CUP

FA	FA
1965-6	1977-8
A 3-1 w	A 1-1 D
	H 0-1 L

SUMMARY	Played	Won	Drawn	Lost	For	Against
Home	24	18	5	1	54	15
Away	24	7	7	10	31	36
Total	48	25	12	11	85	51

LINCOLN CITY

LEAGUE

1960-1
H 5-1 w
A 4-1 w

CUP

F League 1961-2
H 3-2 w

LIVERPOOL

LEAGUE

1960-1	1961-2	1972-3	1973-4	1975-6	1976-7
H 2-1 w	H 1-2 L	H 1-1	H 1-1 D	H 0-1 L	H 2-1 w
A 1-2 L	A 4-5 L	A 1-3 L	A 0-1 L	A 3-1 w	A 0-1 L

1977-8	1978-9	1979-80	1980-1	1982-3	1983-4
H 2-1 w	H 1-4 L	H 3-5 L	H 0-1 L	H 1-0 w	H 0-1 L
A 0-3 L	A 0-6 L	A 0-0 D	A 1-4 L	A 2-0 w	A 1-1 D

1984-5	1986-7	1987-8	1988-9	1989-90	1990-1
H 3-3 D	H 2-1 w	H 0-0 D	H 0 1 L	H 0-0 D	H 1-1 D
A 0-4 L	A 2-6 L	A 0-0 D	A 1-0 w	A 0-0 D	A 0-3 L

1991-2	1992-3	1993-4	1994-5
H 3-0 w	H 1-0 w	H 2-2 D	H 1-2 L
A 1-2 L	A 1-4 L	A 1-0 w	A 0-4 L

CUP

FA 1908-9	FA 1936-7	FA 1950-1	FA 1985-6	FA 1989-90
A 3-2 w	H 3-0 w	H 3-1 w	A 0-5 L	H 0-0 D
				A 1-3 L

F LEAGUE 1979-80	MILK 1982-3
H 1-3 L	A 0-2 L

RESULTS

SUMMARY	Played	Won	Drawn	Lost	For	Against
Home	22	7	7	8	27	29
Away	22	4	4	14	19	50
Total	44	11	11	22	46	79

LOWESTOFT TOWN

CUP

FA 1902-3	FA 1903-4
A 0-5 L	H 4-1 W

LUTON TOWN

LEAGUE

1905-6	1906-7	1907-8	1908-9	1909-10	1910-1
H 1-1 D	H 0-1 L	H 6-1 W	H 3-2 W	H 6-0 W	H 3-2 W
A 1-2 L	A 3-1 W	A 0-0 D	A 0-4 L	A 1-1 D	A 1-3 L

1911-2	1914-5	1919-20	1920-1	1921-2	1922-3
H 2-2 D	H 5-1 W	H 1-1 D	H 3-0 W	H 0-1 L	H 1-2 L
A 1-0 W	A 1-1 D	A 1-1 D	A 0-4 L	A 1-2 L	A 0-4 L

1923-4	1924-5	1925-6	1926-7	1927-8	1928-9
H 2-0 W	H 1-1 D	H 2-0 W	H 3-2 W	H 3-0 W	H 3-0 W
A 1-2 L	A 0-0 D	A 2-3 L	A 2-2 D	A 3-1 W	A 1-2 L

1929-30	1930-1	1931-2	1932-3	1933-4	1937-8
H 1-1 D	H 1-0 W	H 3-3 D	H 2-1 W	H 4-0 W	H 0-4 L
A 1-1 D	A 0-1 L	A 1-7 L	A 1-1 D	A 3-2 W	A 1-1 D

1938-9	1960-1	1961-2	1962-3	1970-1	1971-2
H 2-1 W	H 2-1 W	H 0-4 L	H 3-3 D	H 1-1 D	H 3-1 W
A 1-2 L	A 2-0 W	A 2-1 W	A 2-4 L	A 0-0 D	A 1-1 D

RESULTS

1981-2	1982-3	1983-4	1984-5	1986-7	1987-8
H 1-3 L	H 1-0 W	H 0-0 D	H 3-0 W	H 0-0 D	H 2-2 D
A 0-2 L	A 1-0 W	A 2-2 D	A 1-3 L	A 0-0 D	A 2-1 W

1988-9	1989-90	1990-1	1991-2	1995-6
H 2-2 D	H 2-0 W	H 1-3 L	H 1-0 W	H 0-1 L
A 0-1 L	A 1-4 L	A 1-0 W	A 0-2 L	A 3-1 W

CUP

FA	FA	FA	Milk
1927-8	1958-9	1975-6	1985-6
A 0-6 L	A 0-0 D	H 2-0 W	A 2-0 W
	N 0-1 L		

SUMMARY	Played	Won	Drawn	Lost	For	Against
Home	41	21	12	8	80	48
Away	41	10	13	18	45	70
Total	82	31	25	26	125	118

MANCHESTER CITY

LEAGUE

1938-9	1963-4	1964-5	1965-6	1972-3	1973-4
H 0-0 D	H 1-2 L	H 4-1 W	H 3-3 D	H 1-1 D	H 1-1 D
A 1-4 L	A 0-5 L	A 2-0 W	A 0-0 D	A 0-3 L	A 1-2 L

1975-6	1976-7	1977-8	1978-9	1979-80	1980-1
H 2-2 D	H 0-2 L	H 1-3 L	H 1-1 D	H 2-2 D	H 2-0 W
A 0-3 L	A 0-2 L	A 0-4 L	A 2-2 D	A 0-0 D	A 0-1 L

1982-3	1986-7	1989-90	1990-1	1991-2	1992-3
H 1-2 L	H 1-1 D	H 0-1 L	H 1-2 L	H 0-0 D	H 2-1 W
A 1-4 L	A 2-2 D	A 0-1 L	A 1-2 L	A 1-2 L	A 1-3 L

1993-4	1994-5	1996-7	1997-8	1999-00	2001-2
H 1-1 D	H 1-1 D	H 0-0 D	H 0-0 D	H 1-0 W	H 2-0 W
A 1-1 D	A 0-2 L	A 1-2 L	A 2-1 W	A 1-3 L	A 1-3 L

CUP

FA 1938-9	FA 1962-3	FA 1980-1	F League 1975-6	F League 1978-9	Littlewoods 1989-90
H 0-5 L	A 2-1 W	A 0-6 L	H 1-1 D A 2-2 D N 1-6 L	H 1-3 L	A 1-3 L

SUMMARY	Played	Won	Drawn	Lost	For	Against
Home	24	5	13	6	28	27
Away	24	2	5	17	18	52
Total	48	7	18	23	46	79

MANCHESTER UTD

LEAGUE

1934-5	1935-6	1937-8	1972-3	1973-4	1974-5
H 3-2 W	H 3-5 L	H 2-3 L	H 0-2 L	H 0-2 L	H 2-0 W
A 0-5 L	A 1-2 L	A 0-0 D	A 0-1 L	A 0-0 D	A 1-1 D

1975-6	1976-7	1977-8	1978-9	1979-80	1980-1
H 1-1 D	H 2-1 W	H 1-3 L	H 2-2 D	H 0-2 L	H 2-2 D
A 0-1 L	A 2-2 D	A 0-1 L	A 0-1 L	A 0-5 L	A 0-1 L

1982-3	1983-4	1984-5	1986-7	1987-8	1988-9
H 1-1 D	H 3-3 D	H 0-1 L	H 0-0 D	H 1-0 W	H 2-1 W
A 0-3 L	A 0-0 D	A 0-2 L	A 1-0 W	A 1-2 L	A 2-1 W

1989-90	1990-1	1991-2	1992-3	1993-4	1994-5
H 2-0 W	H 0-3 L	H 1-3 L	H 1-3 L	H 0-2 L	H 0-2 L
A 2-0 W	A 0-3 L	A 0-3 L	A 0-1 L	A 2-2 D	A 0-1 L

CUP

FA 1905-6	FA 1958-9	FA 1966-7	FA 1990-1	FA 1993-4
A 0-3 L	H 3-0 W	A 2-1 W	H 2-1 W	H 0-2 L

F League 1974-5		F League 1979-80
A 2-2 D	1st leg S/F	H 4-1 W
H 1-0 W	2nd leg S/F	

SUMMARY	Played	Won	Drawn	Lost	For	Against
Home	24	6	6	12	29	44
Away	24	3	6	15	12	38
Total	48	9	12	27	41	82

MANSFIELD TOWN

LEAGUE

1931-2	1946-7	1958-9	1959-60
H 1-1 D	H 3-1 W	H 1-0 W	H 5-1 W
A 2-5 L	A 4-4 D	A 1-1 D	A 2-3 L

SUMMARY	Played	Won	Drawn	Lost	For	Against
Home	4	3	1	0	10	3
Away	4	0	2	2	9	13
Total	8	3	3	2	19	16

MERTHYR TOWN

LEAGUE

1912-3	1913-4	1919-20	1920-1	1921-2	1922-3
H 0-0 D	H 5-2 W	H 4-0 W	H 0-0 D	H 2-0 W	H 1-1 W
A 2-2 D	A 0-0 D	A 2-0 W	A 0-0 D	A 0-3 L	A 1-0 W

1923-4	1924-5	1925-6	1926-7	1927-8	1928-9
H 2-0 W	H 1-0 W	H 2-2 D	H 4-0 W	H 4-0 W	H 3-1 W
A 3-2 W	A 2-0 W	A 1-3 L	A 1-1 D	A 1-1 D	A 1-2 L

1929-30
H 5-1 w
A 5-1 w

SUMMARY	Played	Won	Drawn	Lost	For	Against
Home	13	9	4	0	33	7
Away	13	5	5	3	19	15
Total	26	14	9	3	52	22

MERTHYR TYDFIL

CUP

FA
1947-8
H 3-0 w

METROGAS

CUP

FA
1921-2
A 2-1 w

MIDDLESBROUGH

LEAGUE

1960-1	1961-2	1962-3	1963-4	1964-5	1965-6
H 4-1 w	H 5-4 w	H 3-4 L	H 1-1 D	H 2-0 w	H 1-2 L
A 0-2 L	A 1-2 L	A 2-6 L	A 1-0 w	A 0-2 L	A 1-0 w

1967-8	1968-9	1969-70	1970-1	1971-2	1975-6
H 2-1 w	H 0-2 L	H 2-0 w	H 1-1 D	H 2-0 w	H 0-1 L
A 0-2 L	A 0-0 D	A 0-0 D	A 0-5 L	A 0-1 L	A 1-0 L

1976-7	1977-8	1978-9	1979-80	1980-1	1985-6
H 1-0 w	H 1-1 D	H 1-0 w	H 0-0 D	H 2-0 w	H 2-0 w
A 0-1 L	A 2-2 D	A 0-2 L	A 0-1 L	A 1-6 L	A 1-1 D

1988-9	1992-3	1997-8
H 0-0 D	H 1-1 D	H 1-3 L
A 3-2 w	A 3-3 D	A 0-3 L

CUP

F League	Rumbelows
1961-2	1990-1
H 3-2 w	A 0-2 L

SUMMARY	Played	Won	Drawn	Lost	For	Against
Home	21	10	6	5	32	22
Away	21	4	5	12	16	41
Total	42	14	11	17	48	63

MILLWALL

LEAGUE

1905-6	1906-7	1907-8	1908-9	1909-10	1910-1
H 1-1 D	H 3-0 W	H 0-1 L	H 2-2 D	H 4-1 W	H 1-1 D
A 1-0 W	A 2-1 W	A 1-6 L	A 1-2 L	A 0-3 L	A 0-1 L

1911-2	1912-3	1913-4	1914-5	1919-20	1920-1
H 0-2 L	H 2-0 W	H 2-2 D	H 1-3 L	H 1-2 L	H 2-0 W
A 0-0 D	A 0-1 L	A 2-2 D	A 1-0 W	A 0-1 L	A 0-2 L

1921-2	1922-3	1923-4	1924-5	1925-6	1926-7
H 3-1 W	H 3-2 W	H 1-1 D	H 2-2 D	H 1-0 W	H 0-2 L
A 2-2 D	A 0-3 L	A 1-2 L	A 0-0 D	A 1-3 L	A 1-6 L

1927-8	1938-9	1948-9	1949-50	1950-1	1951-2
H 2-0 W	H 0-2 L	H 1-2 L	H 0-2 L	H 2-1 W	H 1-0 W
A 1-2 L	A 0-6 L	A 3-1 W	A 2-1 W	A 1-1 D	A 1-2 L

1952-3	1953-4	1954-5	1955-6	1956-7	1957-8
H 2-2 D	H 4-3 W	H 2-1 W	H 4-1 W	H 2-0 W	H 1-1 D
A 3-2 W	A 3-1 W	A 0-0 D	A 0-1 L	A 1-5 L	A 2-2 D

1966-7	1967-8	1968-9	1969-70	1970-1	1971-2
H 1-1 D	H 5-2 W	H 0-3 L	H 2-1 W	H 1-0 W	H 2-2 D
A 1-2 L	A 0-1 L	A 1-3 L	A 0-1 L	A 2-2 D	A 1-2 L

1974-5	1985-6	1988-9	1989-90	1995-6	2001-2
H 2-0 W	H 6-1 W	H 2-2 D	H 1-1 D	H 0-0 D	H 0-0 D
A 1-1 D	A 2-4 L	A 3-2 W	A 1-0 W	A 1-2 L	A 0-4 L

2002-3	2003-4
H 3-1 W	H 3-1 W
A 2-0 W	A 0-0 D

CUP

FA	F League	F League	Littlewoods
1991-2	1964-5	1973-4	1986-7
H 2-1 W	A 2-1 W	A 1-1 D	H 4-1 W
		H 2-1 W	

SUMMARY	Played	Won	Drawn	Lost	For	Against
Home	44	21	14	9	78	53
Away	44	10	10	24	45	83
Total	88	31	24	33	123	136

NEWCASTLE UNITED

LEAGUE

1934-5	1935-6	1936-7	1937-8	1938-9	1961-2
H 2-0 w	H 1-0 w	H 1-5 L	H 1-1 D	H 1-1 D	H 0-0 D
A 0-2 L	A 1-1 D	A 1-0 w	A 1-0 w	A 0-4 L	A 0-0 D

1962-3	1963-4	1964-5	1972-3	1973-4	1975-6
H 1-2 L	H 3-1 w	H 1-1 D	H 0-1 L	H 1-1 D	H 1-2 L
A 1-2 L	A 0-2 L	A 0-2 L	A 1-3 L	A 0-0 D	A 2-5 L

1976-7	1977-8	1981-2	1984-5	1986-7	1987-8
H 3-2 w	H 2-1 w	H 2-1 w	H 0-0 D	H 2-0 w	H 1-1 D
A 1-5 L	A 2-2 D	A 1-2 L	A 1-1 D	A 1-4 L	A 3-1 w

1988-9	1993-4	1994-5
H 0-2 L	H 1-2 L	H 2-1 w
A 2-0 w	A 0-3 L	A 0-3 L

CUP

FA
1962-3
H 5-0 w

SUMMARY	Played	Won	Drawn	Lost	For	Against
Home	21	8	7	6	26	25
Away	21	4	5	12	18	42
Total	42	12	12	18	44	67

NEWPORT COUNTY

LEAGUE

1919-20	1920-1	1921-2	1922-3	1923-4	1924-5
H 4-1 w	H 3-0 w	H 2-2 d	H 1-1 d	H 3-1 w	H 2-1 w
A 2-5 l	A 0-2 l	A 0-1 l	A 3-1 w	A 0-1 l	A 0-3 l

1925-6	1926-7	1927-8	1928-9	1929-30	1930-1
H 0-0 d	H 1-0 w	H 1-1 d	H 3-1 w	H 4-1 w	H 4-1 w
A 1-1 d	A 0-0 d	A 2-2 d	A 2-2 d	A 4-4 d	A 0-3 l

1932-3	1933-4	1947-8	1948-9	1949-50	1950-1
H 3-1 w	H 2-1 w	H 1-2 l	H 0-0 d	H 4-0 w	H 2-1 w
A 4-3 w	A 0-0 d	A 1-1 d	A 3-4 l	A 2-3 l	A 1-1 d

1951-2	1952-3	1953-4	1954-5	1955-6	1956-7
H 1-2 l	H 2-0 w	H 2-0 w	H 2-0 w	H 2-3 l	H 1-1 d
A 2-2 d	A 1-1 d	A 1-4 l	A 1-1 d	A 2-2 d	A 1-3 l

1957-8	1958-9	1959-60
H 5-2 w	H 3-0 w	H 1-0 w
A 0-1 l	A 2-2 d	A 1-1 d

CUP

FA	FA
1928-9	1950-1
H 6-0 w	A 2-0 w

SUMMARY	Played	Won	Drawn	Lost	For	Against
Home	27	18	6	3	59	23
Away	27	2	14	11	36	54
Total	54	20	20	14	95	77

NORTHAMPTON TOWN

LEAGUE

1905-6	1906-7	1907-8	1908-9	1909-10	1910-1
H 4-0 w	H 3-1 w	H 2-1 w	H 1-0 w	H 2-0 w	H 1-0 w
A 2-0 w	A 1-1 d	A 1-0 w	A 2-1 w	A 1-3 l	A 0-4 l

1911-2	1912-3	1913-4	1914-5	1919-20	1920-1
H 1-0 w	H 2-2 d	H 1-1 d	H 0-1 l	H 3-1 w	H 3-3 d
A 0-1 l	A 0-3 l	A 1-1 d	A 1-4 l	A 0-0 d	A 0-1 l

1921-2	1922-3	1923-4	1924-5	1925-6	1926-7
H 2-0 w	H 1-0 w	H 1-4 l	H 4-0 w	H 2-1 w	H 6-1 w
A 0-3 l	A 1-1 d	A 0-1 l	A 1-1 d	A 2-3 l	A 0-3 l

1927-8	1928-9	1929-30	1930-1	1931-2	1932-4
H 3-4 l	H 1-1 d	H 4-3 w	H 1-1 d	H 0-0 d	H 2-0 w
A 2-4 l	A 0-2 l	A 0-4 l	A 1-3 l	A 2-2 d	A 2-2 d

1933-4	1946-7	1947-8	1948-9	1949-50	1950-1
H 2-0 d	H 2-3 l	H 2-3 l	H 2-1 w	H 2-1 w	H 0-0 d
A 2-2 d	A 0-1 l	A 0-1 l	A 0-1 l	A 1-3 l	A 2-1 w

1951-2	1952-3	1953-4	1954-5	1955-6	1956-7
H 2-1 w	H 1-2 l	H 4-1 w	H 3-2 w	H 4-1 w	H 2-1 w
A 2-1 w	A 3-3 d	A 0-2 l	A 1-1 d	A 1-1 d	A 1-1 d

1957-8	1963-4	1964-5	1966-7
H 2-2 d	H 3-3 d	H 1-1 d	H 1-0 w
A 1-0 w	A 2-3 l	A 0-0 d	A 2-1 w

CUP

FA	Carling
1951-2	2003-4
H 3-2 w	A 0-1 l

SUMMARY	Played	Won	Drawn	Lost	For	Against
Home	40	24	10	6	83	47
Away	40	7	13	20	38	70
Total	80	31	23	26	121	117

NOTTINGHAM FOREST

LEAGUE

1934-5	1935-6	1936-7	1937-8	1938-9	1949-50
H 3-3 D	H 4-0 W	H 4-0 W	H 2-0 W	H 1-0 W	H 1-1 D
A 2-5 L	A 2-2 D	A 4-3 W	A 2-1 W	A 0-1 L	A 1-0 W

1950-1	1974-5	1977-8	1978-9	1979-80	1980-1
H 2-0 W	H 3-0 W	H 3-3 D	H 1-1 D	H 3-1 W	H 1-1 D
A 2-4 L	A 3-1 W	A 1-1 D	A 1-2 L	A 0-2 L	A 1-2 L

1982-3	1983-4	1984-5	1986-7	1987-8	1988-9
H 0-1 L	H 2-3 L	H 0-1 L	H 2-1 W	H 0-2 L	H 2-1 W
A 2-2 D	A 0-3 L	A 1-3 L	A 1-1 D	A 0-2 L	A 0-2 L

1989-90	1990-1	1991-2	1992-3	1994-5	1997-8
H 1-1 D	H 2-6 L	H 0-0 D	H 3-1 W	H 0-1 L	H 1-0 W
A 1-0 W	A 0-5 L	A 0-2 L	A 3-0 W	A 0-1 L	A 1-4 L

1999-00	2000-1	2001-2	2002-3	2003-4	
H 1-0 W	H 0-0 D	H 1-0 W	H 0-0 D	H 1-0 W	
A 1-1 D	A 0-0 D	A 0-2 L	A 0-4 L	A 0-2 L	

CUP

FA	FA	FA
1914-5	1964-5	1990-1
A 4-1 W	A 0-1 L	H 0-1 L

SUMMARY	Played	Won	Drawn	Lost	For	Against
Home	29	14	9	6	44	28
Away	29	6	6	17	29	58
Total	58	20	15	23	73	86

NOTTS COUNTY

LEAGUE

1930-1	1934-5	1946-7	1947-8	1948-9	1949-50
H 2-2 D	H 7-2 W	H 2-2 D	H 0-1 L	H 3-0 W	H 4-3 W
A 0-4 L	A 0-1 L	A 0-3 L	A 2-1 W	A 1-2 L	A 0-5 L

1958-9	1974-5	1982-3	1983-4	1991-2
H 3-3 D	H 3-0 W	H 1-2 L	H 0-1 L	H 0-1 L
A 3-1 W	A 1-1 D	A 2-2 D	A 1-1 D	A 2-2 D

CUP

FA	FA	Milk	Coca-Cola
1924-5	1991-2	1984-5	1994-5
A 0-4 L	H 3-0 W	H 3-0 W	H 1-0 W

SUMMARY	Played	Won	Drawn	Lost	For	Against
Home	11	4	3	4	25	17
Away	11	2	4	5	12	23
Total	22	6	7	9	37	40

OLDHAM ATHLETIC

LEAGUE

1934-5	1974-5	1981-2	1985-6	1991-2	1992-3
H 0-0 D	H 1-0 W	H 1-2 L	H 1-0 W	H 1-2 L	H 1-0 W
A 2-4 L	A 2-2 D	A 0-2 L	A 3-1 W	A 2-2 D	A 3-2 W

1993-4	1995-6	1996-7
H 1-1 D	H 2-1 W	H 2-0 W
A 1-2 L	A 0 2 L	A 0 3 L

CUP

F League
1960-1
H 6-2 W

SUMMARY	Played	Won	Drawn	Lost	For	Against
Home	9	5	2	2	10	6
Away	9	2	2	5	13	20
Total	18	7	4	7	23	26

OXFORD CITY

CUP

FA
1921-2
A 1-1 D
H 3-0 W

OXFORD UNITED

LEAGUE

1968-9	1969-70	1970-1	1971-2	1974-5	1986-7
H 1-1 D	H 2-0 W	H 1-1 D	H 3-2 W	H 1-0 W	H 2-1 W
A 2-0 W	A 0-1 L	A 1-1 D	A 2-0 W	A 1-2 L	A 1-0 W

1987-8	1996-7	1997-8	1998-9
H 4-2 W	H 1-1 D	H 2-1 W	H 1-3 L
A 0-3 L	A 1-0 W	A 0-2 L	A 4-2 W

CUP

Milk	Coca-Cola
1985-6	1996-7
A 1-3 L	A 1-1 D
	H 2-3 L

SUMMARY	Played	Won	Drawn	Lost	For	Against
Home	10	6	3	1	18	12
Away	10	5	1	4	12	11
Total	20	11	4	5	30	23

PETERBOROUGH UNITED

CUP

Littlewoods
1986-7
A 0-0 D
H 1-0 W

PLYMOUTH ARGYLE

LEAGUE

1905-6	1906-7	1907-8	1908-9	1909-10	1910-1
H 2-1 W	H 0-1 L	H 2-1 W	H 0-0 D	H 2-4 L	H 3-1 W
A 0-2 L	A 0-2 L	A 0-1 L	A 1-2 L	A 0-1 L	A 0-1 L

1911-2	1912-3	1913-4	1914-5	1919-20	1920-1
H 1-1 D	H 0-3 L	H 1-1 D	H 2-0 W	H 2-3 L	H 0-0 D
A 0-3 L	A 1-3 L	A 0-2 L	A 2-2 D	A 0-4 L	A 1-1 D

1921-2	1922-3	1923-4	1924-5	1925-6	1926-7
H 1-1 D	H 1-0 W	H 0-1 L	H 1-1 D	H 0-3 L	H 0-2 L
A 1-1 D	A 1-1 D	A 0-2 L	A 0-5 L	A 3-6 L	A 1-2 L

1927-8	1928-9	1929-30	1934-5	1935-6	1936-7
H 2-0 W	H 0-3 L	H 1-2 L	H 3-0 W	H 0-0 D	H 1-2 L
A 2-4 L	A 0-4 L	A 1-4 L	A 1-0 W	A 1-5 L	A 0-2 L

1937-8	1938-9	1950-1	1951-2	1956-7	1957-8
H 4-0 W	H 2-1 W	H 1-0 W	H 3-0 W	H 3-0 W	H 1-0 W
A 1-1 D	A 0-1 L	A 1-2 L	A 1-3 L	A 2-3 L	A 1-0 W

1958-9	1960 1	1961-2	1962-3	1963-4	1964-5
H 1-1 D	H 1-0 W	H 0-2 L	H 2-1 W	H 1-1 D	H 3-0 W
A 1-0 W	A 0-3 L	A 1-3 L	A 0-1 L	A 2-1 W	A 0-1 L

1965-6	1966 7	1967-8
H 0-0 D	H 3-1 W	H 2-0 W
A 0-2 L	A 2-2 D	A 2-2 D

SUMMARY	Played	Won	Drawn	Lost	For	Against
Home	39	18	10	11	52	38
Away	39	4	7	28	30	85
Total	78	22	17	39	82	123

POOLE TOWN

CUP

FA
1927-8

A 1-1 D

H 5-0 W

PORTSMOUTH

LEAGUE

1905-6	1906-7	1907-8	1908-9	1909-10	1910-1
H 1-1 D	H 1-3 L	H 4-0 W	H 0-0 D	H 2-1 W	H 2-0 W
A 1-2 L	A 0-1 L	A 1-1 D	A 1-1 D	A 1-2 L	A 1-1 D

1912-3	1913-4	1914-5	1919-20	1920-1	1921-2
H 0-0 D	H 0-0 D	H 0-0 D	H 1-1 D	H 2-2 D	H 2-1 W
A 0-2 L	A 0-1 L	A 0-0 D	A 0-3 L	A 1-2 L	A 1-0 W

1922-3	1923-4	1960-1	1962-3	1963-4	1964-5
H 0-2 L	H 3-1 W	H 3-1 W	H 5-3 W	H 3-1 W	H 3-1 W
A 1-2 L	A 0-4 L	A 0-3 L	A 2-0 W	A 1-1 D	A 0-4 L

1965-6	1966-7	1967-8	1968-9	1969-70	1970-1
H 1-3 L	H 0-0 D	H 1-3 L	H 0-1 L	H 0-0 D	H 1-1 D
A 3-0 W	A 3-3 D	A 0-3 L	A 2-5 L	A 4-1 W	A 2-0 W

1971-2	1974-5	1985-6	1987-8	1995-6	1996-7
H 3-1 w	H 2-0 w	H 2-0 w	H 0-1 L	H 1-1 D	H 1-0 w
A 1-2 L	A 3-0 w	A 0-2 L	A 2-2 D	A 0-1 L	A 1-0 w

1997-8	1998-9	1999-00	2000-1	2001-2	2002-3
H 2-0 w	H 0-0 D	H 2-1 w	H 0-0 D	H 0-0 D	H 1-0 w
A 1-1 D	A 2-1 w	A 1-2 L	A 0-2 L	A 2-1 w	A 2-3 L

CUP

FA
1949-50
A 1-1 D
H 0-2 L

SUMMARY	Played	Won	Drawn	Lost	For	Against
Home	36	16	14	6	49	30
Away	36	9	8	19	40	59
Total	72	25	22	25	89	89

PORT VALE

LEAGUE

1934-5	1935-6	1946-7	1947-8	1948-9	1949-50
H 0-0 D	H 4-2 w	H 3-0 w	H 1-2 L	H 2-0 w	H 0-1 L
A 1-1 D	A 1-3 L	A 3-1 w	A 0-2 L	A 0-0 D	A 2-2 D

1950-1	1951-2	1957-8	1959-60	1995-6	1996-7
H 2-0 w	H 2-3 L	H 3-0 w	H 5-1 w	H 2-1 w	H 1-1 D
A 1-2 L	A 0-0 D	A 2-2 D	A 1-2 L	A 0-1 L	A 1-6 L

1997-8	1998-9	1999-00
H 1-0 w	H 3-4 L	H 0-0 D
A 2-2 D	A 0-1 L	A 1-0 w

RESULTS

CUP

FA
1988-9
A 3-1 W

SUMMARY	Played	Won	Drawn	Lost	For	Against
Home	15	8	3	4	29	15
Away	15	2	6	7	15	25
Total	30	10	9	11	44	40

PRESTON NORTH END

LEAGUE

1961-2	1962-3	1963-4	1964-5	1965-6	1966-7
H 2-0 W	H 1-1 D	H 2-1 W	H 4-2 W	H 1-1 D	H 1-1 D
A 0-2 L	A 2-2 D	A 0-3 L	A 1-3 L	A 0-0 D	A 1-3 L

1967-8	1968-9	1969-70	1971-2	2000-1	2001-2
H 1-3 L	H 1-1 D	H 1-2 L	H 1-1 D	H 1-2 L	H 3-0 W
A 0-1 L	A 3-1 W	A 1-1 D	A 2-0 W	A 0-1 L	A 0-4 L

2002-3	2003-4
H 2-0 W	H 3-2 W
A 2-1 W	A 0-0 D

CUP

F League	Milk	Milk	Littlewoods		
1982-3	1984-5	1985-6	1988-9		
H 2-1 W	A 3-3 D	A 1-1 D	H 2-0 W	1st legs	
A 2-1 W	H 6-1 W	H 2-1 W	A 3-0 W	2nd legs	

SUMMARY	Played	Won	Drawn	Lost	For	Against
Home	14	6	5	3	24	17
Away	14	3	4	7	12	22
Total	28	9	9	10	36	39

QUEENS PARK RANGERS

LEAGUE

1905-6	1906-7	1907-8	1908-9	1909-10	1910-1
H 4-0 w	H 1-0 w	H 0-1 L	H 3-2 w	H 0-0 D	H 0-0 D
A 0-0 D	A 1-1 D	A 1-3 L	A 2-2 D	A 0-1 L	A 1-1 D

1911-2	1912-3	1913-4	1914-5	1919-20	1920-1
H 1-1 D	H 2-0 w	H 2-3 L	H 2-1 w	H 3-1 w	H 2-0 w
A 2-1 w	A 0-1 L	A 1-1 D	A 1-1 D	A 0-1 L	A 0-2 L

1921-2	1922-3	1923-4	1924-5	1925-6	1926-7
H 0-0 D	H 1-1 D	H 5-0 w	H 5-0 w	H 1-1 D	H 0-1 L
A 0-2 L	A 0-2 L	A 1-2 L	A 2-1 w	A 1-0 w	A 0-4 L

1927-8	1928-9	1929-30	1930-1	1931-2	1932-3
H 3-1 w	H 3-1 w	H 3-0 w	H 1-1 D	H 2-1 w	H 3-2 w
A 0-0 D	A 0-3 L	A 2-3 L	A 1-3 L	A 2-2 D	A 2-2 D

1933-4	1946-7	1947-8	1952-3	1953-4	1954-5
H 1-0 w	H 0-1 L	H 5-2 w	H 2-0 w	H 2-2 D	H 1-1 D
A 2-5 L	A 1-1 D	A 1-3 L	A 1-3 L	A 2-0 w	A 1-2 L

1955-6	1956-7	1957-8	1958-9	1959-60	1967-8
H 1-0 w	H 1-2 L	H 2-0 w	H 5-1 w	H 1-0 w	H 0-0 D
A 3-2 w	A 1-3 L	A 1-1 D	A 1-2 L	A 0-0 D	A 0-2 L

1969-70	1970-1	1971-2	1973-4	1975-6	1976-7
H 1-0 w	H 3-0 w	H 0-0 D	H 0-0 D	H 3-2 w	H 2-0 w
A 0-4 L	A 1-0 w	A 0-0 D	A 2-1 w	A 0-2 L	A 3-2 w

1977-8	1978-9	1981-2	1983-4	1984-5	1986-7
H 1-1 D	H 1-1 D	H 0-1 L	H 0-3 L	H 2-0 w	H 1-0 w
A 1-2 L	A 0-0 D	A 0-2 L	A 0-2 L	A 2-2 D	A 1-1 D

1987-8	1988-9	1989-90	1990-1	1991-2	1992-3
H 1-1 D	H 1-0 w	H 0-0 D	H 1-0 w	H 0-1 L	H 2-1 w
A 0-3 L	A 1-1 D	A 1-2 L	A 3-1 w	A 2-0 w	A 1-3 L

RESULTS

1993-4	1994-5	1996-7	1997-8	1998-9	1999-00
H 3-4 L	H 4-2 W	H 1-1 D	H 0-0 D	H 4-2 W	H 2-1 W
A 2-2 D	A 0-2 L	A 2-3 L	A 1-1 D	A 0-2 L	A 2-2 D

2000-1
H 1-0 W
A 3-2 W

CUP

FA	FA
1909-10	1946-7
H 0-0 D	H 4-4 D
A 0-3 L	A 0-2 L

SUMMARY	Played	Won	Drawn	Lost	For	Against
Home	61	34	18	9	102	48
Away	61	11	20	30	62	105
Total	122	45	38	39	164	153

READING

LEAGUE

1905-6	1906-7	1907-8	1908-9	1909-10	1911-2
H 2-3 L	H 4-2 W	H 0-0 D	H 0-1 L	H 4-2 W	H 3-1 W
A 1-3 L	A 0-3 L	A 1-2 L	A 1-7 L	A 0-3 L	A 1-2 L

1912-3	1913-4	1914-5	1919-20	1920-1	1921-2
H 3-1 W	H 0-0 D	H 0-2 L	H 2-0 W	H 2-0 W	H 4-1 W
A 5-2 W	A 2-3 L	A 0-1 L	A 2-3 L	A 1-0 W	A 1-2 L

1922-3	1923-4	1924-5	1925-6	1926-7	1932-3
H 2-0 W	H 2-2 D	H 0-2 L	H 3-1 W	H 0-0 D	H 2-2 D
A 1-4 L	A 0-3 L	A 0-2 L	A 0-2 L	A 1-1 D	A 2-3 L

1933-4	1946-7	1947-8	1948-9	1949-50	1950-1
H 3-2 W	H 0-2 L	H 2-1 W	H 1-2 L	H 1-1 D	H 2-1 W
A 0-1 L	A 3-4 L	A 4-2 W	A 1-2 L	A 1-4 L	A 1-3 L

1951-2	1952-3	1953-4	1954-5	1955-6	1956-7
H 2-1 w	H 3-0 w	H 2-3 L	H 0-1 L	H 2-1 w	H 2-5 L
A 1-1 D	A 1-0 w	A 4-4 D	A 1-1 D	A 2-2 D	A 1-2 L

1957-8	1958-9	1959-60	1995-6	1996-7	1997-8
H 2-2 D	H 1-0 w	H 4-2 w	H 3-3 D	H 1-1 D	H 0-0 D
A 2-1 w	A 1-3 L	A 2-0 w	A 3-0 w	A 1-2 L	A 1-0 w

2002-3	2003-4
H 0-1 L	H 2-1 w
A 2-0 w	A 1-0 w

CUP

FA 1908-9	FA 1959-60
N 0-0 D	H 1-1 D
A 1-1 D	A 1-2 L
N 3-2 w	

SUMMARY	Played	Won	Drawn	Lost	For	Against
Home	38	18	10	10	66	49
Away	38	10	5	23	52	79
Total	76	28	15	33	118	128

REDHILL

CUP

FA 1957-8
H 6-1 w

RHYL UNITED

CUP

FA 1950-1
A 1-0 w

ROCHDALE

LEAGUE

1958-9
H 2-1 w
A 2-1 w

CUP

FA	FA	F League		
1924-5	1975-6	1961-2		
H 1-0 w	H 1-1 D	A 3-0 w	1st leg Final	
	A 0-0 D	H 1-0 w	2nd leg Final	
	H 2-1 w			

SUMMARY	Played	Won	Drawn	Lost	For	Against
Home	6	4	5	5	28	23
Away	6	2	5	7	13	24
Total	6	6	10	12	41	47

ROTHERHAM UNITED

LEAGUE

1960-1	1961-2	1962-3	1963-4	1964-5	1965-6
H 3-1 w	H 0-1 L	H 4-2 w	H 2-2 D	H 3-0 w	H 1-2 L
A 2-0 w	A 1-3 L	A 3-0 w	A 0-4 L	A 0-4 L	A 1-2 L

1966-7	1967-8	1981-2	2001-2	2002-3	2003-4
H 1-0 w	H 2-2 D	H 2-0 w	H 0-0 D	H 1-1 D	H 2-0 w
A 1-2 L	A 3-1 w	A 1-4 L	A 1-1 D	A 1-1 D	A 4-4 D

CUP

F League	Littlewoods		
1967-8	1989-90		
H 1-1 D	H 1-1 D	1st leg	
A 2-0 w	A 2-0 w	2nd leg	

SUMMARY	Played	Won	Drawn	Lost	For	Against
Home	12	6	4	2	21	11
Away	12	3	3	6	18	26
Total	24	9	7	8	39	37

SCUNTHORPE UNITED

LEAGUE

1960-1	1961-2	1962-3	1963-4
H 0-1 L	H 2-2 D	H 3-3 D	H 2-1 W
A 1-2 L	A 0-2 L	A 1-3 L	A 2-2 D

CUP

FA
1960-1
A 4-1 L

SUMMARY	Played	Won	Drawn	Lost	For	Against
Home	4	1	2	1	7	7
Away	4	0	1	3	4	9
Total	8	1	3	4	11	16

SHEFFIELD UNITED

LEAGUE

1934-5	1935-6	1936-7	1937-8	1938-9	1960-1
H 3-1 W	H 0-1 L	H 1-1 D	H 2-2 D	H 1-2 L	H 1-1 D
A 1-1 D	A 2-3 L	A 0-2 L	A 1-4 L	A 0-4 L	A 1-1 D

1968-9	1969-70	1970-1	1972-3	1973-4	1975-6
H 2-0 W	H 1-1 D	H 1-0 W	H 1-1 D	H 2-1 W	H 1-3 L
A 0-1 L	A 0-1 L	A 0-0 D	A 0-2 L	A 0-1 L	A 1-0 W

1985-6	1990-1	1991-2	1992-3	1993-4	1995-6
H 4-0 W	H 3-0 W	H 2-2 D	H 2-1 W	H 0-1 L	H 0-0 D
A 5-2 W	A 1-2 L	A 0-1 L	A 1-0 W	A 2-1 W	A 1-2 L

1996-7	1997-8	1998-9	1999-00	2000-1	2001-2
H 1-1 D	H 2-1 W	H 1-1 D	H 2-1 W	H 4-2 W	H 2-1 W
A 3-2 W	A 2-2 D	A 1-2 L	A 0-0 D	A 1-1 D	A 1-2 L

2002-3	2003-4
H 2-3 L	H 1-0 W
A 1-0 W	A 0-1 L

CUP

FA	FA	FA	FA	F League
1958-9	1961-2	1988-9	1996-7	1974-5
A 1-1 D	A 1-3 L	H 3-2 W	H 1-0 W	A 2-2 D
H 3-2 W				H 2-1 W

SUMMARY	Played	Won	Drawn	Lost	For	Against
Home	26	12	9	5	42	28
Away	26	6	6	14	25	38
Total	52	18	15	19	67	66

SHEFFIELD WEDNESDAY

LEAGUE

1937-8	1938-9	1970-1	1971-2	1974-5	1981-2
H 3-1 W	H 2-2 D	H 0-0 D	H 1-0 W	H 1-1 D	H 2-3 L
A 0-1 L	A 0-7 L	A 1-2 L	A 1-1 D	A 1-0 W	A 1-2 L

1984-5	1986-7	1987-8	1988-9	1989-90	1991-2
H 1-1 D	H 1-0 W	H 0-3 L	H 1-1 D	H 2-1 W	H 1-0 W
A 2-1 W	A 1-1 D	A 0-1 L	A 2-2 D	A 2-0 W	A 0-2 L

1992-3	1993-4	1994-5	2000-1	2001-2	2002-3
H 1-0 W	H 1-1 D	H 0-0 D	H 1-0 W	H 2-0 W	H 3-0 W
A 0-1 L	A 3-3 D	A 0-0 D	A 2-3 L	A 5-0 W	A 2-2 D

CUP

FA	FA	FA	FA	FA
1907-8	1934-5	1966-7	1988-9	2000-1
H 2-0 W	H 0-1 L	H 1-3 L	A 1-4 L	A 1-2 L

SUMMARY	Played	Won	Drawn	Lost	For	Against
Home	18	9	7	2	23	14
Away	18	4	6	8	23	29
Total	36	13	13	10	46	43

SHEPPEY UNITED

CUP

FA
1905-6
A 2-0 w

SHREWSBURY TOWN

LEAGUE

1951-2	1952-3	1953-4	1954-5	1955-6	1956-7
H 3-2 w	H 2-1 w	H 1-0 w	H 2-0 w	H 3-1 w	H 3-0 w
A 2-0 w	A 8-1 w	A 0-4 L	A 1-2 L	A 0-6 L	A 5-4 w

1957-8	1959-60	1981-2	1985-6
H 2-0 w	H 1-1 D	H 2-1 w	H 3-1 w
A 0-0 D	A 3-1 w	A 2-0 w	A 3-0 w

CUP

F League	F League	
1960-1	1980-1	
A 0-1L	A 1-1 D	Ist leg
	H 2-0 w	2nd leg

SUMMARY	Played	Won	Drawn	Lost	For	Against
Home	10	9	1	0	22	7
Away	10	6	1	3	24	18
Total	20	15	2	3	46	25

SOUTHAMPTON

LEAGUE

1905-6	1906-7	1907-8	1908-9	1909-10	1910-1
H 1-1 D	H 1-1 D	H 0-1 L	H 2-2 D	H 0-3 L	H 2-1 W
A 1-2 L	A 2-2 D	A 3-0 W	A 0-1 L	A 0-0 D	A 1-2 L

1911-2	1912-3	1913-4	1914-5	1919-20	1920-1
H 0-0 D	H 3-0 W	H 2-1 W	H 0-0 D	H 2-1 W	H 0-1 L
A 1-1 D	A 0-1 L	A 0-2 L	A 2-2 D	A 0-3 L	A 0-1 L

1921-2	1934-5	1935-6	1936-7	1937-8	1938-9
H 2-2 D	H 4-0 W	H 5-1 W	H 4-2 W	H 4-3 W	H 2-1 W
A 0-2 L	A 4-1 W	A 1-1 D	A 1-3 L	A 1-3 L	A 1-3 L

1953-4	1954-5	1955-6	1956-7	1957-8	1958-9
H 1-0 W	H 2-0 W	H 1-4 L	H 0-3 L	H 0-2 L	H 3-1 W
A 0-0 D	A 1-3 L	A 5-2 W	A 0-2 L	A 3-7 L	A 0-2 L

1959-60	1960-1	1961-2	1962-3	1963-4	1964-5
H 1-2 L	H 5-0 W	H 1-1 D	H 1-0 W	H 1-1 D	H 2-2 D
A 2-2 D	A 2-2 D	A 2-2 D	A 1-3 L	A 0-3 L	A 0-1 L

1965-6	1972-3	1973-4	1974-5	1978-9	1979-80
H 3-4 L	H 0-0 D	H 2-0 W	H 1-0 W	H 3-1 W	H 2-1 W
A 2-2 D	A 0-1 L	A 2-2 D	A 1-1 D	A 2-2 D	A 0-2 L

1980-1	1982-3	1983-4	1984-5	1986-7	1987-8
H 1-0 W	H 1-1 D	H 1-0 W	H 1-0 W	H 4-3 W	H 0-1 L
A 1-2 L	A 0-4 L	A 0-0 D	A 1-2 L	A 2-1 W	A 0-0 D

1988-9	1989-90	1990-1	1991-2	1992-3	1993-4
H 1-1 D	H 4-4 D	H 3-1 W	H 2-1 W	H 1-0 W	H 4-5 L
A 0-0 D	A 1-4 L	A 0-1 L	A 0-0 D	A 0-3 L	A 1-0 W

1994-5
H 2-2 D
A 1-1 D

CUP

FA 1926-7	FA 1991-2	FA 2002-3	F League 1968-9	F League 1973-4
A 0-3 L	A 0-0 D H 2-1 W	A 0-2 L	H 0-4 L	A 2-0 W

SUMMARY	Played	Won	Drawn	Lost	For	Against
Home	49	25	14	10	88	62
Away	49	5	18	26	48	87
Total	98	30	32	36	136	149

SOUTHEND UNITED

LEAGUE

1908-9	1909-10	1910-1	1913-4	1914-5	1919-20
H 2-0 W	H 3-0 W	H 1-0 W	H 6-0 W	H 1-1 D	H 1-1 D
A 0-3 L	A 5-2 W	A 0-1 L	A 2-2 D	A 1-4 L	A 1-2 L

1920-1	1921-2	1922-3	1923-4	1924-5	1925-6
H 3-1 W	H 1-1 D	H 2-1 W	H 3-1 W	H 0-1 L	H 1-2 L
A 1-3 L	A 1-0 W	A 1-3 L	A 1-3 L	A 1-0 W	A 1-0 W

1926-7	1927-8	1928-9	1929-30	1930-1	1931-2
H 1-1 D	H 2-1 W	H 2-5 L	H 1-1 D	H 0-1 L	H 1-1 D
A 3-3 D	A 1-1 D	A 3-5 L	A 1-1 D	A 0-2 L	A 0-2 L

1932-3	1933-4	1946-7	1947-8	1948-9	1949-50
H 1-0 W	H 0-0 D	H 1-5 L	H 1-1 D	H 3-0 W	H 0-0 D
A 1-2 L	A 0-0 D	A 0-3 L	A 1-0 W	A 2-2 D	A 0-1 L

1950-1	1951-2	1952-3	1953-4	1954-5	1955-6
H 3-0 W	H 1-0 W	H 3-1 W	H 1-0 W	H 3-3 D	H 7-2 W
A 2-0 W	A 1-2 L	A 2-1 W	A 2-5 L	A 1-4 L	A 1-3 L

1956-7	1957-8	1958-9	1959-60	1995-6	1996-7
H 1-2 L	H 0-2 L	H 4-0 W	H 4-3 W	H 0-1 L	H 0-0 D
A 0-0 D	A 2-5 L	A 0-1 L	A 0-1 L	A 1-1 D	A 1-1 D

RESULTS

CUP

FA
1922-3
A 2-2 D
H 2-1 W

SUMMARY	Played	Won	Drawn	Lost	For	Against
Home	36	17	11	8	64	39
Away	36	7	9	20	40	69
Total	72	24	20	28	104	108

STOCKPORT COUNTY

LEAGUE

1937-8	1958-9	1997-8	1998-9	1999-00	2000-1
H 1-0 W	H 1-3 L	H 1-1 D	H 0-2 L	H 2-0 W	H 4-0 W
A 1-1 D	A 3-2 W	A 2-2 D	A 2-0 W	A 2-2 D	A 3-1 W

2001-2
H 2-0 W
A 1-2 L

CUP

FA	League
1923-4	1972-3
H 2-0 W	A 5-1 W

SUMMARY	Played	Won	Drawn	Lost	For	Against
Home	7	4	1	2	11	6
Away	7	3	3	1	14	10
Total	14	7	4	3	25	16

STOKE CITY

LEAGUE

1911-2	1912-3	1960-1	1961-2	1962-3	1972-3
H 2-1 w	H 1-0 w	H 1-0 w	H 1-0 w	H 6-0 w	H 2-0 w
A 1-1 d	A 1-0 w	A 1-1 d	A 1-3 l	A 0-3 l	A 0-2 l

1973-4	1975-6	1976-7	1979-80	1980-1	1982-3
H 4-0 w	H 0-1 l	H 1-1 d	H 2-2 d	H 5-1 w	H 4-2 w
A 0-2 l	A 2-0 w	A 0-0 d	A 1-2 l	A 1-3 l	A 0-1 l

1983-4	1984-5	1985-6	1995-6	1996-7	1997-8
H 2-2 d	H 0-0 d	H 1-1 d	H 0-1 l	H 2-0 w	H 0-0 d
A 0-2 l	A 3-2 w	A 1-1 d	A 1-1 d	A 2-1 w	A 0-2 l

2002-3	2003-4
H 2-2 d	H 1-0 w
A 1-1 d	A 1-1 d

CUP

FA	F League	F League
1981-2	1965-6	1987-8
A 1-0 w	A 1-2 l	A 1-2 l

SUMMARY	Played	Won	Drawn	Lost	For	Against
Home	20	11	7	2	37	14
Away	20	4	7	9	17	29
Total	40	15	14	11	54	43

SUNDERLAND

LEAGUE

1960-1	1961-2	1962-3	1963-4	1970-1	1971-2
H 3-0 w	H 3-1 w	H 4-2 w	H 2-3 l	H 3-0 w	H 1-1 d
A 3-0 w	A 0-2 l	A 1-7 l	A 0-0 d	A 1-2 l	A 1-1 d

1974-5	1976-7	1980-1	1982-3	1983-4	1984-5
H 0-0 D	H 2-2 D	H 1-0 W	H 2-0 W	H 3-0 W	H 1-3 L
A 0-0 D	A 1-0 W	A 0-3 L	A 1-4 L	A 1-1 D	A 1-2 L

1985-6	1990-1	1995-6	1997-8	1998-9	2003-4
H 0-0 D	H 3-2 W	H 0-0 D	H 2-1 W	H 2-2 W	H 1-0 W
A 2-0 W	A 2-1 W	A 1-0 W	A 1-0 W	A 0-1 L	A 0-1 L

CUP

FA	FA	FA	FA	FA	FA
1910-1	1950-1	1955-6	1960-1	1967-8	1991-2
H 3-1 W	A 1-3 L	A 2-4 L	H 0-1 L	H 1-1 D	N 0-1 L
				A 1-0 W	

F League	Milk	Milk	Milk
1961-2	1982-3	1983-4	1984-5
A 4-1 W	A 0-0 D	H 0-0 D	N 1-0 W
	H 3-1 W	A 2-1 W	

SUMMARY	Played	Won	Drawn	Lost	For	Against
Home	18	11	5	2	33	17
Away	18	6	4	8	16	25
Total	36	17	9	10	49	42

SUTTON UNITED

CUP

FA
1988-9
H 8-0 W

SWANSEA TOWN (as Swansea City from 1982)

LEAGUE

1919-20	1920-1	1921-2	1922-3	1923-4	1924-5
H 1-1 D	H 1-1 D	H 3-2 W	H 1-4 L	H 2-0 W	H 2-0 W
A 0-2 L	A 2-5 L	A 1-1 D	A 1-3 L	A 0-1 L	A 0-2 L

1934-5	1935-6	1936-7	1937-8	1938-9	1947-8
H 2-2 D	H 0-1 L	H 3-0 W	H 1-1 D	H 3-0 W	H 1-2 L
A 1-1 D	A 3-4 L	A 1-2 L	A 0-1 L	A 1-0 W	A 2-3 L

1948-9	1960-1	1961-2	1962-3	1963-4	1964-5
H 1-0 W	H 0-0 D	H 2-1 W	H 5-0 W	H 3-0 W	H 2-1 W
A 1-2 L	A 1-4 L	A 3-0 W	A 0-2 L	A 1-3 L	A 0-0 D

1982-3
H 1-0 W
A 0-4 L

CUP

FA	Coca Cola		Worthington	
1982-3	1994-5		1998-9	
H 2-1 W	H 3-0 W	1st leg	A 1-1 D	1st leg
	A 0-1 L	2nd leg	H 1-0 W	2nd leg

SUMMARY	Played	Won	Drawn	Lost	For	Against
Home	19	11	5	3	34	16
Away	19	2	3	14	18	40
Total	38	13	8	17	52	56

SWINDON TOWN

LEAGUE

1905-6	1906-7	1907-8	1908-9	1909-10	1910-11
H 1-0 W	H 1-1 D	H 3-1 W	H 0-0 W	H 1-3 D	H 1-2 L
A 3-1 W	A 1-3 L	A 1-1 D	A 2-10 L	A 1-7 L	A 1-5 L

1911-2	1912-3	1913-4	1914-5	1919-20	1920-1
H 4-3 W	H 0-2 L	H 1-2 L	H 1-1 D	H 4-1 W	H 3-2 W
A 3-5 L	A 0-3 L	A 0-2 L	A 0-4 L	A 1-0 W	A 2-4 L

1921-2	1922-3	1923-4	1924-5	1925-6	1926-7
H 1-2 L	H 0-0 D	H 2-0 W	H 4-0 W	H 2-2 D	H 2-1 W
A 1-6 L	A 2-1 W	A 2-4 L	A 0-1 L	A 1-3 L	A 2-3 L

RESULTS

1927-8	1928-9	1929-30	1930-1	1931-2	1932-3
H 1-3 L	H 1-1 D	H 1-5 L	H 2-0 W	H 4-2 W	H 5-2 W
A 1-1 D	A 2-1 W	A 1-2 L	A 2-5 L	A 0-2 L	A 4-2 W

1933-4	1946-7	1947-8	1948-9	1949-50	1950-1
H 3-2 W	H 1-5 L	H 2-2 D	H 0-0 D	H 4-0 W	H 2-0 W
A 0-0 D	A 1-1 D	A 2-3 L	A 3-3 D	A 1-1 D	A 0-1 L

1951-2	1952-3	1953-4	1954-5	1955-6	1956-7
H 2-0 W	H 1-1 D	H 2-2 D	H 2-1 W	H 4-1 W	H 2-4 L
A 1-1 D	A 1-2 L	A 0-0 D	A 0-1 L	A 1-1 D	A 1-1 D

1957-8	1958-9	1959-60	1963-4	1964-5	1969-70
H 1-1 D	H 1-1 D	H 3-2 W	H 3-2 W	H 3-1 W	H 1-0 W
A 2-1 W	A 3-4 L	A 1-0 W	A 2-2 D	A 1-0 W	A 0-2 L

1970-1	1971-2	1993-4	1996-7	1997-8	1998-9
H 1-0 W	H 1-0 W	H 0-0 D	H 2-0 W	H 5-0 W	H 2-1 W
A 2-3 L	A 1-0 W	A 3-3 D	A 3-0 W	A 0-1 L	A 1-1 D

1999-00
H 0-2 L
A 0-0 D

CUP

FA 1930-1	FA 1958-9	FA 1987-8	FA 1990-1
H 2-0 W	A 1-1 D	A 0-0 D	H 3-1 W
	H 1-0 W	H 0-2 L	

SUMMARY	Played	Won	Drawn	Lost	For	Against
Home	49	27	13	9	93	64
Away	49	10	14	25	63	108
Total	98	37	27	34	156	172

THAMES

LEAGUE

1930-1	1931-2
H 0-0 D	H 7-0 W
A 0-2 L	A 0-1 L

TONBRIDGE

CUP

FA 1952-3
A 2-2 D
H 1-0 W

TORQUAY UNITED

LEAGUE

1927-8	1928-9	1929-30	1930-1	1931-2	1932-3
H 4-0 W	H 3-0 W	H 2-0 W	H 3-0 W	H 2-0 W	H 1-2 L
A 2-4 L	A 3-0 W	A 2-2 D	A 0-2 L	A 4-2 W	A 2-2 D

1933-4	1946-7	1947-8	1948-9	1949-50	1950-1
H 0-2 L	H 2-0 W	H 1-1 D	H 0-0 D	H 3-3 D	H 1-1 D
A 2-1 W	A 1-2 L	A 1-1 D	A 1-2 L	A 1-1 D	A 5-1 W

1951-2	1952-3	1953-4	1954-5	1955-6	1956-7
H 7-0 W	H 3-0 W	H 0-1 L	H 5-1 W	H 0-0 D	H 1-2 L
A 2-1 W	A 1-4 L	A 4-2 W	A 0-2 L	A 1-1 D	A 1-7 L

1957-8
H 3-1 W
A 1-1 D

CUP

FA	F League
1948-9	1995-6
A 1-3 L	H 6-1 w
	A 3-2 w

SUMMARY	Played	Won	Drawn	Lost	For	Against
Home	19	10	5	4	41	14
Away	19	6	6	7	34	38
Total	38	16	11	11	75	52

TOTTENHAM HOTSPUR

LEAGUE

1905-6	1906-7	1907-8	1935-6	1936-7	1937-8
H 4-1 w	H 5-0 w	H 2-1 w	H 1-0 w	H 2-3 L	H 2-1 w
A 0-3 L	A 2-2 D	A 0-3 L	A 1-2 L	A 3-2 w	A 0-4 L

1938-9	1972-3	1973-4	1975-6	1976-7	1978-9
H 1-2 L	H 2-1 w	H 1-1 D	H 3-1 w	H 1-3 L	H 2-2 D
A 1-4 L	A 0-3 L	A 0-0 D	A 2-2 D	A 1-1 D	A 0-0 D

1979-80	1980-1	1982-3	1983-4	1984-5	1986-7
H 4-0 w	H 2-2 D	H 0-0 D	H 2-1 w	H 1-2 L	H 2-1 w
A 2-3 L	A 3-2 w	A 0-0 D	A 0-2 L	A 1-3 L	A 0-3 L

1987-8	1988-9	1989-90	1990-1	1991-2	1992-3
H 2-1 w	H 3-1 w	H 2-2 D	H 2-1 w	H 0-1 L	H 0-0 D
A 3-1 w	A 1-2 L	A 0-4 L	A 1-2 L	A 0-3 L	A 1-5 L

1993-4	1994-5
H 1-2 L	H 0-2 L
A 3-1 w	A 0-1 L

RESULTS

CUP

FA 1914-5	FA 1958-9	FA 1983-4	FA 1992-3	F League 1972-3	Rumbelows 1991-2
H 3-2 w	A 1-1 D	A 0-0 D	H 0-2 L	N 0-1 L	A 1-2 L
	H 1-0 w	H 2-1 w			

SUMMARY	Played	Won	Drawn	Lost	For	Against
Home	26	13	6	7	47	32
Away	26	4	6	16	25	58
Total	52	17	12	23	72	90

TRANMERE ROVERS

LEAGUE

1938-9	1958-9	1959-60	1995-6	1996-7	1997-8
H 2-0 w	H 0-0 D	H 3-0 w	H 1-1 D	H 1-1 D	H 0-2 L
A 1-0 w	A 1-0 w	A 0-0 D	A 1-1 D	A 1-3 L	A 0-2 L

1998-9	1999-00	2000-1
H 2-2 D	H 1-1 D	H 1-0 w
A 3-1 w	A 2-1 w	A 1-0 w

CUP

League 1994-5
A 1-1 D
H 4-2 w

SUMMARY	Played	Won	Drawn	Lost	For	Against
Home	9	3	5	1	11	7
Away	9	5	2	2	10	8
Total	18	8	7	3	21	15

TUNBRIDGE WELLS RANGERS

CUP

FA 1905-6
H 1-1 D
A 5-0 W

WALSALL

LEAGUE

1927-8	1928-9	1929-30	1930-1	1946-7	1947-8
H 1-4 L	H 2-1 W	H 3-0 W	H 3-1 W	H 0-2 L	H 1-0 W
A 1-1 D	A 3-3 D	A 0-1 L	A 0-7 L	A 2-2 D	A 2-3 L

1948-9	1949-50	1950-1	1951-2	1952-3	1953-4
H 1-2 L	H 3-2 W	H 1-0 W	H 8-0 W	H 3-0 W	H 3-0 W
A 1-4 L	A 1-1 D	A 1-0 W	A 0-4 L	A 2-3 L	A 4-1 W

1954-5	1955-6	1956-7	1957-8	1961-2	1962-3
H 2-1 W	H 3-2 W	H 2-2 D	H 2-1 W	H 3-1 W	H 2-1 W
A 1-2 L	A 0-2 L	A 3-6 L	A 1-2 L	A 0-5 L	A 1-3 L

1999-00	2001-2	2002-3	2003-4
H 1-1 D	H 1-1 D	H 2-1 W	H 5-0 W
A 2-2 D	A 0-2 L	A 0-0 D	A 3-1 W

CUP

FA 1947-8	FA 1965-6
H 2-2 D	H 3-2 W
A 2-3 L	

RESULTS

SUMMARY	Played	Won	Drawn	Lost	For	Against
Home	22	16	3	3	52	23
Away	22	3	6	13	28	55
Total	44	19	9	16	80	78

WALTHAMSTOW GRANGE

CUP

FA
1913-4
H 6-0 w

WATFORD

LEAGUE

1905-6	1906-7	1907-8	1908-9	1909-10	1910-1
H 1-1 d	H 2-0 w	H 2-0 w	H 2-2 d	H 2-2 d	H 5-1 w
A 0-1 l	A 2-1 w	A 0-1 l	A 1-1 d	A 1-1 d	A 0-3 l

1911-2	1912-3	1913-4	1914-5	1919-20	1920-1
H 1-1 d	H 1-1 d	H 3-1 w	H 2-0 w	H 1-0 w	H 1-1 d
A 1-3 l	A 0-2 l	A 0-2 l	A 1-2 l	A 1-0 w	A 0-2 l

1921-2	1922-3	1923-4	1924-5	1925-6	1926-7
H 1-1 d	H 2-0 w	H 0-0 d	H 2-1 w	H 1-1 d	H 4-0 w
A 2-4 l	A 1-2 l	A 0-0 d	A 2-0 w	A 1-3 l	A 1-1 d

1927-8	1928-9	1929-30	1930-1	1931-2	1932-3
H 1-1 d	H 5-2 w	H 3-1 w	H 0-1 l	H 4-1 w	H 1-2 l
A 0-2 l	A 2-2 d	A 1-2 l	A 2-2 d	A 1-1 d	A 2-1 w

1933-4	1946-7	1947-8	1948-9	1949-50	1950-1
H 3-1 w	H 4-2 w	H 1-0 w	H 0-1 l	H 2-1 w	H 3-1 w
A 3-1 w	A 1-4 l	A 2-2 d	A 1-1 d	A 0-0 d	A 2-0 w

1951-2	1952-3	1953-4	1954-5	1955-6	1956-7
H 3-0 w	H 5-3 w	H 4-1 w	H 3-1 w	H 4-1 w	H 1-2 L
A 1-1 D	A 2-3 L	A 3-1 w	A 2-2 D	A 1-1 D	A 3-3 D

1957-8	1969-70	1970-1	1971-2	1981-2	1982-3
H 1-1 D	H 1-1 D	H 2-1 w	H 1-1 D	H 4-2 w	H 3-0 w
A 4-1 w	A 1-1 D	A 0-2 L	A 1-1 D	A 0-3 L	A 2-2 D

1983-4	1984-5	1986-7	1987-8	1995-6	1998-9
H 6-1 w	H 3-2 w	H 1-3 L	H 0-0 D	H 1-2 L	H 1-1 D
A 3-1 w	A 0-2 L	A 1-1 D	A 1-0 w	A 2-0 w	A 1-1 D

2000-1	2001-2	2002-3	2003-4
H 2-1 w	H 3-1 w	H 4-0 w	H 1-2 L
A 1-4 L	A 1-2 L	A 1-2 L	A 2-1 w

CUP

FA	League
1950-1	1990-1
H 2-0 w	H 2-0 w
	A 3-0 w

SUMMARY	Played	Won	Drawn	Lost	For	Against
Home	52	30	15	7	114	54
Away	52	12	19	21	64	82
Total	104	42	34	28	178	136

WEST BROMWICH ALBION

LEAGUE

1938-9	1972-3	1974-5	1976-7	1977-8	1978-9
H 2-3 L	H 2-0 w	H 3-2 w	H 1-0 w	H 1-1 D	H 1-1 D
A 2-4 L	A 1-0 w	A 1-1 D	A 0-2 L	A 0-0 D	A 2-2 D

1979-80	1980-1	1982-3	1983-4	1984-5	1995-6
H 1-1 D	H 0-2 L	H 1-3 L	H 2-0 w	H 2-1 w	H 2-2 D
A 1-2 L	A 0-3 L	A 0-1 L	A 0-0 D	A 1-0 w	A 4-1 w

1996-7	1997-8	1998-9	1999-00	2000-1	2001-2
H 2-4 L	H 1-1 D	H 1-1 D	H 2-1 W	H 0-1 L	H 2-0 W
A 1-5 L	A 0-1 L	A 0-2 L	A 1-1 D	A 3-2 W	A 0-1 L

2003-4
H 0-0 D
A 0-1 L

CUP

FA	FA	FA	F League	F League
1906-7	1968-9	1981-2	1974-5	1979-80
A 0-1 L	A 0-3 L	A 0-1 L	A 1-1 D	A 0-0 D
			H 2-0 W	H 3-0 W

SUMMARY	Played	Won	Drawn	Lost	For	Against
Home	19	7	7	5	26	24
Away	19	4	5	10	17	29
Total	38	11	12	15	43	53

WELLINGTON TOWN

CUP

FA
1948-9
H 1-0 W

WEST HAM UNITED

LEAGUE

1905-6	1906-7	1907-8	1908-9	1909-10	1910-1
H 1-0 W	H 3-2 W	H 1-1 D	H 6-3 W	H 1-3 L	H 2-0 W
A 1-6 L	A 1-3 L	A 0-3 L	A 1-2 L	A 0-5 L	A 1-2 L

1911-2	1912-3	1913-4	1914-5	1934-5	1935-6
H 2-2 D	H 2-0 W	H 1-0 W	H 0-0 D	H 1-2 L	H 4-3 W
A 0-4 L	A 1-2 L	A 1-1 D	A 1-1 D	A 0-1 L	A 2-3 L

1936-7	1937-8	1938-9	1972-3	1973-4	1975-6
H 3-3 D	H 2-2 D	H 2-6 L	H 0-1 L	H 2-2 D	H 1-0 W
A 1-4 L	A 3-3 D	A 0-2 L	A 0-4 L	A 2-4 L	A 1-0 W

1976-7	1977-8	1982-3	1983-4	1984-5	1986-7
H 1-0 W	H 2-2 D	H 1-1 D	H 1-0 W	H 1-0 W	H 1-1 D
A 0-1 L	A 3-1 W	A 0-1 L	A 0-0 D	A 0-1 L	A 2-0 W

1987-8	1988-9	1991-2	1993-4	1994-5	2003-4
H 4-1 W	H 2-1 W	H 2-1 W	H 0-0 D	H 1-0 W	H 1-1 D
A 0-2 L	A 2-0 W	A 0-4 L	A 3-3 D	A 2-2 D	A 1-1 D

CUP

FA	FA	Rumbelows
1984-5	1988-9	1991-2
A 1-2 L	A 0-0 D	H 2-1 W
	H 3-1 W	

SUMMARY	Played	Won	Drawn	Lost	For	Against
Home	30	15	11	4	51	38
Away	30	4	7	19	29	66
Total	60	18	18	24	80	104

WEST NORWOOD

CUP

FA
1903-4
H 1-1 D

Scratched

WIGAN

LEAGUE

2003-4
H 2-0 W
A 1-1 D

RESULTS

CUP

FA	Worthington	
1986-7	1998-9	
A 0-1 L	H 1-0 w	1st leg
	A 3-2 w	2nd leg

WIMBLEDON

LEAGUE

1985-6	1986-7	1987-8	1988-9	1989-90	1990-1
H 1-2 L	H 0-0 D	H 0-1 L	H 1-0 w	H 0-1 L	H 0-4 L
A 1-2 L	A 0-2 L	A 0-1 L	A 2-0 w	A 1-1 D	A 0-0 D

1991-2	1992-3	1993-4	1994-5	2000-1	2001-2
H 1-1 D	H 2-1w	H 0-1 L	H 0-1 L	H 1-2 L	H 2-1 w
A 1-3 L	A 0-3 L	A 1-3 L	A 0-1 L	A 0-0 D	A 1-0 w

2002-3	2003-4
H 1-0 w	H 3-2 w
A 2-4 L	A 1-0 w

CUP

FA
1931-2
A 3-1 w

SUMMARY	Played	Won	Drawn	Lost	For	Against
Home	14	5	2	7	12	17
Away	14	3	3	8	10	20
Total	28	8	5	15	22	37

WOLVERHAMPTON WANDERERS

LEAGUE

1965-6	1966-7	1972-3	1973-4	1975-6	1977-8
H 0-3 L	H 1-2 L	H 1-1 D	H 1-1 D	H 1-1 D	H 2-1 W
A 1-2 L	A 1-4 L	A 0-3 L	A 1-3 L	A 0-1 L	A 3-3 D

1978-9	1979-80	1980-1	1983-4	1995-6	1996-7
H 0-0 D	H 0-4 L	H 1-1 D	H 3-0 W	H 2-3 L	H 1-0 W
A 0-1 L	A 0-1 L	A 0-3 L	A 0-2 L	A 2-0 W	A 2-3 L

1997-8	1998-9	1999-00	2000-1	2001-2	2002-3
H 0-2 L	H 0-0 D	H 1-0 W	H 1-0 W	H 2-0 W	H 0-3 L
A 0-5 L	A 2-2 D	A 0-1 L	A 0-4 L	A 0-0 D	A 0-1 L

CUP

FA	FA	F League		
1970-1	1979-80	1973-4		
A 1-5 L	H 2-3 L	H 1-1 D	Ist leg S/F	
	A 1-1 D	A 0-1 L	2nd leg S/F	

PLAY OFF

2001-2	
H 3-1 W	1st leg
A 0-1 L	2nd leg

SUMMARY	Played	Won	Drawn	Lost	For	Against
Home	18	6	6	6	17	22
Away	18	1	3	14	12	39
Total	36	7	9	20	29	61

WORKINGTON

CUP

F League
1964-5
A 0-3 L

WREXHAM

LEAGUE

1958-9	1959-60	1981-2
H 2-2 D	H 3-1 W	H 4-0 W
A 2-1 W	A 2-1 W	A 3-2 W

CUP

FA	F League	F League	F League
1961-2	1969-70	1973-4	1978-9
H 3-1 W	H 1-2 L	H 6-2 W	A 3-1 W

SUMMARY	Played	Won	Drawn	Lost	For	Against
Home	3	2	1	0	9	3
Away	3	3	0	0	7	4
Total	6	5	1	0	16	7

WYCOMBE WANDERERS

CUP

FA
1993-4
A 2-0 W

YARMOUTH TOWN

CUP

FA
1903-4
A 2-1 W

YEOVIL TOWN

CUP

FA	FA
1953-4	1979-80
A 2-0 w	A 3-0 w

YORK CITY

LEAGUE

1959-60	1974-5
H 1-0 w	H 2-3 L
A 2-1 w	A 0-1 L

CUP

FA
1960-1
H 1-0 w
A 1-1 D